DIVINE INCARNATION

Although the pharaoh was considered to be divine, and was deified after death, he was never the equal of the great gods such as Horus or Amun. It was thought that, in the form of the falcon god, the king flew to be crowned by the sun god—that is, he was an incarnation of Horus and the sun god and could take the name "Re the Horus of the Two Horizons." Ramesses II claimed, "I am born of Re, though raised by Sethos" [Sethos I, his father].

At the same time, when a pharaoh and a god were depicted in art, facing each other, the pose of the former was one of prostration or receiving the gift of life, or else of making an offering. The king was more the image of Horus than Horus himself; "Son of Re" implied that the king was of lower status than Re, his father and protector. The ruler was very much a physical, living person, becoming a deity at death when he journeyed to the horizon to be assimilated by Re, the sun.

It is because of his divine qualities that the pharaoh was said to have "creative utterance" and "superhuman understanding" and, most important, thought to be ruling according to the *maat*, or cosmic principle of harmony—in brief, the law. Especially in the New Kingdom, kings were war leaders and their heroism was commemorated in art and narrative. But in essence the king was "father and mother of all men, alone by himself, without a peer."

c. 2900 BCE Egyptians begin to wear the *wesekh* or broad collar (made of three or four strings of long beads, or faience in the earliest period) that will later become a standard Egyptian ornament.

c. 2900–2600 BCE Study of mathematics begins, with methods devised for the accurate calculation of complicated fractions, the use of unknown quantities, and calculation of the area of a circle or the volume of a cylinder or pyramid.

2900 BCE (onward) Copper artifacts are either beaten into shape or cast in open molds. Early Egypt's material technology is based largely on copper.

c. 2900 BCE A perforated ivory label for a pair of sandals illustrates how writing and picture overlap. It reads: "First time of smiting the East." King Den of Dynasty I is shown clubbing a fallen desert man.

c. 2900 BCE At Gebel Shaikh Suleiman, at the Second Cataract on the Upper Nile in Nubia, an Egyptian relief is made commemorating a military victory—probably little more than a slave raid.

- Cedar wood from Lebanon begins to be used in Egypt for special construction and furniture, and for boats.

c. 2813–2663 BCE Dynasty II prevails; its rule centered on Memphis as its kings are buried at Saqqara and Abydos.

c. 2800 BCE Turquoise from Sinai and lapis lazuli from northern Afghanistan are in use in Egypt.

c. 2800 BCE The dedication of votive and funerary objects with elaborate symbolism gradually gives way to massive monuments to commemorate the dead.

c. 2750 BCE Ninetjer is the first known pharaoh to celebrate the Sed festival, a ritual renewal of his royal powers.

2700 BCE The cult of Re, the sun god, is established at Heliopolis and from now on dominates Egyptian civilization. Re, the sun, is

thought to cross the sky each day, as do the moon and stars. The ruler is seen as an incarnation of Re and of the falcon god Horus (a bird that flies exceptionally high).

The deceased at the table was part of the ritual associated with the concept of the afterlife.

RENEWAL OF KINGSHIP

Divine kingship was exercised amid imposing architecture, in the context of a rich mythology, and in the public realm. At sunrise, immediately following the death of a king, his successor took part in a ritual

that symbolized the restoration of maat–order, stability, and the prevalence of truth and justice. In this ritual of coronation the pharaoh received his regalia, ran along a marked path indicating that he was taking possession of his realm, and chose the fivefold titles by which he would be known as the new monarch. Before he prepared to tour his kingdom, his accession was announced and his names (by which his subjects would now be taking oaths) were sent to senior officials in the provinces.

Some of the rituals of the coronation were repeated during the Sed festival, usually celebrated after thirty years on the throne, as a symbolic renewal of the kingship. New obelisks were built for the festival, along with new halls for the ceremony and feast; images of the gods of Upper and Lower Egypt were assembled; rewards were given to trusted "friends of the ruler"–the priests and ministers.

At the Opet festival at Luxor, a big procession followed the pharaoh to the doors of a temple; he entered with a few priests and moved into the dark and incense-fragrant rooms at the back into the presence of the great god Amun. Transformed, the king reappeared in the open air, before his subjects as a divine being.

Like the Sed festival, the Opet festival celebrated the renewal of kingship.

ROYAL RESIDENCES

The hieroglyph for "palace" is a rectangular outline with buttresses. There are very few archaeological remains of palaces in Memphis or Thebes, partly because, as texts reveal, the site of royal residences could be shifted during the reign of a king, and also because the royal residences were not necessarily in city centers.

We can tell from the remains of a late palace, that of Apries (589–570 BCE) at Memphis, that it dominated the urban landscape. In western Thebes the palace of Amenophis III is known to have had a pleasant artificial lake, columned open halls for assembly, and an upper floor, probably for the women. Ceiling paintings in bright colors depicted the joys of nature.

As kings toured their realms frequently, many riverside halting places were prepared for them. These may have been temporary, but they were still luxurious. Local people had the onus of bringing in at least some of the supplies for the royal party.

Written evidence records that the palace collected and stored goods for later distribution; papyrus records refer to grain being removed from various places for the palace stores, and to baking hundreds of loaves in the palace–a senior official was in charge of the royal bakery. One text refers to thirty women milling grain into flour. Leftover food was handed over to the ka-priests ("soul servants") to offer to the dead.

THE HISTORY OF
ANCIENT EGYPT

THE HISTORY OF
ANCIENT EGYPT

SHEREEN RATNAGAR

WORTH
PRESS

First published 2017 by Worth Press Ltd., Bath, England
worthpress@btconnect.com

British Library Cataloguing in Publication Data
A catalogue record for this book is available from the
British Library

ISBN: 978-1-84931-140-3

10 9 8 7 6 5 4 3 2 1

Designed and produced by DAG Publications Ltd., London.

Printed and bound in China.

3.

HOW TO USE THE BOOK

Features section:
Provides information on various aspects of
ancient Egyptian history.

Timeline section:
Entries on significant
events flow down in
chronological order (on
blue background).

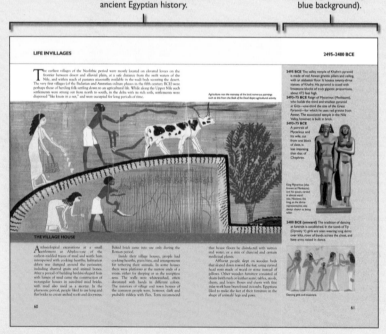

Cover (front): Sphinx (top, left to right): Narmer palette, Djoser, Mentuhotep, Tutankhamun as sun god, glass mosaic.
Cover (back): Luxor Temple.
Front endpaper: Detail of gilt shrine of Tutankhamun.
Back endpaper: Banqueting scene from the tomb chapel of Nebamun.
Title page: Great Temple of Ramesses II, Abu Simbel.

CONTENTS

The pharaoh Taharqa (690–664 BCE),
shown as a man-lion.

INTRODUCTION TO EGYPTOLOGY

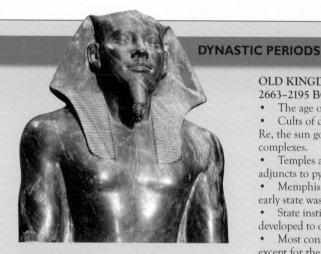

Dynasty IV pharaoh Chephren

DYNASTIC PERIODS

OLD KINGDOM (DYNASTIES III–VI) 2663–2195 BCE
- The age of pyramid building.
- Cults of dead kings—associated with Re, the sun god—instituted at the pyramid complexes.
- Temples are mostly sun temples and adjuncts to pyramids.
- Memphis is an important center but the early state was not city-centered.
- State institutions must have been highly developed to organize mass labor on pyramids.
- Most construction is in sun-dried brick, except for the stone pyramids.
- The Great Sphinx at Giza.
- Military adventures in Nubia.
- Gold mining begins in the Eastern Desert.
- The technology of blue-green faience, typical of Egypt, is mastered.
- The autobiography becomes an important literary genre.
- Orthography of the hieroglyphic script is established.
- Pyramid Texts (spells and incantations for the dead) are inscribed on pyramid chamber walls.
- Hieratic (joined-up) writing comes in use.

PREHISTORIC PERIOD TO c. 3050 BCE
- For the most part, this is the stone age.
- The farming and animal herding that were to sustain this prosperous civilization take their shape; the donkey is put to use.
- Linen cloth is made; eye cosmetics come into use.
- The pattern of leaving rich offerings with the dead begins.
- People live in reed and mud houses.
- Pottery making is advanced by the end of this period.
- After 3400 BCE, copper technology begins to develop.
- Hieroglyphic writing begins late in this period.

ARCHAIC OR EARLY DYNASTIC PERIOD 3050–2663 BCE
- Trade with Lebanon for fine cedar wood.
- Tombs of the nobility of sun-dried brick.
- Papyrus in evidence.
- Boats with cabins and oars on the Nile.
- The unification of Egypt under one king.
- The institutions of the state begin to take form.

A pair of cranes; the bird was associated with the god Thoth.

THE AGE OF EGYPTIAN IMPERIALISM, when Egypt held territories in Palestine and Syria (that is, they had garrisons stationed in towns there), began around 1480 BCE with the military successes of Tuthmosis II of Dynasty XVIII and ended around 1180 BCE, when Ramesses III (Dynasty XX) removed the Egyptian garrisons in Canaan.

THE AMARNA PERIOD was the age of radically new developments in politics, religion, and art that began in the last years of Amenophis III (r. 1388–1348 BCE) but the religious changes did not survive Akhenaten (1360–1343 BCE) and the artistic innovations ended with the reign of Tutankhamun (1343–1333 BCE). This is also the age of international diplomacy, as is evident from an archive of royal correspondence unearthed at Tell el-Amarna, the new capital built by Akhenaten.

THE RAMESSIDE PERIOD covers Dynasty XIX (beginning c. 1298 BCE) and part of Dynasty XX, up to the end of Ramesses V's rule (c. 1140 BCE). Although there were later rulers named Ramesses (VI to XI, up to 1064 BCE), they did not have very distinguished reigns and the prestige of Egypt sank low in the Mediterranean world.

NUBIAN RULE was in the time of Dynasty XXV (752–656 BCE). With Egypt weak after 1100 BCE, the Nubian kingdom grew in power and prosperity, and annexed Upper Egypt (752 BCE). The aristocrats of the Nile delta were also subject to their hegemony. Some superb statuary was produced for the Nubian or Kushite kings, who were eventually defeated by the Assyrians.

THE SAITE PERIOD refers to Dynasty XXVI (664–525 BCE), when the center of power was Sais in the delta. This was a time of increasing immigration (Syrian, Greek, Jewish) into the country, and at the same time a harking back to old traditions on the part of the rulers. The period is therefore called the Egyptian renaissance. Dark and very hard stones, polished to a gloss, were preferred for the portraits of the rulers, who were shown with idealized features rather than aged and worn down by care, as in the following period.

THE BRONZE AGE was when bronze was developed for tools and weapons and the metalsmith became a specialist in society. This age runs parallel to the pharaonic age.

THE IRON AGE came relatively late to Egypt, probably in the sixth century BCE. Iron was a cheaper metal to smelt and was more abundant in the crust of the earth (although not very much so in Egypt), and iron technology replaced copper and bronze technology in many countries of the world.

THE POST PHARAONIC PERIOD signaled the end of Egypt's independence. First the Persians made her a province of their empire, until Alexander's invasion; Alexandria replaced Memphis as the capital. The Ptolemies followed; Greek took precedence over the Egyptian language. With Roman rule, the economic system changed; taxes were henceforth paid in cash or kind to Rome. Byzantine rulers continued foreign oppression, and from 640 CE onwards, Egypt became part of the Arab world.

Gold head of a cult statue of the god Horus.

FIRST INTERMEDIATE PERIOD
2195–2160 BCE

- State political control declines.
- Most tombs are small.
- Relief sculpture becomes less well-finished.
- Many make do with a memorial stela inscribed with a prayer to ensure a good life after death.

MIDDLE KINGDOM (DYNASTIES XI AND XII) 2160–1650 BCE

- El Lahun (Kahun) and Thebes gain in importance.
- A period of political centralization and administrative consolidation.
- Many and varied missions to procure raw materials from the world around Egypt.
- A vested interest in Nubia and its resources.
- The "Tod treasure," a tribute of precious metals and jewels from as far away as Afghanistan, sent by the ruler of Byblos to the pharaoh.
- The temple-tomb of Mentuhotep II (Nebhepetre) at Deir el-Bahri.
- Massive statues of pharaohs at their temple sites.
- Investment in the Faiyum depression.
- Amun, the god of Thebes, is assimilated to Re.
- Abydos becomes the pilgrimage center associated with the myth of Osiris.
- Golden age of secular literature.
- Ushabti figurines in burials.

SECOND INTERMEDIATE PERIOD
1650–1550 BCE

- Hyksos invaders and conquerors rule from Avaris in the delta.
- Seth is worshipped at Avaris.
- Asiatic incursions continue.
- Nubia is independent of Egypt and its own dynasties grow in power.
- The war chariot is introduced into Egypt.
- Scarabs become popular.

NEW KINGDOM 1550–1064 BCE

- The pharaonic state is at its peak of maturity.

Top left: Fighting and hunting scene from a painting on a box found in Tutankhamun's tomb.
Left: The unfinished head of Nefertiti.

- Amun is the state deity at Karnak (Thebes).
- Religion changes for a short period when Aten, the sun god, is the only officially recognized deity.
- International diplomacy as the kings of Anatolia, Syria, Babylon, and Egypt correspond with one another in Akkadian.
- Pharaohs marry Babylonian and Mitannian royal women.
- Tuthmosis II begins Egypt's military involvement in Asia.
- Hatshepsut, female "king" of Egypt, organizes trade down the Red Sea.

- Tiy and Nefertiti are important queens.
- Extensive construction in the Biban el-Moluk, the Valley of the Kings.
- Hatshepsut's temple at Deir el-Bahri.
- Ramesses II's temple (the Ramesseum) at Thebes.
- Ramesses II's great temples at Abu Simbel.
- *Book of the Dead.*
- Period of great sculpture and reliefs.
- Voluminous literary output.
- Importance and influence of the high priests of Amun.

Below: Ointment container from Tutankhamun's tomb.
Overleaf: The Temple of Luxor.

Top: Painting detail from a coffin (Roman period).
Right: Wooden statue of Osiris covered with
silver and gold.

THIRD INTERMEDIATE PERIOD 1064–656 BCE
• There are two centers of power, in Middle Egypt and in the delta.
• A few forays into Palestine.
• A Nubian dynasty rules.
• Bubastite Portal in Karnak temple precinct.
• Colossus of Pinudjem I at Luxor.
• The bodies of rulers buried in the Theban necropolis are removed and cached to prevent vandalism.
• Animal gods become popular.
• Demotic script comes into use.
• Bronze casting in quantity; sculpture takes on new stylistic elements.
• Cartonnage (layers of papyrus and linen in gypsum plaster) becomes a cover for mummified burials.

SAITE PERIOD 664–525 BCE
• Assyrian conquest of Egypt.
• Greek mercenaries fight for the pharaoh.
• Achaemenid Persian conquest of Egypt.
• Palace of Apries at Memphis.
• Royal burials and temples in the delta.
• Jews fleeing from the Babylonian king Nabuchadnezzar seek sanctuary in Egypt.
• Substantial iron smelting in Egypt.

PERSIAN AND MACEDONIAN RULE 525–332 BCE
• Herodotus is a tourist in Egypt.
• Egypt is a province of the Persian empire.
• A Jewish settlement develops near Elephantine.
• Construction begins at Philae.
• Massive immigrations of Greeks, Persians, Jews. Aramaic language in use.
• Greek literature is recorded on papyrus.
• Coins are minted in Egypt.
• Glass technology is at its peak.

INVASION OF ALEXANDER THE GREAT 332 BCE
• Alexander consults the oracle of Amun.
• Construction of Alexandria as the capital.

PTOLEMAIC PERIOD 310–30 BCE
• Three centuries of rule by a Hellenistic dynasty that does not speak Egyptian, with one exception—Cleopatra VII.

• Ptolemies promote intellectual activity in Alexandria.
• A Ptolemaic decree is inscribed on the Rosetta stone—in hieroglyphics, demotic, and Greek.
• Elephants used in warfare.
• An embassy sent to India.
• Developments in irrigation technology.
• Manetho writes a history of the pharaohs in Greek.
• Lighthouse in Alexandria harbor.
• Temple of Isis on Philae.
• Emerald mining begins in the east.

ROMAN PERIOD 30 BCE–395 CE
• Egypt supplies a large proportion of the city of Rome's grain, and all of its papyrus.
• Christianity comes to Egypt.
• Coptic literature.
• Cult of Isis is popular in the early Roman empire.
• Persecution of Christians up to the fourth century.
• Pagan religions banned by Roman emperor in the late fourth century.
• Last hieroglyphic inscription.
• Serapeum at Memphis.
• Class stratification becomes marked.
• Many farmers become impoverished.

BYZANTINE PERIOD 395–640 CE
• Imposing churches built in Egypt.
• With the old religion banned, Egypt becomes Christian.
• Coptic Christians disagree with those of Constantinople over theology.
• Christian monasteries are established across Egypt.
• Poverty worsens in the countryside.
• The codex (bound book) replaces the scroll of papyrus.

ARAB RULE BEGINS 640 CE
• Coptic soon ceases to be a spoken language.
• Arab rule begins with Al Fustat (modern Cairo) as the new capital; Islam slowly replaces Coptic Christianity as the majority religion.

■ ARCHAIC PERIOD

Dynasty I 3050–2813 BCE

Narmer (Menes?)

Aha (Menes?)

Djer

Djet

Den

Anedjib

Semerkhet

Qaa

Dynasty II 2813–2663 BCE

Hotepsekhemwy

Nebre

Ninetjer

Weneg

Sened

Sekhemib/Peribsen

Neferkare

Neferkasokar

Khasakhemy/Khasekhemwy

Khasakhemy

■ OLD KINGDOM
2663–2195 BCE

Dynasty III

Sanakht 2663–2654 BCE

Djoser 2654–2635 BCE

Sekhemkhet
2635–2629 BCE

Khaba 2629–2623 BCE

Nebkhare 2623–2621 BCE

Huni 2621–2597 BCE

Dynasty IV

Snoferu 2597–2547 BCE

Cheops (Khufu)
2547–2524 BCE

Djedefre 2524–2516 BCE

Chephren
(Khafre)
2516–2493 BCE

Mykerinus
(Menkaure)
2493–2475 BCE

Shepseskaf
2475–2471 BCE

Mykerinus
and wife

Dynasty V

Userkaf
2471–2464 BCE

Sahure
2464–2452 BCE

Neferirkare 2452–2442 BCE

Shepseskare 2442–2435 BCE

Neferefre 2435–2432 BCE

Niuserre 2432–2421 BCE

Menkauhor 2421–2413 BCE

Isesi (Djedkare)
2413–2385 BCE

Unas 2385–2355 BCE

Dynasty VI

Teti 2355–2343 BCE

Pepy I 2343–2297 BCE

Nemtyemsaf I (Merenre)
2297–2290 BCE

Pepy II 2290–2196 BCE

Nemtyemsaf II
2196–2195 BCE

■ FIRST INTERMEDIATE
PERIOD

**Dynasty VII/VIII
2195–2160 BCE**

Netjerkare

Nitokris

Neferkare

Neby

Shemay

Khendu

Merenhor

Nikare

Tereru

Neferkahor

Pepysonbe

Neferkamin

Ibi

Wajjare

Khuihapy

Neferirkare

Ammenemes III

**Dynasties IX/X
2160–2040 BCE**

Akhtoy I/Ankhtify

Neferkare

Akhtoy II (Wahkare)

Senenen

Akhtoy III

Akhtoy IV

Meryhathor

Akhtoy V

Merykare

Dynasty XIa

Mentuhotep I 2160– ? BCE

Inyotef I ? –2123 BCE

Inyotef II 2123–2074 BCE

Inyotef III 2074–2066 BCE

■ MIDDLE KINGDOM

Dynasty XIb

Mentuhotep II
(Nebhepetre)
2066-2014 BCE

Mentuhotep III
(S'ankhkare)
2014-2001 BCE

Mentuhotep IV
2001-1994 BCE

Dynasty XII

Ammenemes I
1994-1964
BCE

Mentuhotep II

Sesostris I 1974-1929 BCE

Ammenemes II
1932-1896 BCE

Sesostris II 1900-1880 BCE

Sesostris III 1881-1840 BCE

Ammenemes III
1842-1794 BCE

Ammenemes IV
1798-1785 BCE

Sobekneferu 1785-1781 BCE

Dynasty XIII 1781-1650 BCE

Wegaf

Amenemhatsonbef

Sekhemre-khutowi

Ammenemes V

Ameny-Qemau

Ameny-Inyotef-Ammenemes VI

Nebnuni

Hornedjhiryotef-sa-Qemau

Swadjkare

Nedjemibre

Sobekhotep I

Rensonbe

Sobekhotep V

Hor

Kay-Ammenemes VII

Sobekhotep II

Khendjer

Imyromesha

Inyotef IV

Sobekhotep III

Neferhotep I

Sihathor

Sobekhotep IV

Sobekhotep V

Iaib

Ay I

Sobekhotep VI

Neferhotep II

Sobekhotep VII

Dedumose

Senebmiu

■ SECOND INTERMEDIATE PERIOD

(Dynasty XIV was a series of unrelated and often competing kings of fragmented, small provinces. Dynasty XVI kings were contemporary with and vassals of Dynasty XV.)

Dynasty XV (Hyksos) 1650-1535 BCE

Sheshi

Yakobher

Khyan

Yansas

Apophis 1585-1545 BCE

Khamudy 1545-1535 BCE

Dynasty XVII (Thebes) 1650-1550 BCE

Rehotep

Djehuty

Mentuhotep VII

Nebiriau I

Nebiriau II

Seuserenre

Sobekemsaf I

Inyotef V

Inyotef VI

Inyotef VII

Sobekemsaf II

Taa I (Senakhtenre)

Taa II (Seqenenre)
1558-1554 BCE

Kamose 1554-1550 BCE

■ NEW KINGDOM

Dynasty XVIII

Amosis (Ahmose)
1550-1524 BCE

Amenophis I 1524-1503 BCE

Tuthmosis I 1503-1491 BCE

Tuthmosis II 1491-1479 BCE

Tuthmosis III 1479-1424 BCE

(Hatshepsut 1472-1457 BCE)

Amenophis II
1424-1398 BCE

Tuthmosis IV 1398-1388 BCE

Amenophis III
1388-1348 BCE

Amenophis
IV/Akhenaten
1360-1343
BCE

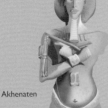

Akhenaten

Ramesses II

(Smenkhkare/Neferneferuaten 1346–1343 BCE)

Tutankhaten/amun 1343–1333 BCE

Ay (II) 1333–1328 BCE

Horemheb 1328–1298 BCE

Dynasty XIX

Ramesses I 1298–1296 BCE

Sethos I 1296–1279 BCE

Ramesses II 1279–1212 BCE

Merenptah 1212–1201 BCE

Sethos II 1201–1195 BCE

(Amenmesse 1200–1196 BCE)

Siptah 1195–1189 BCE

Tawosret 1189–1187 BCE

Dynasty XX

Sethnakhte 1187–1185 BCE

Ramesses III 1185–1153 BCE

Ramesses IV 1153–1146 BCE

Ramesses V (Amenhirkopshef I) 1146–1141 BCE

Ramesses VI (Amenhirkopshef II) 1141–1133 BCE

Ramesses VII (Itamun) 1133–1125 BCE

Ramesses VIII

(Sethhirkopshef) 1125–1123 BCE

Ramesses IX (Khaemwaset I) 1123–1104 BCE

Ramesses X (Amenhirkopshef III) 1104–1094 BCE

Ramesses XI (Khaemwaset II) 1094–1064 BCE

■ THIRD INTERMEDIATE PERIOD

Dynasty XXI

Psusennes I

Smendes 1064–1038 BCE

Amenemnesu 1038–1034 BCE

(Pinudjem I 1049–1026 BCE)

Psusennes I 1034–981 BCE

Amenemopet 984–974 BCE

Osokhor 974–968 BCE

Siamun 968–948 BCE

(Psusennes II 945–940 BCE)

Dynasty XXII

Shoshenq I 948–927 BCE

Osorkon I 927–892 BCE

(Shoshenq II 895 BCE)

Takelot I 892–877 BCE

Osorkon II 877–838 BCE

Shoshenq III 838–798 BCE

Shoshenq IV 798–786 BCE

Pimay 786–780 BCE

Shoshenq V 780–743 BCE

"Theban Dynasty XXIII"

Harsiese 867–857 BCE

Takelot II 841–815 BCE

Pedubast I 830–799 BCE

(Iupet I 815–813 BCE)

Osorkon III 799–769 BCE

Takelot III 774–759 BCE

Rudamun 759–739 BCE

Iny 739–734 BCE

Taharqa

Peftjauawybast 734–724 BCE

Dynasty XXIII (Tanis)

Pedubast II 743–733 BCE

Osorkon IV 733–715 BCE

Dynasty XXIV (Sais)

Tefnakhte 731–723 BCE

Bokkhoris 723–717 BCE

Dynasty XXV

Piye 752–717 BCE

Shabaka 717–703 BCE

Shabataka 703–690 BCE

Taharqa 690–664 BCE

Tanutamun 664–656 BCE

■ SAITE PERIOD

Dynasty XXVI

Psammetikhos I
664–610 BCE

Nekho II
610–595 BCE

Psammetikhos
II
595–589 BCE

Apries 589–570 BCE

Amasis 570–526 BCE

Psammetikhos III
526–525 BCE

Cambyses

■ LATE PERIOD
Dynasty XXVII (Persians)

Cambyses 525–522 BCE

Darius I 521–486 BCE

Xerxes I 486–465 BCE

Artaxerxes I 465–424 BCE

Xerxes II 424 BCE

Darius II 423–405 BCE

Dynasty XXVIII

Amyrtaios 404–399 BCE

Dynasty XXIX

Nepherites I 399–393 BCE

Psamuthis 393 BCE

Akhoris 393–380 BCE

Nepherites II 380 BCE

Dynasty XXX

Nektanebo I 380–362 BCE

Alexander III

Teos 362–360 BCE

Nektanebo II 360–342 BCE

Dynasty XXXI (Persians)

Artaxerxes III Okhos
342–338 BCE

Arses 338–336 BCE

Darius III 335–332 BCE

■ HELLENISTIC PERIOD
Dynasty of Macedonia

Alexander III 332–323 BCE

Philippos Arrhidaeos
323–317 BCE

Alexander IV 317–310 BCE

Dynasty of Ptolemy

Ptolemy I Soter
310–282 BCE

Ptolemy II Philadelphos
285–246 BCE

Ptolemy III Euergetes I
246–222 BCE

Ptolemy IV Philopator
222–205 BCE

Ptolemy V Epiphanes
205–180 BCE

Ptolemy VI Philometer
180–164 BCE

Ptolemy VIII Euergetes II
170–163 BCE

Ptolemy VI (again)
163–145 BCE

Ptolemy VII Neos Philopator
145 BCE

Ptolemy VIII (again)
145–116 BCE

Ptolemy IX Soter II
116–110 BCE

Ptolemy X Alexander I

110–109 BCE

Ptolemy IX (again)
109–107 BCE

Ptolemy X (again)
107–88 BCE

Ptolemy IX (again)
88–80 BCE

(Ptolemy XI 80 BCE)

Ptolemy XII Neos Dioysos
80–58 BCE

Ptolemy XII (again)
55–51 BCE

Cleopatra VII Philopator
51–30 BCE

Ptolemy XIII 51–47 BCE

(Ptolemy XIV 47–44 BCE)

(Ptolemy XV Kaisaros
41–30 BCE)

■ ROMAN PERIOD
30 BCE–395 CE

■ BYZANTINE PERIOD
395–640 CE

■ ARAB PERIOD
640–1517

■ OTTOMAN PERIOD
1517–1805

■ KHEDIVAL PERIOD
1805–1914

■ BRITISH PROTECTORATE
1914–1922

■ MONARCHY
1922–1953

■ REPUBLIC
1953–

OLD KINGDOM

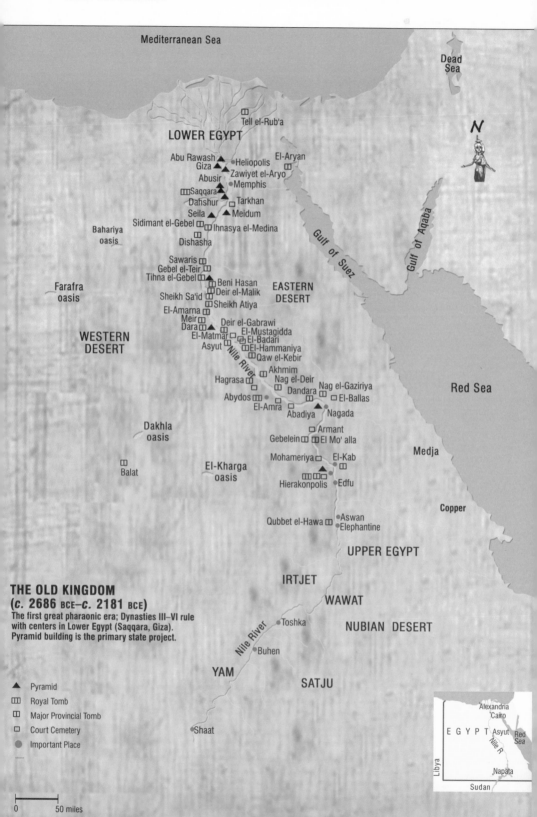

Mediterranean Sea

Dead Sea

Tell el-Rub'a

LOWER EGYPT

Abu Rawash
Giza
Heliopolis
El-Aryan
Zawiyet el-Aryo
Abusir
Memphis
Saqqara
Dahshur
Tarkhan
Seila
Meidum
Sidimant el-Gebel
Ihnasya el-Medina
Bahariya oasis
Dishasha

Gulf of Suez

Gulf of Aqaba

Sawaris
Gebel el-Teir
Tihna el-Gebel
Beni Hasan
Deir el-Malik
EASTERN DESERT
Sheikh Sa'id
Sheikh Atiya
El-Amarna
Meir
Dara
Deir el-Gabrawi
El-Matmar
El-Mustagidda
El-Badari
Asyut
El-Hammaniya
Qaw el-Kebir

Farafra oasis

WESTERN DESERT

Akhmim
Hagrasa
Nag el-Deir
Dandara
Nag el-Gaziriya
Abydos
El-Ballas
El-Amra
Abadiya
Nagada

Red Sea

Dakhla oasis

Armant
Gebelein
El Mo' alla

Medja

Mohameriya
El-Kab
Balat
El-Kharga oasis
Hierakonpolis
Edfu

Copper

Qubbet el-Hawa
Aswan
Elephantine

UPPER EGYPT

IRTJET

WAWAT

THE OLD KINGDOM
(*c.* 2686 BCE–*c.* 2181 BCE)
The first great pharaonic era; Dynasties III–VI rule
with centers in Lower Egypt (Saqqara, Giza).
Pyramid building is the primary state project.

Toshka

NUBIAN DESERT

Nile River

Buhen

YAM

SATJU

▲ Pyramid
🏛 Royal Tomb
▤ Major Provincial Tomb
□ Court Cemetery
● Important Place

Shaat

0   50 miles

Alexandria
Cairo
E G Y P T Asyut
Red Sea
Libya
Nile R
Napata
Sudan

TJEHENYU

Mediterranean Sea

Dead Sea

Raqttote
Buto
Esbet Rushdi
Sais
Tell-Nabasta
Sebennytos
Komel-Hisn
Athribis
Tell el-Daba
Tell el-Yahudiya
Giza
Heliopolis
Saqqara
Memphis
Dahshur
El-Lisht
Hawara
El-Lahun (Kahun)
Medinet Ma'adi
Kom Medinet Ghurab
Heracleopolis
Beni Hasan
El-Ashmunein
El-Sheikh Ibada
Deir el-Bersha
Tell-Amarna
Meir
Asyut
Qaw el-Kebir
Akhmim
Abydos
Valley of the Kings
Thebes
Armant
El-Kab
Hierakonpolis
Edfu
Wadi Beiza
Elephantine
Aswan

Serabit el-Khadim

Gulf of Suez

Gulf of Aqaba

Nile River

Mersa Gawasis

Red Sea

Wadi Kharit

Head of Nekheb
(Berenike)

Bahariya
Oasis

Farafra
Oasis

WESTERN
DESERT

Dakhla
Oasis

El-Kharga
Oasis

TJEMEH

Dunqul
Oasis

Beit el-Wali
Amada
Gerf Husein
El Sebua
Abu Simbel
Aniba
El-Derr
Abahuda
Buhen

WAWAT

Wadi Allaqi

THE NEW KINGDOM
(c. 1550 BCE–c. 1069 BCE)

Era of prosperity, expansion. Dynasties XVIII–XX
rule from Thebes. Valley of the Kings becomes
the royal necropolis.

Faras
Semna
Uronarti
Aksha
Kumma
Amarra
Sedeinga
Sdeb
Sesebi

NMAY

Temple
Royal Tomb
Major Provincial Tomb
Court Cemetery
Fortification
Important Place

KUSH

Kawa

IREM

Gebel Barkal
Napata

0   50 miles

THE CIVILIZATION OF EGYPT

The ancient Egyptians have fascinated the rest of the world long after the demise of their civilization. Roman emperors, though they did not understand the culture of their Egyptian subjects, were in awe of Egypt's "ancient wisdom" and had its obelisks transported to Rome. The modern tourist visiting Highgate Cemetery in London, after paying his respects to Karl Marx in the eastern part, may be taken aback by the obelisks, lotus columns, and "Egyptian Avenue" that added to the ostentation of the Victorian burials in the western part of this nineteenth-century cemetery. Intellectuals such as Sigmund Freud, born in the mid-nineteenth century and a great collector of antiquities, were also captivated by some aspects of ancient Egypt.

Osiris, the god of the dead, painted on a coffin, Dynasties XXI–XXII.

EGYPT'S GREAT TRADITION

Only some societies in the past attained the level of culture we call "civilization." Such societies developed their distinctive "great traditions," or codes of high culture (such as literary expression, sculptural modeling, and building construction), along with economic organization across regions and technological breakthroughs. These cultural elements were shared over a large area by several disparate communities.

With the coming of metal (copper and bronze) technology, many great river valleys of the world witnessed the early rise of such civilizations, among them the valleys of the Euphrates in Mesopotamia, of the Nile, the Indus in southern Asia, and the Huang Ho (Yellow River) in northern China. Each had its own personality and bequeathed its particular legacy to the world.

Colored glass containers found in graves at north Saqqara, 1430 BCE.

TIMELINE OF ANCIENT EGYPT

11,000–5000 BCE Tools of Stone Age hunter-gatherers are found in the Western Desert and at a few sites such as Sebil in Upper Egypt; others may be buried under the Nile alluvium.

10,000–5000 BCE Rock art found at sites in Libya (Uweinat, Gilf Kebir) in the Western Desert, showing scenes of hunting and animal herding.

c. 7000–6000 BCE Late Paleolithic and early Neolithic food-producing sites in the Western Desert, e.g., Nabta. Hunting of gazelle and hare. Later, stone tools used in agriculture and animal herding.

c. 7000–5000 BCE Early farming and animal-raising cultures occur in both the Western Desert and Nile Valley; grazing on vegetation in wadi beds and in oases. As settlement in the valley progresses and its population grows, a distinctive pastoral culture develops.

Herdsmen leading cattle across a canal.

Above: An iconic image of ancient Egyptian civilization, the Sphinx at Giza, 2500 BCE.
Left: Another typical image of ancient Egypt, a painted interior of a wooden coffin, c. 950 BCE.

21

A VARIEGATED PERSONALITY

City-states first developed in Mesopotamia, where the kings constantly fought each other. However, in Egypt (the Nile valley downstream of Aswan), the country was politically unified under one king around 3000 BCE. Because the branches of the lower Euphrates have gradually shifted west, dozens of Mesopotamian villages and towns can be excavated unimpeded by current cultivation, but in Egypt the narrow valley of the Nile has been tilled for millennia, so the only sites of past activity that have survived were located on the edge of the deserts to the east or west.

The arid soil conditions of these deserts ensured the survival of corpses and artifacts to a degree that is not possible in the other great river valleys, but we do not know much about towns within the narrow alluvial plain. So far, Egypt has revealed no urban architecture to match Mohenjodaro on the lower Indus plain. Yet, in the Indus valley culture there was no ideology that encouraged the burial of the elite in lavishly equipped tombs. In ancient China, although the mortuary offerings of the Shang rulers included enormous numbers of bronze vessels, in Egypt copper was a metal for craft tools, and the memorials for pharaohs were pyramids, statues, stelae, and temples.

Today we think of ancient Egypt as simply mummies, pyramids (there are almost a hundred pyramids in all), scarabs, the beaded *wesekh* collar, and the sex appeal of Nefertiti or Cleopatra. However, Egypt offers much more:

- Peasants wore circlets of grass and flowers as body ornaments.
- Sandals were made of grass fiber and rope.
- The Egyptians were so attached to their cats that families went into full mourning when their pet cat died.
- They rested their heads on high, curved rests as they slept.
- In village wells, they did not raise water up but lowered themselves to the level of the water.
- Members of the nonroyal elite had long autobiographies written on their tomb walls; these developed into distinct literary genres.

PROSPERITY

Food shortages were rare. A few reliefs show people during a famine, but on the whole Egyptian agriculture was productive without making excessive demands on the labor of the peasant family and their livestock. Egyptians quite possibly made more use of gold than did any other Old World civilization, and they produced more stone statuary than either ancient Greece or India.

Yet high levels of artistic and technological production and the prolific stone statuary were not the result of prosperity alone. First there was the ideology that statues were the home of the living spirit of a god or a dead person. Also, much of the monument construction, relief sculpture, painting, and furniture making was centrally organized by royal and temple workshops. This ensured that craftspersons and artists had access to suitable raw materials and to the right tools and instruments of measurement. The state also organized central management, supplying supervisors for workshops and priests, members of the royal family, or men of similar social status to set the local standards.

A funerary papyrus written in Hieratic c. 525–343 BCE.

ACCESSIBILITY

After about 650 BCE, there was widespread immigration of mercenaries, intellectuals, traders, and rulers from Greece, so Greek interpretations of Egyptian culture became the standard throughout Europe. Europeans had easier access to this ancient civilization than they did to the civilizations of Mesopotamia, India, or China.

ENJOYMENT OF LIFE

At first glance ancient Egyptians seem to be obsessed with pessimism and death. The archaeological record consists of almost nothing except funerary texts, mortuary temples, tombs, and mummies. Yet alongside all this anxiety over death can be found an enjoyment of life and sensuality. The common symbol of the lotus flower was actually an erotic reference, and there is the well-known painting on a large piece of stone (c. 1300 BCE), for example, that depicts

PRECIOUS OFFERINGS

Of all ancient civilizations, Egypt used the most gold. Gold was extracted from the Eastern Desert wadi sands and gravels (carried on donkey back to the Nile for washing), and also from veins in rocks. Later, gold came to Egypt from Nubia. All Egyptian sources of gold have now been depleted, and possibly ran short after about 1000 BCE, when Egypt's gold exports and gifts abroad came to an end. The Eastern Desert also provided semiprecious stones such as carnelian, garnet, and amazonite; natron (used for adding to food preservatives and as an industrial material for faience), glass, and metals came from the Wadi Natrum to the west of the delta; diorite came from the Western Desert (and Nubia); gypsum from the Faiyum. There was limestone in several shades at Tura on the east bank of the Nile opposite Giza. Translucent alabaster came from the Wadi Hammamat in the Eastern Desert.

- **c. 7000–3000 BCE** A "repopulation" of the Sahara desert, brought about by a period of higher rainfall (over 2 inches per year); growth of vegetation (where today nothing grows). The floodplain of the Nile is a habitat for rhinoceroses, elephants, and hippopotamuses.
- Climatic change allows hunters and trappers to settle in the oases of the desert and take to agriculture; some settlements are on high ground in and around the floodplain.
- **c. 6000 BCE** Food-producing economies begin on wadi beds in the Western Desert: wheat, barley, and flax are grown; sheep, goat, cattle, pig, and geese are herded. Sites: Merimdeh on the western edge of the delta, Faiyum-A, Deir Tasa in Upper Egypt.
- **c. 5500 BCE** Copper-using cultures at el-Amra near Abydos, at Badari, and at Hemamieh in Middle Egypt, with agriculture and animal domestication, stone tools, coiled pottery, animal skins for clothing, bone tools, basketry, the throwstick, and the mace.
- In the Badarian culture in Middle Egypt, cemeteries are set aside where the dead are buried in shallow graves.
- **c. 5000 BCE** A long-lasting tradition begins of (a) the use of fine hollow-based arrowheads of flaked flint; these are found in settlements and cemeteries for centuries to come; (b) the use of ivory from hippopotamuses and elephants for ornaments, combs, and needles; and (c) the use of powdered malachite (a green mineral, an ore of copper) for painting the eyes, and a prophylactic against eye infections. Special grinding palettes are used by the affluent for this cosmetic.
- **c. 5000–4000 BCE** Merimdeh is perhaps the first village in the delta settled by desert herders. Remains of houses of wooden posts found; also wickerwork and mud, baskets with mud lining for grain storage; pottery in simple shapes.
- **c. 5000 BCE (onward)** Pottery continues to be made by hand but Upper Egypt has technical refinements: it is baked hard, burnished to a sheen

Early Egyptian pottery, which was often used for funerary purposes and typically colored red ocher and a metallic black.

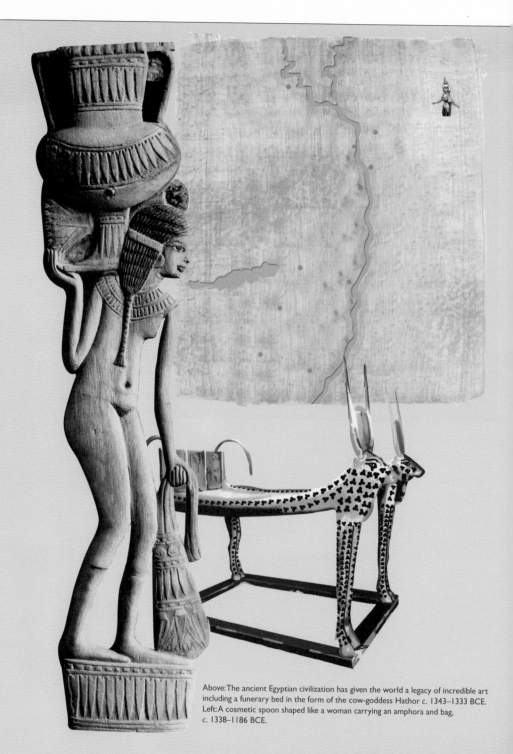

Above: The ancient Egyptian civilization has given the world a legacy of incredible art including a funerary bed in the form of the cow-goddess Hathor c. 1343–1333 BCE.
Left: A cosmetic spoon shaped like a woman carrying an amphora and bag, c. 1338–1186 BCE.

a dancer clad only in an embroidered waist cloth making a back bend, her very curly hair in a cascade down to the ground. Women are often portrayed in diaphanous pleated dress and long, heavy wigs. The natural world is celebrated in joyful paintings of rural landscapes, where a monkey ruffles the feathers of a crane, or where a mimosa tree is shown in full flower together with a brown and white bird.

Humor is also seen in many literary texts; for example, in the story of King Neferkare and General Sasenet, a high court official stumbles upon a royal family member sneaking to the general's house, throwing a brick up at the window to announce his presence, and climbing in via a rope ladder hastily thrown down. The official notes that the king is "going out at night, all alone, nobody with him," but every time he tries to recount at court this scandalous news, his voice is drowned out by "the singers' songs, the musicians' music, the acclaimers' acclamations, and the whistlers' whistling."

RESPECT FOR WOMEN

In ancient times Egyptian women enjoyed rights to property inheritance and to the bestowal of property, to bear witness in the law courts, and to wield political power in the way no ancient Mesopotamian or Greek woman could. However, the peasantry, the anonymous people of the countryside that created the wealth that the pharaohs enjoyed, remained almost voiceless and faceless through the centuries.

AN ENDURING LEGACY

Egypt was a land that provided plenty for its inhabitants, a society that portrayed the joys of family life, respected women, and did not ignore the erotic in its mortuary art. Ancient Egyptians absorbed immigrants from the deserts and Asia into their fold, and there were occasional intermarriages and adoption of items of other cultures. Even when the Greeks migrated in large numbers, conflict was rare.

Sigmund Freud, who used archaeology as a metaphor for psychoanalysis, said that conscious thoughts are soon lost, but that the unconscious endures. He illustrated this by pointing out to his patients the antiques that cluttered his study, many of them from Egypt. As he put it, they were only objects found in a tomb, but "their burial had been their preservation."

with smooth pebbles; often it is two-tone, the upper part blackened and the lower red-brown.

- *c.* **5000–4000 BCE** In the Nile Valley, there is use of ostrich eggshell from the deserts, and shells from the Mediterranean and Red Sea regions.
- *c.* **4000 BCE** Use of copper; the making of stone containers begins, along with weaving flax into cloth, and using spindles and loom weights.
- Potters develop new skills and produce a lustrous red ware fired with the mouths of pots placed on the ash of the fire to smear the upper portion black.

Early Egyptian art focused on objects of everyday life, including items of personal adornment, such as these combs found in graves at Naqada.

- *c.* **4000 BCE (onward)** Amratian culture in various sites in Upper Egypt, and the Buto-Maadi culture in the delta.
- The stone mace (of hard stone) appears as a weapon associated with Egyptian rulers.
- Cultural expansion of the Amratian/Badari tradition is evident, firmly rooted in Upper Egypt; it begins to influence the delta.
- *c.* **4000 BCE** Occurrence of very large oblong cosmetic stone palettes—possibly votive or ceremonial artifacts.
- *c.* **4000 BCE (onward)** Small carved figures of animals, including the elephant and hippopotamus, are frequent finds in temple precincts.
- *c.* **4000 BCE** People are now depicted in sculpture in the round.
- *c.* **3550–3200 BCE** Gerzean culture of Upper Egypt. Hierakonpolis and Naqada are the main centers, with a great many burial sites.

25

It was Homer who first referred to the Nile and its valley as *Aigyptos*. Its own inhabitants called it the Black Land. In his *Historia*, an enquiry into the cultures and pasts of various peoples known to his world, the Greek intellectual Herodotus (fifth century BCE) wrote that "the Egypt to which we sail nowadays is, as it were, the gift of the river."

The two life forces of Egypt were the Nile, provider and protector, and the sun, the source of much of its religious and metaphysical ideology.

GEOGRAPHY OF THE RIVER

The Nile is an enormously long river that collects the waters of the Blue Nile and the White Nile near Khartoum (Sudan) and then flows north to be joined by its last tributary, the Atbara.

The source of the White Nile is the lakes region of central Africa, whereas the Blue Nile (on which the height and duration of the flood in Egypt is dependent) and the Atbara rise in the Abyssinian mountains, which receive heavy monsoon rainfall in the summer. The combined Nile River enters Egypt from Nubia at Aswan, and travels about 560 miles to the head of the delta, where the waters flow into several branches emptying into the Mediterranean Sea.

The valley of the Nile is narrow, hemmed in by high desert to its east and west. Rainfall is negligible, about 1.2 inches per year near Cairo (falling between January and March) at the head of the delta, and even less in the upper valley.

- "Black Land" Egypt: *order*
- "Red Land" bordering Egypt: *chaos*

Pharaoh's Two Lands (both fertile):
- *Upper Egypt (narrow Nile valley)*
- *Lower Egypt (delta)*

Sinai Peninsula: east of the delta, accessible by land bridge; source of abundant copper and turquoise

---

NOURISHER AND PRESERVER

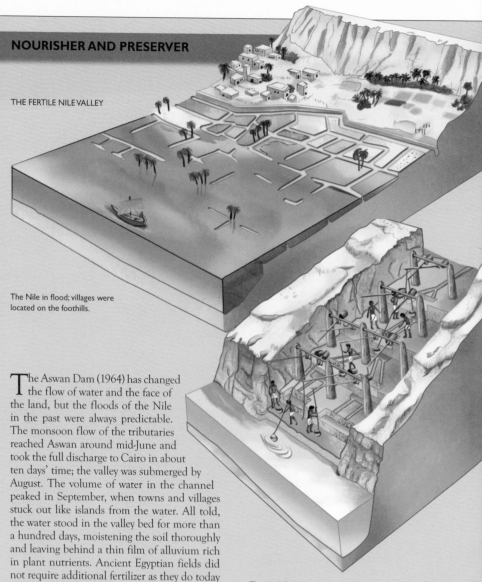

THE FERTILE NILE VALLEY

The Nile in flood; villages were located on the foothills.

The *shaduf* was a pulley system in which water was lifted in leather bags and carried upward.

The Aswan Dam (1964) has changed the flow of water and the face of the land, but the floods of the Nile in the past were always predictable. The monsoon flow of the tributaries reached Aswan around mid-June and took the full discharge to Cairo in about ten days' time; the valley was submerged by August. The volume of water in the channel peaked in September, when towns and villages stuck out like islands from the water. All told, the water stood in the valley bed for more than a hundred days, moistening the soil thoroughly and leaving behind a thin film of alluvium rich in plant nutrients. Ancient Egyptian fields did not require additional fertilizer as they do today or as did other places in the rest of the ancient world.

The Nile gives the land its fertility, unlike the Euphrates and the Indus rivers of Mesopotamia, India, and Pakistan— other rivers that witnessed the early rise of civilization and cities. The Nile has seldom destroyed the settlements in its valley. Flooding was gradual and predictable. One of the most fertile agricultural lands in the world, the Nile valley and delta also lay in the close vicinity of fisheries and the high desert and its wadi beds with their pastures. Herodotus remarked in the fifth century BCE that the Egyptians were one of the healthiest societies in the world. When it was made a part of the Roman Empire, a large proportion of the grain that fed the huge population of the city of Rome, later of Constantinople, was supplied by Egypt.

c. 3550–3400 BCE A length of painted linen (that took modern restorers four years to repair) shows narrative scenes that include two boats with cabins and a man in the stern steering; one boat has multiple rowers. The heads and bodies are brown and the men are shown with short black beards.

c. 3500 BCE A settlement of Elephantine, at the First Cataract (near Aswan); here and at Buto on the delta, artifacts with Palestinian connections are found.

c. 3500–3000 BCE A settlement flourishes at Maadi, on the fringes of present-day Cairo. Its economic base was probably overland trade to Sinai and beyond for copper. This is suggested by the Palestinian-type underground houses and pottery jars from this time found at Maadi, as well as remnants of metallic copper, copper ores, and donkey bones.

c. 3400–3300 BCE Tomb 100 at Hierakonpolis, the burial site of a local chief, has painted plaster on the walls. The painting depicts a hunt, men fighting, and a procession of boats, some with cabins.

c. 3400–3300 BCE Besides being hammered into shape, copper is now cast as axes and daggers; the metal is used increasingly for containers and tools.

c. 3400–3300 BCE Rich burials at Naqada and Hierakonpolis indicate the emergence of chiefships.

c. 3300–3200 BCE A strong Upper Egyptian cultural influence is also discernible at Buto (in pottery, flint tools, building methods); it may indicate some measure of domination from the south.

c. 3300 BCE The first burials at Abydos.

c. 3300 BCE (onward) Pressure flaking, perhaps with wooden punches, is used to produce flint knife blades with exquisite rippled surfaces; they also have carved ivory handles.

• Population of the delta increases steadily.

• Upper Egyptian black-topped pottery comes into use at Maadi, together with pigment palettes.

c. 3250 BCE Writing begins as small and isolated images of birds, snakes, plants, and diverse objects inserted in a picture. A small scorpion in front of the figure of a man reads "Scorpion," the name of an early king.

Predynastic pottery shows crude depictions of boats with human figures, probably the deceased, on a journey to the realm of the dead.

MANAGING THE WATERS

The challenge to the ancient farmer was to manage the floodwater on the narrow plain in such a way that the maximum area was submerged. The ceremonial mace head of Scorpion, perhaps the first king, depicts the role of the ruler in caring for the irrigation: with a pick in his hand, he ceremonially starts water management for the year. The plain was divided by earth banks into basins; the banks were cut open to let water into a few basins at a time, each holding more than three feet of river water for forty to sixty days. This annual phenomenon was part of the cosmology of ancient Egypt: it was believed that the land arose from the primeval waters (symbolizing chaos) in an act of creation. As the primeval mound emerged, the universe was fashioned. The basins were then drained one at a time, proceeding downstream. The land now ready, the sowing of wheat commenced in late October or November, and then barley was sown; neither of these sowings required deep plowing. Both crops were ripe around March. Thus there were three seasons: inundation, growing, and drought (after March). Not surprisingly, the Nile was commonly called Iteru, or "the Seasonal One." If it became necessary to sow another crop after the March harvest, or if the inundation had not been adequate in summer, water was raised from wells with the use of the weighted lever, or shaduf.

CROPS AND FOOD

The crops that nourished Egypt were wheat and barley. The staple foods were bread and a thick beer valued more for its nutrition than for its intoxication. People ate cucumbers, lettuce, beans, lentils, and onions; oil came from sesame and castor; dates, melons, the fig of the sycamore tree, and grapes were their fruits. Honey came from the meadows beyond the delta. Water lilies and cornflowers were used to decorate objects and to wear as garlands. Beef was offered to the gods and eaten along with wild game; people herded

PLANTS

- Palms, acacias, tamarisk, and sycamore fig–main local trees, not suitable for boats or choice furniture.
- Reeds–used for basketry, boxes, stands, and stools.
- Papyrus–used for rope, sandals, and paper (Egypt exported it for writing purposes by 1000 BCE).
- Flax–fiber of the stem used to weave cloth. From early days, fine linen was often painted with narrative scenes, as for example in an early tomb at Gebelein in the middle Nile valley.

Geese, cranes, and ducks were found in abundance.

pigs, cattle, and sheep as well; but the beloved cat, as a pet, emerges comparatively late. Cranes were captured and fed with flour pellets until they were fat enough to eat; migratory birds were also netted for their meat. Fish, however, may have been more a food for the peasantry than for the elite.

ANIMALS

- Donkey–domesticated after 4000 BCE. The major draft animal of Egypt.
- Scarab–a dung beetle that rolls its eggs along on the ground; symbolically associated with the movement of the sun across the sky.
- Crocodile (along low edges of Nile plain); cobra and viper; eye-infecting flies.
- Royal men hunted lions and antelopes. The Egyptians tried to domesticate antelopes, gazelles, and even hyenas, but were not successful.

REGENERATING THE FAIYUM

An important adjunct to the Nile valley is the Faiyum depression, in the center of which lies a shallow lake about 164 feet below sea level. In the period from 7000 to 5000 BCE, when the climate was much wetter than today, this lake received overflows from the Nile through the Hawara channel. But as the climate settled to its present aridity, the Nile cut down its bed, and its discharge could no longer reach the lake. Around 1840 BCE, the pharaoh had the Hawara channel cleaned and

a huge area in the Faiyum became productive, with exceptionally fertile soil. The Fayum constituted a major administrative district or nome: here was the town of Shedet, where the crocodile god Sobek was worshipped, and as the Faiyum area gained importance during the Middle Kingdom, shrines for Sobek were built in several other places as well. The area of

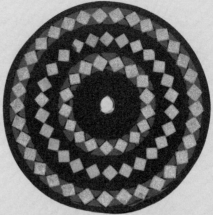

These game disks were found in the tomb of an important official at Saqqara; made of stone, they were associated with the sport of the rich.

- **c. 3250–3050 BCE** At Abydos, in one of the twelve chambers of the Tomb U-j, more than a hundred Palestinan wine jars are found from this era.
- **c. 3200–3050 BCE** Referred to by some as the "Protodynastic" period, when Scorpion, and then Narmer, are believed to be the first kings, ruling around 3100 BCE.
- A period of political ferment, a struggle for the control of Upper and Lower Egypt. Political units expand and the rural population clusters in larger villages; ultimately, the leaders of Upper Egypt reign supreme.
- **c. 3200–3050 BCE** Abydos and Hierakonpolis burial sites have all kinds of stone and metal tools, cosmetic palettes with malachite lumps, shell and stone beads, pottery, and figurines.
- **c. 3200 BCE (onward)** By now, farmers along the Nile know how to calculate the onset of floods by the appearance of Sirius, the dog star.

In Egypt, Sirius vanishes from the sky in the summer, but its first dawn reappearance heralds the rise of the river. Each year of the Egyptian calendar begins at the heliacal rising of Sirius.

- **c. 3200–3000 BCE** At Hierakonpolis (also called Nekhen), a temple on the west bank, a town develops with a building that is possibly a temple in the shape of a U, with brick walls recessed at intervals. There are also at least three large tombs, with pottery, ivory, and clay figurines, beads, and amulets.
- **c. 3200–3000 BCE** Scholars see this as a brief period of Mesopotamian influence in Egypt in terms of brick buildings with recessed facades, cylinder seals, and perhaps the idea of writing. Brick construction is particularly evident at Abydos.
- **c. 3150–3050 BCE** The first writing occurs on pottery, jar sealings, wooden and ivory labels, and plaques or palettes. The writing often includes a personal name.
- Pottery found with human burials occasionally bears the names of individuals such as Qa and Aha, written on the surface in ink.
- **3100 BCE (onward)** The funerary monument assumes importance as the site of rituals for the dead; a relief depicting food offerings at a table is an invariable fixture.
- **c. 3100–3000 BCE** Carving of stone vases and bowls begins to grow into a major industry with high standards of finish and aesthetics, especially for goods to be placed in graves.
- Electrum, a natural alloy of silver and gold, probably from Nubia, begins to be used.

arable land in the depression was increased by blocking the flow through the feeder channel from the Nile, and near the neck of this channel two colossi of quartzite were installed by Ammenemes III. Later, after 300 BCE, the Faiyum was again revived for agriculture under the Ptolemies and Romans. Today the lake is called the Birket Qarun and still sees the annual migration of beautiful birds, the subject of several wall paintings in antiquity.

THE NARMER PALETTE

RIVERLANDS UNITED

The early Egyptians used malachite and galena as cosmetics for painting their eyelids and to protect their eyes from infection and glare. They may have thought that these materials had mystic properties, for many stone palettes, used for grinding, were large and impractical, and were more like votive objects.

The large Narmer Palette (c. 3050 BCE), made of dark green slate, is a significant document of the period of state emergence. The top corners on the obverse and reverse carry the image of the goddess Hathor, and in the top center on both sides are hieroglyphs for a pharaoh, Narmer.

On the obverse the pharaoh is shown in the Red Crown of the delta, his name written again before his face; he is preceded by a priest and four standard-bearers and is on his way to inspect the slain enemy after a battle. A boat carved above the beheaded bodies may indicate this was a river or sea battle. Note the bull's tail worn by the pharaoh from the left shoulder to the waist and then hanging below the waist.

In the center of the palette is a depression for grinding the pigment, made by the curving necks of two mythical beasts, probably signifying danger that has been brought under control. At the bottom, the pharaoh as a bull breaks down the houses and town wall of a foreign enemy.

On the reverse of the palette is the pharaoh in the White Crown of Upper Egypt, dispatching an enemy chief with his mace. Above the enemy is depicted in picture and hieroglyphs the hawk Horus taking captive bearded men of the papyrus (delta) region. His sandal-bearer and foot-washer appears behind the pharaoh. Beneath are two corpses with signs for two kinds of fortresses.

The palette appears to signify the unification of the south and north.

A raised relief in siltstone, the Narmer Palette is among the earliest examples of two-dimensional Egyptian art. It is a symbolic depiction of the undisputed status of the king.

THE SCORPION MACE HEAD

Made to commemorate the deeds of a possible predecessor of Narmer, this lentoid limestone ceremonial weapon (c. 3050 BCE) is carved in low relief. It shows the ruler in the White Crown of Upper Egypt cutting the soil, perhaps ritually inaugurating the agricultural season. An officer kneels to receive the first clod. On the top is a row of standards, the emblems of different provinces. There are fan bearers, and the flow of water is indicated.

Following the Predynastic period, the mace becomes more of a ceremonial object than a weapon, conveying a religious concept or reinforcing the preeminent status of the pharaoh.

c. 3100–3000 BCE Evidence of dozens of tall jars containing the ash of vegetable matter suggests that funerary ritual items are placed in graves.

c. 3050–2663 BCE The practice of burying wives, servants, guards, even pet animals, in pits around the grave of a ruler is in vogue.

- Religious belief in the permanence of the realm of the dead does not prevent looters from pillaging graves or desecrating dead bodies. (In one grave at Abydos only the linen-wrapped and bejeweled arm of a queen survives.)

A beaker with goats and sheep, discovered in a grave at Naqada.

c. 3050 BCE A ceremonial limestone mace head in the Hierakonpolis main deposit depicts the legendary king Scorpion.

- The Narmer Palette of dark green slate is made in Hierakonpolis.
- The Narmer Palette has signs and relief carving that together convey the message, "The King, the incarnation of Horus, makes captive the marsh dwellers."

c. 3050 BCE Political unification of Upper and Lower Egypt, when, according to a priest, Manetho (c. 3000 BCE), writing the history of Egypt under the rule of thirty-one dynasties, Menes is the first king. Other chronicles too begin with Menes, a culture hero whose name does not occur on any artifact, but who is possibly the same individual as Narmer. (Manetho and other sources ascribe the building of a new capital at Memphis to Menes, who gives it white-washed walls.)

c. 3050 BCE Changes occur in burial practices; at Abydos each burial has several underground rooms containing offerings; it is capped by a mound of earth. By 2700 BCE the superstructure becomes larger and is made of mud bricks, with a niched facade.

c. 3050–2900 BCE The ceremonial cosmetic palette dedicated in a temple is typical of the period of the political unification of Upper and Lower Egypt.

MOVEMENT ALONG THE WATERWAY

It was easy to transport grain, fish, and oil from villages to towns because of the waterways. To sail down the Nile a boat needed oars, but it mainly took advantage of the current; coming upstream meant going against the current, but taking advantage of the prevalent wind that blows from the north. Wheeled carts and wagons appeared later in Egypt than in western Asia and Mesopotamia, not because of technological backwardness, but because the Nile provided a means of cheap transport.

Boats and other river vessels were an essential part of daily life.

People traveled by boat for pleasure and for work, to transport livestock or merchandise, and also for religious processions to pilgrim centers and burial places. Boats were classified as fishing boats, traveling boats, kitchen boats, freight boats, and pleasure boats. Huge blocks of stone were transported by boat, which indicates the use of clever design and careful construction. Sometimes, rafts were made of tied-up logs and used to float heavy material downstream. Papyrus boats with high prows were used for ritual journeys, but also by fishermen.

Sails were rectangular and made of linen, and required a great deal of rope length. Occasionally the mast for the sail was bipod, to spread the weight. Red Sea boats are shown with very broad sails. There were two fixed paddles on either side of the stern or else there was a single steering oar. Near Heliopolis, a boat was buried sometime in the fifth century BCE—it was made of local sycamore wood, shaped like a spoon, and had a length of about 36 feet.

Left: The papyrus reed, found along the Nile, supplied the material for numerous writings, such as this funeral text, written in Hieratic c. 525-343 BCE.
Overleaf: A Nubian slave.

THE CATARACTS
AND BEYOND

Egyptian life was rarely sealed off from the Eastern and Western deserts. In these there were oasis dwellers and pastoralists who moved between the chain of oases, particularly in the Western Desert. If Egypt was never entirely cut off from desert life, it was not culturally or politically separate from Nubia, the "land of Kush" south of Aswan, either. Throughout history, the southern frontier of Egypt has been near Aswan, with Elephantine Island on the First Cataract or waterfall. (There are four more cataracts upstream, in Nubia.) The cataracts were stretches on the Nile bed, with huge protruding granite rocks and rapids that made navigation difficult.

Nubians often enlisted in the army and their cemeteries are found here and there in the valley. The name Medjay, which was used for a group from lower Nubia, ultimately came to mean "policeman." The pharaohs who were interested in ivory, ebony, ostrich feathers, monkeys, animal skins and, above all, gold, built frontier posts to guard the Upper Nile beyond Aswan when circumstances allowed. Slave raids and military incursions were frequent.

Several immigrant groups settled in the Nile valley and were assimilated in the local society. Agricultural prosperity and access to gold are factors that made for the greatness of Egypt. After the harvest in March and April, there was a large workforce available for construction sites of the pharaohs.

Egyptian life and culture centered on the fertile alluvial valley with its black soil, while the red deserts were the locale of the Other, associated with wild animals, a source of danger.

c. **3050–2800 BCE** Craftsmen make beads and also animal and human figurines of faience and master the technique of polychromy by blending two faience mixtures.

c. **3050–2813 BCE** Most Dynasty I rulers, from Narmer/Menes onward, are buried at Saqqara, with cenotaphs at Abydos.

c. **3000 BCE** Perhaps a brief Egyptian expansion into south Palestine: Egyptian pottery is found there.

- Faience figure of a baboon, an animal of tropical Africa, is found at Abydos.

- Evidence of ivory coming from Nubia. It is used for furniture legs and labels occasionally inscribed with rulers' names.

c. **3000 BCE** Houses are mainly of mud plastered over reeds, with posts supporting the roof. Later, there is evidence of building with mud bricks, with massive roof logs (often of cedar wood).

c. **3000 BCE (onward)** Memphis on the west bank of the Nile is associated with royalty and is the political and administrative center. It is the place of the pharaoh's coronation and anniversary celebrations. Pharaohs ritually circumambulate its perimeter.

c. **3000–2665 BCE** Royal tombs are built of brick at Abydos and Saqqara in large, deep pits, roofed with wooden planks. Some burial chambers are paneled with Lebanese cedar; others are stocked with provisions for the afterlife.

c. **3000 BCE** Gold is increasingly used for artifacts to be buried with the dead at Abydos and Saqqara.

c. **3000 BCE** The tradition is born that Abydos is the place where the god Osiris lies buried.

- From now on rippled-surface flint knives with carved handles are possibly used to sacrifice animals in temples; some of these are quite large (26 inches long).

c. **3000 BCE (onward)** Hierakonpolis and Naqada lose their old importance. Buto and Maadi on the delta will soon be abandoned. At Maadi the most recent layer in the archaeological record is nothing but a scattering of ash and human bones.

c. **3000 BCE (onward)** Wooden buildings are constructed, covered with mats, reeds, or wooden slats, such as the "tent" of Queen Hetepheres at Giza.

c. **3000–2870 BCE** The earliest papyrus scrolls from this period are in a storeroom in a tomb at Saqqara. They are blank, ready for writing.

THE PHARAOH

"Pharaoh" has come to us from the term used in the Old Testament for the Egyptian ruler. It comes from the word *per-'o*, meaning the "great house" from which all of Egypt was ruled. In the second millennium BCE, *per-'o* came to mean the king himself, but the convention in modern Egyptology has been to refer to all rulers up to the Roman annexation as "pharaoh." In an inscription in the sarcophagus chamber of the pyramid of Unas (2385–2355 BCE), the last king of Dynasty V, the sky-goddess tells the king, "Re-Atum, your son comes to you, this Unas comes to you! May you cross the sky united in the dark, May you rise in lightland, the place where you shine! Make your seat in heaven, among the stars of heaven, for you are the Lone Star, You shall look down on Osiris as he commands the spirits [in the netherworld]."

Statues of the deified pharaoh Ramesses II on the rock-cut temple of three state deities at Abu Simbel.

The pharaoh as a lion, symbol of power, devours his enemies.

A STRING OF NAMES

In the heyday of pharaonic power, a king could have five separate names, which were personal, royal, religious, or secular: (1) as the reincarnation of Horus, the falcon god, the king had a "Horus name" written in a rectangle showing the vertical recesses of a palace facade (the serekh) with the falcon on top. After the name would be the standard phrase "Horus strong bull arisen in Thebes"; (2) the Two Ladies name, written with the signs of the female vulture and the cobra deities, signifying rule over Upper and Lower Egypt ("The Two Ladies Enduring of Kingship"); (3) a name followed by the phrase "Powerful of strength, holy of appearance"; (4) a name referring to the sedge of Upper Egypt and the bee of Lower Egypt combined, written in a cartouche (in the case of Tuthmosis III, it was "Menkheperre," his first name); (5) the Nomen, or personal name, given at birth, with the phrase "Son of Re" also written in a cartouche (such as "Tuthmosis, Ruler of Truth").

Pharaohs of the New Kingdom emphasized Amun, the ancient god of Thebes, their capital, sometimes merging him with Re: Amun-Re gave victory to a king, or Amun impregnated a royal wife. Theogamy is claimed with great delicacy in one scene, with the royal wife seated opposite Amun, his left hand touching her hand, and his right hand offering the hieroglyph meaning "life." The accompanying inscription states that Amun "found her as she slept in the innermost part of the palace. She awoke on account of a divine fragrance and turned toward the king [the god Amun had taken the form of the reigning king] ... his love, it entered her body."

- It is believed that after death, the pharaoh, the Son of the Sun (Re), is assimilated into the sun by journeying across the waters to the horizon. Therefore, boats are buried in pits at pyramid sites.

c. 2700 BCE (onward) The agricultural estate is an institution that organizes the cultivation of tracts for the benefit of particular royal persons, cults of dead rulers, or of deities.

2700–2190 BCE As earlier, *mastabas* are built for dead priests, officers, and nobility. These are boxlike, aboveground structures, like the mud benches in present-day house courtyards, where statues of the owner, inscribed with his name, are placed.

- A funerary ritual at the mastabas develops, beginning with relatives bringing food and assembling for a ritual meal soon after the burial.

2700–2200 BCE In spite of the use of copper, stone remains important: huge numbers of flint tools indicate the perforation and shaping of stone beads.

c. 2680 BCE Upper Egypt is ascendant and pharaoh Peribsen discards the Horus epithet (associated with the delta) and uses the symbol of Seth. Egypt is now organized into provinces or nomes, with regionally controlled irrigation. Each has its own emblem and is often ruled by a nomarch.

2680 BCE The great sage Imhotep, believed to be an architect and astronomer, designs the Step Pyramid at Saqqara; he is a priest of the sun god at Heliopolis. From this time to the end of the pharaonic period, the priesthood at Heliopolis are the intellectuals who observed the passage of the sun and stars through the sky and laid the foundations of astronomy.

c. 2670 BCE Khasekhemy, the last ruler of Dynasty II, finally unites the land and has both the Horus and the Seth symbols written with his name.

2670 BCE (onward) Hieroglyphic writing of the Horus-names of early rulers is enclosed in *serekhs*, which also showas the palace-facade motif.

2670 BCE (onward) For several centuries, Heliopolis (Cairo) remains the intellectual center of Egypt. Imhotep is an early figure, and the historian Manetho, one of the later priests. Priests of the sun god observe the movement of the sun and lay the foundations of Egyptian cosmogony.

THE KING AND PROTOCOL AT COURT

The pharaoh's Red Crown of Upper Egypt and White Crown of Lower Egypt were carefully kept in a special shrine when not in use. His regalia also included a long staff or crook symbolizing dominion, a mace, a bull's tail, and a false beard signifying divinity. Headdresses could be depicted with the uraeus, symbol of Wadjet, and/or the hood of the cobra goddess.

People could have an audience with the king only at set hours. His personal routine was also arranged according to a strict schedule. His jewels, clothes, and boxes were the king's alone, and were consecrated before use. Early depictions show his sandal-bearer and foot washer in attendance.

The people would kiss the ground before the feet of the pharaoh—it was a great privilege to be allowed to kiss his feet. The king would move around his city in a formal procession. He would make "appearances" at a balcony, looking down on his people greeting and revering him, and on such occasions would have gifts distributed to them. On certain public occasions, the pharaoh would make offerings to the gods.

There was an elaborate etiquette and a hierarchy of court personnel. A "sole friend" was of higher status than a "royal acquaintance." There were overseers of the palace and overseers of the audience hall. In New Kingdom times, the position of royal scribe may have meant being a kind of secretary to the king, and there now appeared the post of "fan-bearer on the right side of the king." All senior officials were dependent on the king's permission for procuring slabs of good stone (limestone, granite) for their own mastabas, and all inscriptions on such tombs refer to this in the opening sentence, "A boon that pharaoh gives." High officials were also bestowed with sumptuous royal gifts of gold or chariots at the pleasure of the pharaoh.

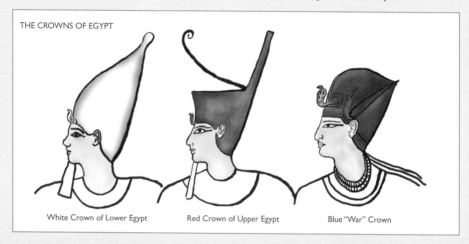

THE CROWNS OF EGYPT

White Crown of Lower Egypt   Red Crown of Upper Egypt   Blue "War" Crown

RESPECTED IN DEATH

For the most part the pharaoh was distant from the people in daily life. As for death, his privileged and exclusive afterlife is best conveyed by the great pyramids of the Old Kingdom. A New Kingdom text reveals that a "statue of the lord (life, prosperity, health!)" was kept by the chief treasurer in a shrine in his home. At Amarna, a stela depicting Amenophis III and his queen has been found in a residential house. Kings themselves can be shown making offerings to earlier kings of Egypt, and on many occasions they had the tombs of their predecessors repaired or conserved. In a wall carving in the temple at Abydos, Sethos I (c.1290 BCE) is depicted in low relief with his son, both of them making

SCARABS

Shaped like the dung beetle (Scarabaeus sacer), scarabs were amulets, seals, and ornaments–often all three together. They were first made of the soft steatite, glazed in shades of green and blue; later, a range of materials, including red stones, malachite, terra-cotta, and faience were used to make scarabs.

As ornaments, scarabs were incorporated in necklaces and rings, or worn as pendants. As charms they protected the wearer against demons or evil thoughts. They could carry a message: "Firm of heart," or "Amun is strength," or "May Amun give a good new year." This protection was good even for the afterlife, so scarabs were sewn onto mummy cloths or placed on a corpse. Known as "heart scarabs," these came into use in the period of the Hyksos, and one of the earliest heart scarabs was found on the mummy of a priest of Amun. They were typically of green material.

A lapis lazuli scarab inset in a gold amulet.

Some of the prayers written on them are echoes of the spells in the Pyramid Texts. One prayer inscribed on a heart scarab reads:

"O my heart which I received from my Mother, my heart which I received from my Mother, do not testify against me! Do not create opposition to me among the judges, do not tip the scales against me in the presence of the Keeper of the Balance!"

Scarabs of very large size were inscribed for the Dynasty XVIII pharaoh Amenophis III (1388–1348 BCE) with news of five events in the first eleven years of his reign. They mention how heroic he was with wild cattle and lions; the creation of a lake or allocating land for his queen, Tiy; a statement of the boundaries of his kingdom; and the "miraculous" arrival in his kingdom of the daughter of Nahrina (the Mitannian kingdom), with more than 300 young women in her party. The scarabs were copied by the dozens and spread throughout the kingdom of Amenophis III.

When used as seals (generally from the time of Dynasty XII), scarabs were pressed on wet clay closing jars, boxes, the doors of rooms, or official letters. These seals were inscribed with the name of the ruling pharaoh or a high official, such as the keeper of the royal seal.

Right: Scarab of King Amenemhet II.
Far right: A human-headed scarab.

offerings. The text states that the offerings are made to seventy-five royal ancestors. Each of these previous kings is named in a cartouche; the seventy-sixth cartouche carries the name of Sethos. This was a common temple ritual, as offerings were often made to the statues of past kings (here they were made to their names).

An inscription on a wall of the mortuary temple of Pepy I (2343 2297 BCE) gives an indication of the deification of the pharaoh at death: "Command the Living One, the son of Sothis, To speak for this Pepy, To establish for Pepy a seat in the sky! Pepy is one with these four gods: Pepy frees himself from the fetters of the earth."

PRIVATE LIVES

There are few portraits of the pharaoh as a private person, and most of these are of the radical Akhenaten, who is shown in family scenes with his wife and daughters. Written sources do, however, give us many clues about the personal foibles of pharaohs—they could be given to cruelty, encourage sycophants, rage against their servants, indulge themselves, and escape their royal life in secrecy at night. There is also a genre of literature called the "royal story," in which a regular incident is the consultation and discussion by the pharaoh with his courtiers when contingencies arise.

Akhenaten kissing his daughter (below right), and with Nefertiti and their daughters (below left).

What the ancient Egyptians called the "Great House" or "Residence" may often be understood as the state. The head of the state was the pharaoh, and its many arms were the army or king's bodyguard, officialdom, and the scribes (for the administration of such a large area and the imposition of a central authority could not but depend on a detailed written record). At least until the New Kingdom, there was also a priesthood, dependent on the pharaoh for its appointment and for its connections with the sources of power. After Dynasty XVIII, however, the priests gradually moved away from the apparatus of the king and became powerful in their own right, partly on account of the huge landed estates that the temples had come to own.

The pharaoh dispensed justice, law, and order, personified by the figure of the goddess Maat, whose statue he offers in an act designed to ensure that the world will be safe and secure.

TRADE

The state was the major agency to engage in trade. Mediterranean sea boats were constructed in state boat yards. In one version of the official annals (the Palermo stone), one of the years of the reign of Snoferu (2597–2547 BCE), the first ruler of Dynasty IV, was remembered for the arrival of forty ships laden with cedar logs from Byblos.

Ramesses II gave a sea ship and personnel for trade to a temple at Abydos. Most temples had, among their staff, "traders" who saw to the exchange of grain, linen, papyrus, and oil in such a way that the temple could maintain adequate stocks of a range of goods. Paintings in the tomb of one of the nomarchs of the Oryx Nome show him receiving a group of traders from southern Palestine. There is little evidence of the existence of private trade and no separate merchant class ever emerged in pharaonic times.

INFRASTRUCTURE

Some quarrying expeditions were so large (about 17,000 skilled and unskilled workers) that only the central administration could manage their recruitment and provisioning for the duration of the work. Unskilled stonecutters were grouped in tens and hundreds. Occasionally local Nubians were recruited. All these workers out in their camps in the Eastern Desert required the protection of soldiers. There was some degree of actual road surfacing near some mines: from the Hatnub alabaster quarry to the right bank of the Nile, a distance of about twelve miles, the way was paved with stones to facilitate transportation.

Masters of the roads ensured that land routes in the desert were kept safe.

In the beginning there was no standing army staffed by men who were soldiers for life. The army was raised for a particular campaign and among the recruits were desert Nubians (Medjay) as well as Egyptian peasants. Nomarchs and provincial officials would raise the levy. Perhaps only the king's bodyguard was properly equipped as a strong force—a small standing army.

Once there were sustained imperial ambitions, however, the pharaohs had to have a military organization that could equal that of the Mitannians and Hittites in Asia. Besides, chariot warfare required trained warriors. Thus, a professional army came into existence.

In all periods, an army, however levied, had work other than fighting to do. Companies could be sent out to mines and quarries to procure specified materials. The forts built around the Second Cataract during the reign of Sesostris III (1881–1840 BCE) were certainly defensive posts, sending recruits out for surveillance and to search for human and animal tracks. Their garrisons or forts kept contact with one another by using smoke signals or through regular written messages. Nubians carrying goods could enter Egypt by river or on foot only through one of these forts, which thus became conduits of trade and diplomacy.

A SOLDIER'S LIFE

Specialist scribes kept recruitment records, and many texts of the New Kingdom refer to military matters: training young men; placing soldiers on garrison duty over the course of their careers; replacement or reappointment of the palace guard every ten days. On retirement from the army some soldiers were granted small plots of land. When foreign soldiers—Libyans, Greeks, or others—were employed, they too appear to have been entitled to land on retirement.

By the end of Dynasty XVIII, the general Horemheb was strong enough to seize political power and the throne.

A literary text refers to the lot of the ordinary soldier: he marches to Palestine carrying his bread and water on his back as if he were a donkey. He has to drink foul water when his supply runs out. By the time he returns to the homeland, he is like "worm-eaten wood," himself on the back of an ass. Yet other sources say that soldiers could share in war booty: cattle and weapons, if not also gold, silver, and jewelry.

Models of soldiers were buried as part of the funerary goods for protection of a person in the afterlife, but in later periods they also represented the growing need for an organized army, composed of both local and Nubian mercenaries.

STATE-ORGANISED PRODUCTION

A cattle census taken every two years is recorded in the Old Kingdom and the years of a reign remembered as "Time Four of the Count."

Pharaohs sent expeditions out to procure materials, or else gave the rights to temples. Sethos I gave the temple of Abydos the rights to extract gold from certain mines in the Eastern Desert, providing a well at the mines for the workers. The Amun temple at Karnak was also granted such rights, and in the time of the New Kingdom, was a major employer of goldsmiths.

The high standards of Egyptian craftsmanship can, in large part, be ascribed to the organization of craft workshops under state or temple management, with a managerial infrastructure to handle written records, state deliveries of materials and tools, and supervision. In boat construction yards on the banks of the Nile, each stage of work was supervised and documented. Artisans were provided with basic food rations, fish, meat, firewood, and water supplies, and also with cloth. They enjoyed a better standard of life than peasants, but with less independence in making production decisions.

CRAFT WORKSHOPS
- Furnished the temples.
- Made items for pharaoh's personal use.
- Made items for tombs of the elite.

SOME TITLES OF OFFICIALS
- Chief of all Craftsmen.
- Chief of the Goldworkers of the Estate of Amun.
- Chief of the Makers of Thin Gold.
- Overseer of the Treasury of Gold and Silver.

2670 BCE By this time, mud bricks are being used for constructing houses, palaces, town walls, and altars. Niches or recesses in outer walls are characteristic features.

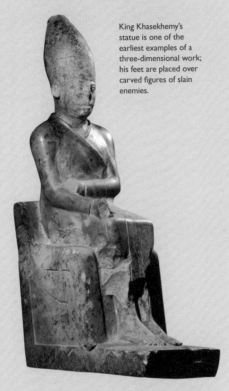

King Khasekhemy's statue is one of the earliest examples of a three-dimensional work; his feet are placed over carved figures of slain enemies.

c. 2670 BCE Stone statues of Khasekhemy seated on a throne begin the tradition of portraying the pharaoh in three-dimensional and monumental stone sculpture.

2663–2195 BCE Age of the Old Kingdom, Dynasties III to VI. Most of the distinctive features of the pharaonic civilization fall into place during this age.

2663–2470 BCE Cemeteries exist at Saqqara, Dahshur, and Giza, west of the Nile, near Memphis.

2663–2470 BCE Shallow reliefs and paintings on the walls of funerary monuments provide the major sources of information on everyday life (as occupation debris of settlements of the period does not exist in any substantial measure).

2663–2200 BCE A huge number of *mastabas* are built at Saqqara.

2663–2597 BCE Dynasty III. The first ruler, Sanakht, reigns till 2654 BCE. He is the grandson of Khasekhemy.

2663–2195 BCE Small painted stone statues (less than 8 inches high), portraying servants, are deposited in tombs to "serve" the deceased in the afterlife.

c. 2663–29 BCE Reliefs in Wadi Maghara, Sinai, show Sanakht, Djoser, and Sekhamkhet smiting enemies and are proof of Dynasty III expeditions into that desert for turquoise.

2660–2470 BCE Ivory is extensively used for furniture parts and ownership labels, which are often pictorially inscribed.

2660 BCE (onward) Stone comes into use for lintels and doorways, later for funerary monuments. Imhotep is credited with the first building in stone.

2654–1300 BCE This is the age of pyramids being built exclusively for the ruler. Because of

The Step Pyramid of Djoser at Saqqara, with adjacent shrines and chapels built for ritual celebrations.

49

OFFICIALS AND THE LAW

Egypt has not produced the range of laws, statutes, and legal codes that Mesopotamia has done, and we thus have to make inferences about the legal principles behind the state infrastructure. Written documents were drawn up when property was sold, when an inheritance was decided by a parent, and in similar matters. When a king made an endowment of land that would yield an income adequate for the maintenance of offerings to his soul in perpetuity, such property does not seem to have been alienable, but we do not know enough about the laws concerning landholdings.

The last chief minister of Tuthmosis III (d. 1424 BCE) at Thebes was Rekhmire, and his tomb depicts the scene of his law court. Rolls of papyrus are displayed to him as judge, purported to contain all the laws of Egypt. We know that a chief minister took "an oath of office," administered by the ruler. Among his duties was the maintenance of records of legal papyri, called "house documents"— earlier, these had been lodged with local officials. However, for the commoner, for whom a journey to Thebes merely to lodge a sealed contract in the official residence of this minister was a difficult task, the way out was to use the "scribe and witness" document in place of the "house document." The former was not sealed, but was written in a prescribed format so that no one could make additions at a later date.

People took loans, especially in the Ptolemaic period when the economy began to be monetized. Rates of interest could be as high as 10 percent. A man could offer his readiness to receive a hundred blows should he fail to return the loan as security. Another interesting practice was that a legal dispute did not end with the issue of a written judgment: the defeated party was required to state in writing that he or she submitted to the judgment—and thus would do as the judgment required.

Statues were made of important officials such as this life-sized one of Chancellor Nakht, found in his tomb at Asyut (c. 2050 BCE).

NOMES AND NOMARCHS

From about 2700 BCE the long strip of the Nile Valley was divided into nomes, or provinces, for administrative purposes. Each was perhaps originally a natural basin irrigated by the annual flood, starting out as an independent polity until unification by Narmer. In subsequent history, the hereditary nobles of the respective localities were in charge and their powers waxed and waned in inverse proportion to that of the pharaohs. In Lower Egypt there were twenty nomes, beginning with Memphis; in Upper Egypt there were twenty-two nomes, beginning with Elephantine, making forty-two nomes in all.

The administrative division of the nomes survived until 308 CE; Nomes in the Roman period even minted their own coins. The pharaohs of Dynasty XII established their capital on the boundary of Upper and Lower Egypt at el Lisht (Itj-tawi), and enjoyed unprecedented power. However, the founder, Ammenemes I (1994–1964 BCE), had come to power with the support of certain nomarchs, and restored their privileges as a reward. They retained titles such as Great Chief of the Oryx Nome. In other nomes, however, heads of new families were installed as chiefs.

For their part, nomarchs were required to provide ships, supplies, and soldiers for the pharaoh's resources or military expeditions. They could be made to accompany the pharaoh on a campaign upstream to Lower Nubia, or on a tour of inspection in the delta. There was much emulation of the pharaoh's behavior and culture.

After about 1850 BCE, the title of great chief for a nome was rarely used. Instead, there were town districts and all administration emanated from the pharaoh's residence, where a hierarchy of ministers, high-status officials, lower-level administrators, and scribes are known to have functioned. This phenomenon, in its turn, made it possible for provincial landowners, craftsmen, and traders to rise in wealth and influence in their own provinces.

the widespread belief that after death the ruler travels in a boat to the horizon and joins Re, the sun god, the royal *mastaba* is transformed into the pyramid, which contains solar and religious symbolism to help launch the pharaoh on his journey.

2654–35 BCE Stone walls continue to have half-columns, a remnant of older construction techniques that used reed columns.

2654–35 BCE Reign of Djoser, brother of Sanakht. He begins the tradition of funerary architecture in stone, and is buried under the Step Pyramid at Saqqara, a funerary complex of monumental scale, overlooking the city of Memphis.

2654 BCE The Step Pyramid of Djoser is built 205 feet high, with six unequal stages of brick-size stones; the temples, sarcophagi, and royal burial chambers are placed deep down in the complex, and are all built of stone slabs. Its perimeter wall has buttresses and recesses at regular intervals, perhaps an echo of Mesopotamian influences perceptible in an earlier period.

Seated life-size statues of Prince Re-hotep and his wife, painted in typical brown for the man and cream for the woman.

2654–35 BCE Relief carvings are made in wood, as well as large painted stone statues, such as those of Re-hotep, high priest of Heliopolis, and his wife.

• A larger-than-life limestone statue is made of Djoser, in a royal robe and seated on a throne, at Saqqara.

COMPULSORY LABOR

More than a harvest tax, what the state demanded from the people was labor. An inscription of Ramesses III refers to a custom of calling up one man in every ten for the army and perhaps the same custom prevailed for unskilled labor. Temples had lands granted to them in the course of the centuries, and people could be recruited to work on these lands.

Labor was an Egyptian's compulsory obligation to the state: if one tried to abscond, he could be imprisoned. Thus, the logic of the ushabti figures buried with the dead, so that the latter may not have to sweat and strain in the afterlife.

A quarrying expedition to the desert might be comprised of unskilled workers, officials to supervise them, scribes to record, as well as people to mill, bake, brew, hunt, supply fish, and carry water. Sometimes it could be Asiatic prisoners of war who were employed in the stone quarries. Laborers could be sent from one part of Egypt to another for plowing or harvesting lands in the state sector. Land surveyors and tax collectors demanded grain from farmers. Before the time when the temple of Amun

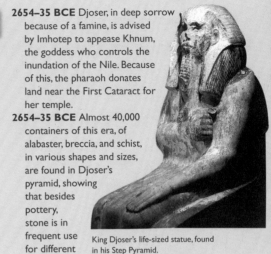

2654–35 BCE Djoser, in deep sorrow because of a famine, is advised by Imhotep to appease Khnum, the goddess who controls the inundation of the Nile. Because of this, the pharaoh donates land near the First Cataract for her temple.

2654–35 BCE Almost 40,000 containers of this era, of alabaster, breccia, and schist, in various shapes and sizes, are found in Djoser's pyramid, showing that besides pottery, stone is in frequent use for different items and that the drill is now used.

King Djoser's life-sized statue, found in his Step Pyramid.

2650 BCE The names and titles of Imhotep are carved, along with those of the ruler Djoser, on a statue plinth. This is an important indication of the respect that Egyptian society shows to intellectuals.

2650–2400 BCE Pyramid building at Giza involves the use of local limestone for the core construction, Tura limestone from across the Nile for the casing, and pink granite from Aswan for the burial chambers.

2650 BCE (onward) Copper wire is now in use. It is made from flat, thin strips or is drawn out of rolled copper through progressively narrower perforations.

• From now on, the lunar calendar of twelve months of thirty days each is adjusted to the solar cycle, and the new civil calendar is given an additional five feast days in the year.

2640 BCE A wall painting in the tomb of a high official indicates that capacity measures for grain have been standardized: it shows two sets of measures, in wood and leather.

2635 BCE The mortuary temple of Djoser at Saqqara is oriented to the north to enable the dead pharaoh to reach the northern skies and guide the north star.

2635 BCE Technique of blue-green faience is mastered. It decorates the walls of the Step Pyramid of Djoser at Saqqara. Tiles are made to look like rush mats.

2635–29 BCE Reign of Sekhemkhet. He is buried in an unfinished pyramid at Saqqara; his name

became autonomous, it could, on occasion, be required to supply to the royal household in Thebes a hundred loaves of bread a day—which would be a fraction of the amount consumed. Much of the temple's land was held as small farms that surrendered about six percent of the yield to the temple authorities, leaving enough to feed a family of four or five people. Such tenants in any case also received supplies when they worked as soldiers, herdsmen, and junior priests for one month in every four.

Above: Models of workers testify to a robust system of labor, as depicted in this carpenters' workshop.

REWARD AND PUNISHMENT

A delinquent taxpayer is caught and receives punishment.

Temples owned a great area of arable land and there were many people, such as artisans, who were totally dependent on the state for their subsistence. It was a custom for officials to be assigned land for the duration of their tenure.

Supplying provisions for all involved in state projects required expert management.

HONORARY TITLES

This was not a bureaucratic system in the strict sense. Titles were honorific in nature (vizier, governor of Upper Egypt, chief seal bearer) and did not literally reflect on the work a senior official actually carried out. The state through the agency of the pharaoh made maat prevail. Yet this was not a welfare state. There were no laws to protect either a community or individual.

The post of overseer of granaries of Upper and Lower Egypt was a senior and prestigious position. Many ration lists on papyrus have been found, listing jugs of beer and loaves of bread. Workers were given wooden tokens shaped like loaves of bread on which were inscribed numbers or quantities of grain, and they would present these tokens when they collected their rations. More than the standard ration of perhaps a jug of beer and ten loaves (for senior officials) could be held on credit, or else—in the absence of coined money—exchanged by the recipient for something else.

Once, the system failed. In Year 29 of the reign of Ramesses III, a formal complaint was made by the residents of Deir el-Medina to the temple administrators that their rations had not been paid. When this was of no avail, workers protested at one of the royal mortuary temples. Written petitions were sent, and there was a further wait until the provisions arrived.

also occurs on a relief in Wadi Maghara in Sinai, in which he smites a local man.

2635–29 BCE A burial deposit of Sekhemkhet includes twenty-one gold bracelets, a gold necklace, a gold box, and tweezers of electrum.

2623–21 BCE Nebkhare rules only two years.

2621–2597 BCE Rule of Huny, the last king of Dynasty III.

2600 BCE (onward) The belief appears that the waters of Chaos gave rise to a primeval mound (the *benben*), on which the Creator appears as the bird of light, dispelling the darkness. In the course of religious syncretism there is then a series of gradual creations of the gods Osiris, Isis, Seth, and Nephthys.

2600 BCE Quarrying of huge stone blocks begins, and copper saws, wedges, chisels, and wet sand are used for this purpose, together with flaked stone tools which, however, break easily.

• Gold mining begins in the Eastern Desert.

2597–2470 BCE In the pyramid temple, food and drink are regularly offered to the dead by priests and administrators. The staff who take care of the maintenance and rituals are paid in bread, beer, grain, sometimes cloth and meat. These provisions come from estates endowed by rulers for each pyramid complex.

• Pyramid rituals also involve the use of boats, perhaps as a metaphor for the crossing over into the land of the dead. Boats are used, dismantled, and then buried in pits near the pyramid.

2597–2471 BCE Dynasty IV, builders of five great pyramids.

2597–47 BCE Snoferu, founder of Dynasty IV, is the son-in-law of Huny, the last king of Dynasty III (his wife bears the title "Daughter of the God," i.e., the ruler). He builds the Bent Pyramid at Dahshur but is interred under the Red Pyramid. A pyramid is built for Snoferu at Dahshur, but during construction its shape was changed, with a more gentle angle introduced about halfway up. It therefore appears to have a "bent" profile. (It may be sinking because its foundation is not adequately firm.)

2597 BCE (onward) The construction of *mastabas* changes. The body is now buried deep undergound, recessed in a chamber that contains a pit for the viscera; a *serdab* in the complex, that cannot be entered but only has a peep-hole, contains statues of the dead person.

c. 2597–47 BCE Snoferu, the founder of Dynasty

IV, leaves his imprint at the turquoise quarry in Sinai.

• According to the Palermo stone, Snoferu leads a campaign to Kush (Nubia) and brings back thousands of prisoners of war as well as 200,000 head of cattle. He also fights the Tjehenyu people of Libya and receives 40 boats laden with cedar wood, probably from Lebanon.

2590 BCE An Egyptian settlement is established at Buhen near the head of the Second Cataract.

2560 BCE The cult of the god Min begins. He is the thunderbolt, shown standing ithyphallic in a tall, feathered headdress, brandishing a flail in one hand. He is associated with the town of Coptos.

2550–2475 BCE Thousands of peasants are recruited on a rotating basis for the construction of royal funerary complexes. Enormous skills in management are needed to coordinate the teams of men working on different tasks at the site; sometimes the heir to the throne takes over the supervision.

2550–25 BCE In a deep shaft at Giza, with the burial equipment for the mother of Cheops (possibly Queen Mother Hetepheres), lie superb examples of Egyptian wooden furniture: a bed, chairs, a sedan chair, and a canopy for a bed net, along with twenty-six silver bracelets inlaid with butterflies of carnelian, lapis, and turquoise. The burial chamber also contains her embalmed internal organs placed in a special chest. The science of mummification has begun.

Queen Hetepheres's armchair, found at Giza and restored in wood, copper, and gold.

2547 BCE Snoferu is buried not under the Bent Pyramid, but under the Red Pyramid at Dahshur.

2547–24 BCE Reign of Cheops (Khufu), builder of the Great Pyramid. Enclosed with subsidiary tombs and shrines within a massive wall, the pyramid itself contains a complex system of burial chambers and corridors.

2547–24 BCE True pyramids—smooth-sided, not stepped, on a square base with three equal triangular sides—are built at Giza from

Above: Etching of a chariot, to be made into a tomb relief.
Overleaf: The horse-drawn chariot, from which archers could easily fire their arrows, became indispensable to Egypt's military and was part of the elite troop.

The horse that we know now is a species of *Equus* that was domesticated from the wild *Equus ferus*. The natural habitat of *Equus ferus* is the dry steppe of Eurasia. It is an animal that can cope with very little water (it is second only to the camel in this), and is a swift creature with keen sight and hearing, so that it could take off at the least sign of danger, and in the wild would live in loose herds of around 300.

The domesticated horse, *Equus caballus*, is not markedly different from its wild stereotype, and thus it is not possible to be precise from the study of excavated skeletons about the exact date of domestication. Generally it is accepted that the horse was domesticated for its milk and meat in Eurasia (perhaps first on the lower Dnieper) as early as 4000 BCE. At this stage, there could have been some horse riding, but there were no stirrups or saddles.

Gradually, after 3000 BCE, pastoralism developed on the steppe; the winters were spent in base villages near rivers, after which the people moved out with flocks of sheep, cattle, and horses. As pastoralism became more specialized, the people of the steppe learned to build the wheeled wagon drawn by horses. A fully nomadic lifestyle, based on the herding of horses, dates to about 1000 BCE.

Domesticated horses came to western Asia early: about 2000 BCE, representations in terra-cotta were made of horse riders in Mesopotamia. Also in the early second millennium BCE, the Hurrians of northern Syria, under their Mitannian rulers, were perhaps the first to use the horse-drawn war chariot. When the Egyptians developed imperialistic ambitions in Asia, they were compelled to use chariots against their Hittite and Mitannian opponents. Whereas the Hittites developed a heavy vehicle, the chariot in Syria and in Egypt was light enough to be carried by one man, with a long pole attached under the body to the axle, and hitched to two horses; the wheels were large, but because they were spoked they were light.

During one charge led by Tuthmosis III, the enemy Qadesh king saw that all the Egyptian horses were stallions, and let loose a mare in heat. The Egyptian general Amenemhab only averted disaster by quickly slaying the mare.

In war the chariot was a mobile platform that gave an archer a high vantage point from which to shoot his arrows (as he looped the reins around his waist after stopping the horses); the horses were controlled with reins attached to a nose band. A chariot charge could split up a close infantry formation.

Chariots, and the horses that pulled them, were obviously expensive to maintain. Their construction required the right kinds of wood and skilled carpentry; also, they needed repeated repairs. Ultimately, they were of no use against the massed infantries of the Sea Peoples who invaded Egypt after 1200 BCE, with their lances, throwing spears, and other weapons. True cavalry was perhaps only introduced around 940 BCE by Pharaoh Shoshenq I against Israel.

huge blocks of stone. The sides of the largest pyramid have an incline of fifty-one degrees.

2547–2475 BCE Each pyramid complex contains, besides the huge structure, a valley temple on the shore of the Nile, a covered causeway leading to the pyramid enclosure, and a mortuary temple at the east foot of the pyramid for remembrance rites and festivals. Thousands of men transport the huge stone blocks to the building site, and haul them up ramps to position them on the monument.

2547–2200 BCE When a king is interred in a pyramid complex, an entire administrative complex is created to maintain the sanctuaries and carry out the commemorative rituals. All staff work for one month in ten, so that the burden of work is spread. Attendance and ration registers are maintained.

2545 BCE Life-size statues of ordinary people are made in this period.

2540 BCE Pyramid building activity moves north to Giza.

2525 BCE Cheops's son and daughter-in-law are shown in shallow relief, one of the last monumental reliefs to be carved on fine limestone without plaster or paint.

2525 BCE The Great Pyramid stands 480 feet high on a 12-acre base and is constructed of some two million blocks of limestone, many of them 15 tons in weight. Stone of the core is quarried locally; the casing blocks come from Tura on the opposite bank of the Nile. Pink granite comes from Aswan for the burial chambers. (In the medieval period, the casing stones of the Great Pyramid were carried off to build Cairo.)

2524–16 BCE Djedefre is the relatively unknown successor of Cheops.

2524 BCE Cedar wood from Lebanon is used to make a boat placed in the Great Pyramid's enclosure.

2516–2493 BCE Reign of Chephren (Khafre), who lies under the second pyramid of Giza (about 10 feet shorter than Cheops's).

2516–2493 BCE The colossal Sphinx (almost 72 feet high and 230 feet long) is carved out of rock near the second pyramid of Giza. A human-headed recumbent lion, he is protector of the threshold of the royal complex. The royal headdress is puzzling.

2510–2493 BCE A life-size statue of Chephren, in diorite, a very hard stone from Nubia, depicts him seated on a high-backed throne,

The great pyramid complex at Giza.

on which is perched the falcon Horus. The modeling of his face captures his pride.

2500 BCE In a tomb of Chephren's wife at Giza is a representation of copper workers using blowpipes on a burning charcoal pile, and a man hammering a copper plate with a rounded stone.

2500 BCE (onward) The massive, rectangular stone pillar, undecorated, gives way to graceful red granite columns in the form of bunches of papyrus stalks, or with capitals in the form of palm leaves.

2500–2190 BCE Ordinary houses continue to be of either reeds and poles, or mud bricks, and are multiroomed but small, with circular brick silos for grain storage.

2500–2200 BCE Mathematicians and engineers write down exercises and calculations. One piece of stone has an inked diagram showing parallel lines, decreasing in length, which produce the arc of a circle when their ends are joined.

2500–2195 BCE At Coptos there are traces of a temple and a collection of votive items that include huge stone figures of bald and bearded men, ithyphallic, totally different from court sculpture, roughly modeled and depicting some provincial custom.

• Rich and poor use pottery in their day-to-day lives, but it receives no artistic decoration, even though some orange-burnished bowls are attractive.

2500 BCE (onward) Wealthier people use unguents and perfumes on a regular basis, as is evident from tomb offerings of containers and spoons for the purpose.

59

The earliest villages of the Neolithic period were mostly located on elevated levees on the frontier between desert and alluvial plain, at a safe distance from the swift waters of the Nile, and within reach of pastures seasonally available in the wadi beds scouring the desert. The very first villages (of the Badarian and Amratian culture phases in the fifth century BCE) were perhaps those of herding folk settling down to an agricultural life. While along the Upper Nile such settlements were strung out from north to south, in the delta with its rich soils, settlements were dispersed "like knots in a net," and were occupied for long periods of time.

THE VILLAGE HOUSE

Archaeological excavations at a small settlement at Abydos—one of the earliest—yielded traces of mud and wattle huts interspersed with cooking hearths; habitation debris was dumped around the perimeter, including charred grain and animal bones. After a period of building beehive-shaped huts with lumps of mud came the construction of rectangular houses in sun-dried mud bricks, with mud also used as a mortar. In the pharaonic period, people liked to use long and flat bricks to create arched roofs and doorways.

Baked brick came into use only during the Roman period.

Inside their village houses, people had cooking hearths, grain bins, and arrangements for tethering their animals. In some houses there were platforms at the narrow ends of a room: either for sleeping or as the reception area. The walls were whitewashed, often decorated with bands in different colors. The interiors of village and town houses of the common people were, however, dark and probably ridden with flies. Texts recommend

Agriculture was the mainstay of the land; numerous paintings such as this from the *Book of the Dead* depict agricultural activity.

2495 BCE The valley temple of Khafre's pyramid is made of red Aswan granite pillars and ceiling, with an alabaster floor. It houses twenty-three statues of Khafre. His pyramid is cased with limestone blocks of truly gigantic proportions, about 472 feet high.

2493–75 BCE Reign of Mycerinus (Menkaure), who builds the third and smallest pyramid at Giza—one-third the size of the Great Pyramid—for which he uses red granite from Aswan. The associated temple in the Nile Valley, however, is built in brick.

2493–75 BCE A portrait of Mycerinus and his wife, cut from one block of slate, is less imposing than that of Chephren.

King Mycerinus (also known as Menkaure) and his queen, carved in almost equal size. However, the king, as the divine representative, was always shown as being taller.

2480 BCE (onward) The tradition of dancing at funerals is established. In the tomb of Tiy (Dynasty V) girls are seen wearing long skirts over kilts, rows of bands across the chest, and have arms raised in dance.

Dancing girls and musicians.

that house floors be disinfected with natron and water, or a mix of charcoal and certain medicinal plants.

Affluent people slept on wooden beds that sloped down toward the feet, using curved head rests made of wood or stone instead of pillows. Other wooden furniture consisted of chairs (with rush or leather seats), tables, stools, chests, and boxes. Boxes and chests with fine inlay work have been found in tombs. Egyptians liked to make the feet of their furniture in the shape of animals' legs and paws.

DAILY LIFE

Linen weaving on the horizontal loom was an activity in both the village and the town household. Tapestry weaving began in the time of Dynasty XVIII. Activities such as making ropes and baskets and milling grain took place in the courtyard. Women swept their floors with reed brooms, while children played with wooden rattles and spinning tops, animals with movable heads or on wheels, and balls of leather. For adults there were board games, as in many parts of western and southern Asia. As boys grew up, a common rite of passage was circumcision, said to symbolize the transition from boyhood to manhood.

Peasantry as a rule could not afford burial at death, and their corpses may have been thrown in the river, to be devoured by crocodiles. Peasants rarely entered the large temples, confining their worship to visits to local roadside shrines of deities.

HUNTING

Besides engaging in agriculture, rural Egyptians hunted in the dense reed thickets for birds, and also caught fish. Agricultural life in Egypt was easier than in many other regions of the world. The Nile took care of much of the watering and fertilization of fields, and the farmer did not have to plow deeply or deploy lots of oxen to raise water. The scribe would register the output and the tax. No one was exempt from labor on a public project or a temple estate.

The marshes and banks of the Nile yielded rich returns from hunting and fishing.

IMPLEMENTS AND GADGETS

The household probably used implements of flaked and ground stone, and also of copper. Iron was not the universal material of tools and weapons until very late in the pharaonic period. Among the early gadgets and technology was the shaduf, or lever, often seen at the well head; notched rods of stone or wood which were used like modern rulers; weights of different materials—copper, stone and, in the countryside, terra-cotta—which took the shape of a hemisphere or else an animal head. In addition, people weighed things with pans of equal-arm balances, while to measure grain, there was the capacity measure made of wood.

ESSENTIAL ROPE

Ropes of various materials and strengths were used for yoking oxen, climbing date palm trees, pulling water up from wells, and towing boats upstream. Ropes were made of flax, palm fiber (also thick and strong), and halfa grass, the latter used for lashing the planks of a boat together. Sandals were made of rope but in the art we see that many Egyptians went about barefoot.

Knotted ropes were used for measuring land; the main unit, a royal cubit (approximately the length of a man's forearm) was divided into smaller lengths the width of the palm, and subdivided further into finger widths.

Above: Models of men using tools were commonplace in tombs and indicated a hardworking lifestyle.

2475–71 BCE Shepseskaf, last ruler of Dynasty IV, rules in a period of decline. He is buried not under a pyramid but in a sarcophagus-shaped tomb in Saqqara (an indication that something has gone wrong).

2471–64 BCE A colossal statue in hard red granite is made of Userkaf, the stone being so hard that the surviving head shows little detail. The statue would have been 16 feet high.

2471–2355 BCE Dynasty V. Its kings are buried mainly at Abusir and Saqqara. The founder, Userkaf (2471–2464 BCE), builds a sun temple at Abusir, establishing the practice of building sun temples in honor of Re.

• The rulers build distinctive obelisk shrines in their pyramid complexes.

2470–2196 BCE At Byblos on the Lebanese coast, there is a shrine to Hathor, the equivalent of the local goddess Astarte, and objects inscribed with the names of pharaohs up to Pepy II.

2470–2355 BCE Dynasty V relief of birds and other marsh-life is executed with enormous delicacy and accuracy.

2470–2190 BCE This is the high point of court art in the form of reliefs and paintings on pyramid and *mastaba* walls, depicting aspects of everyday life and narratives about individual lives.

2470 BCE (onward) The owner of a *mastaba* or private tomb—but not the pharaoh—is often depicted in a statue as a scribe, seated with a scroll of papyrus, writing or reading.

• Two literary genres, the prayer—for a good reception in the world of the dead and/or for offerings—and the autobiography of the nobleman, take form; pyramid spells continue.

2470–2195 BCE During this period the pharaoh is generally served by his sandal-bearer, barber, keeper of robes and crowns, scribes, and his personal lector-priest.

2470–2196 BCE All aspects of everyday life are depicted on the walls of pyramids and *mastabas* of the nonroyal elite, in relief or in painting.

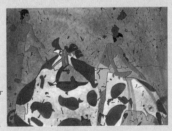

The slaughter of cows, a scene from everyday life.

FOOD AND DRINK

Basic fare for the family consisted of bread, oil, and vegetables. In early Egypt, baking bread and brewing beer from wheat or barley were linked processes. The grain was thoroughly ground, and some of it was soaked in water and set in the sun to ferment. The rest was made to rise with the use of beer and water and then baked in flat loaves on mud trays (or on the hot sand), or else in loaves in long pottery molds (other shapes were also sometimes used). To complete the brewing process, crumbled bread and water were added, as well as old beer, for the right amount of fermentation, and then the nutritious mixture was strained. Its flavor could be improved with dates or spices. Besides beer, wine was also drunk. It is uncertain as to whether this was palm or grape wine during the time of the Old Kingdom, but thereafter vines and wine are attested. Literature and pictures refer to drunkenness in a good-humored way: a Ramesside tomb painting shows an upper-class woman clad in a pleated robe vomiting—it was not considered disgraceful to be intoxicated.

Right: Grape cultivation and wine making was a common occupation.
Below: Craftsmen often worked together in factories.

THE CRAFT WORKERS

Many crafts were practiced in the countryside. Judging from excavated remains and the labels on tomb paintings, there were carpenters, joiners, polishers, leatherworkers, potters, bricklayers, sandal makers, and many others. The process of leathermaking involved a division of labor: tanning the skin in a vat, scraping it clean, stretching it out properly, and then cutting it into strips and using awls for perforating the strips, ready for making into sandals or furniture parts. The many and varied tools of the carpenter have been preserved at many Egyptian sites: the axe, adze, chisel, saw, scraper, and awl, together with instruments for accuracy of line and angle: the measure, the square, and the plumb line. Local woods were used for general purposes, and the imported cedar, yew, and ebony had more restricted uses. Early carpenters made very fine joints and could inlay and overlay with delicacy. At an early date, they also made plywood with six different layers.

As a general rule, pottery was either of Nile silt that was baked to a rich brown-red and was painted in the New Kingdom period in shades of blue, or else there was a better, glossy, "marl clay" pottery, used in Upper Egypt. Pottery was used for dining; there were amphorae for wine and jugs for beer, storage jars, bread molds, lamps, and vases, and also canopic jars for the internal organs to be stored in tombs.

CLOTHING

Out of doors, men and women dressed in linen that was often bleached white in the sun. This set off any stone or faience jewelry worn by the person. Wool was not a popular fabric as it was in contemporary Mesopotamia. Cotton came to Egypt in the first century as a result of trade with India. Silk came with the Rome–China trade.

Garments were simple. For a long time Egyptian women wore simple tight shifts, with a single side seam down the length of the leg, whether calf- or ankle-length. In the early period men, rich and poor, wore kilts, leaving the knees bare. Some of the better ones had fringed or decorated edges. (Men wore wesekh collars just as women did.) During the New Kingdom, modes of attire changed. Women's dresses had stitched sleeves and many fine pleats along the skirt and sleeve ends. Men wore belts and often sashes across the chest.

Both men and women wore wigs, keeping their hair short but cool and free of lice. Wigs were often tightly braided across the top and down the head, but many other styles have been noticed in the art. People applied fragrant oils to the body, not hesitating to compound these with extracts from the bodies of cats, crocodiles, or hippos. For special occasions, cones of animal fat or else of wax were impregnated with myrrh and worn in the hair. As the fat or wax slowly melted, it released the scent of the myrrh. The Egyptians welcomed guests to their homes with garlands of flowers around their necks and perfumed wax cones to put in their hair.

The poor wore simple, sleeveless dresses to stay cool while working.

2470–2355 BCE The priests of Heliopolis wield great influence and the personal names of pharaohs of Dynasty V often contain the word "Re." "Son of Re" is also an epithet frequently mentioned along with the pharaoh's name.

- In pyramid complexes south of Giza obelisks are built on a truncated pyramid (to symbolize the *benben*), with an altar and place for animal sacrifice nearby. It all stands on a platform decorated with reliefs and painting.
- The Sed festival becomes a tradition; after the span of a generation an anniversary of enthronement is celebrated, when the pharaoh is ritually recharged with his magical powers.

2470 BCE (onward) Pyramids for rulers, built at Abusir and Saqqara, are on a much smaller scale than those of the preceding dynasty at Giza.

2470–2355 BCE Six pharaohs of Dynasty V build sun shrines at Abu Gurob near Abusir. These are obelisks with gilded tips placed on truncated pyramids, with adjacent stone altars for animal sacrifice.

2470–2195 BCE Old Kingdom royal inscriptions take three forms: the record of an event, the annalistic record (a year remembered by a particular event), and the decree.

- Pyramid Texts continue to be written: "Your son comes to you [Re], May you cross the united in the dark, May you rise in lightland, the place in which you shine!"

2470–2040 BCE At Elephantine, at the shrine among the cataract boulders, hundreds of small objects in baked clay, faience, stone, and ivory are offered, revealing aspects of a popular, rather than state, cult.

2464–52 BCE Sahure, Userkaf's successor, is buried in a pyramid at Abusir. It is much smaller than those of the preceding dynasty at Giza, but has a wealth of reliefs in white limestone.

2464–52 BCE Sahure's pyramid has a wealth of reliefs depicting the hunt, hippo-baiting, the capture of Libyan chiefs and their cattle, and the return of ships from the Levant with captive Asiatics. (Art historians consider his statue to be of inferior workmanship.) After him, royal statuary is not regularly produced.

2460–20 BCE The sun temples have a valley temple linked by a causeway to the courtyard containing the obelisk, and, as in a true pyramid, there is also a large boat (which may be made of bricks).

2452–42 BCE Neferirkare rules. His pyramid at Abusir is unfinished.

2452–42 BCE Local people take turns to work on the lands, at the storehouses, and for the cult of the dead ruler (as evident from the archive of a pyramid estate). All are paid in grain, bread, and beer.

2450–20 BCE In the tomb of a high official at Abusir are buried large quantities of small blue tablets of faience, with writing and images of the pharaoh and deity.

2450–40 BCE The capacities of different shapes of containers facilitates the systematic accounting of stocks and rations of a temple estate.

- The method of counting is peculiar—only one fraction, that being $\frac{2}{3}$, was ever written with a numerator other than 1. Thus, $\frac{6}{7}$ was written as $\frac{1}{2} + \frac{1}{4} + \frac{1}{14} + \frac{1}{28}$.

2450–2196 BCE Several royal decrees are passed, granting to the priests and dependents of temples and cult centers across the land immunity from compulsory labor and hospitality for official visitors.

2450 BCE Didactic literature comes into being in the form of "instructions" issued by a legendary figure, perhaps a fictional person in some cases, of which the earliest known is the "Instructions of Hardjedef" (Dynasty V).

Ruins of the Step Pyramid complex at Saqqara.

PERFORMING ARTISTS

There were village dancers and musicians who could be hired for entertainment. Musical instruments included the wood or reed flute and other wind instruments blown from the end. There were large harps as in ancient Mesopotamia and, in the New Kingdom, smaller handheld ones. The rhythm could be given by the sistrum rattle or by bone clappers. Drums were played with the hands. The Greeks may have introduced the oboe and panpipes to Egypt.

A painting on an ostracon (potsherd or tile) of a female acrobat/dancer.

BUYING AND SELLING

Art and text reveal that people would visit open-air markets to exchange their wares. Grain could be exchanged for fish or vegetables. The balance of an exchange could be written on an ostracon—a coffin in return for a pig, two goats, two logs, and a certain weight of copper. A seller of property had to draw up a "house document" on papyrus, naming the buyer and giving the names of three witnesses to the sale. An official would roll up the papyrus and seal it. A will also required a house document.

Literature and tomb art also afford glimpses of lively social interactions. One minor ruler exhorts his son to be a craftsman in speech: "Power is in the tongue, speech is mightier than fighting." A silver figurine made in the land of the Hittites was found in a thief's cache near a public well at the town built by Akhenaten. The find included gold and silver that had been melted into long, crude bars and into rings. The archaeologist Flinders Petrie wrote indignantly about an ancient fraud that he happened upon when he excavated the coffin of an infant. On opening the latter he found that the bones were those of an adult knee joint and not of an infant. The "rascal undertaker" had "not troubled to mummify the little brat at all."

2442–13 BCE The reigns of Shepseskare, Neferefre, Niuserre, and Menkauhor, about whom there is little information other than the pyramid of Niuserre at Abusir.

2432–21 BCE Reliefs of Niuserre show the stages of temple building, including placing sacrifices in the foundations and then sealing them.

2420–2196 BCE The burials of high officials at Saqqara are stone complexes of burial and ritual chambers, with additional provisions for the family; Mereruka's tomb has thirty-two decorated chambers.

2413–2385 BCE Isesi (Djedkare) rules and is buried in a pyramid near Saqqara. His vizier, Ptah-hotpe, is the legendary author of a tract of maxims, and is also buried at Saqqara.

2400 BCE The Palermo stone, a stela of black diorite, is inscribed with important historical records. Written horizontally in hieroglyphic script on both sides of the stone are details of the events, festivals, statue making, victories over foreigners, and overseas expeditions for every year of all the previous kings. It also records the annual height of the Nile.

2400 BCE The first glass beads appear in Egypt, but glass as a material gains importance only later. Egyptian pottery is now thrown on the fast wheel.

2385–55 BCE The long reign of Unas (Wenis).

2360 BCE (ONWARD) Not only royal pyramids but *mastabas* are also decorated with excellent examples of court art.

2360 BCE Skilled sculptors work on the tomb of Tiy. One example of their art shows craftsmen making a boat, accurately depicting the tools and the movements of the workers.

2355–2195 Dynasty VI. The rulers do away with the single-minded worship of Re and concentrate their activities around Memphis. Their pyramids are at Saqqara.

- Memphis is the administrative and religious capital, its core a palace complex with a temple. (The site has been silted over by Nile floods and subsoil water makes deep digging impossible.)

2355 BCE Unas is buried in a small pyramid at Saqqara. The 2,296-foot-long causeway of his pyramid has some of the period's best court sculpture (reliefs).

2355 BCE The first known Pyramid Texts are written on the walls of Unas's burial chamber. These hieroglyphic texts are spells, incantations, and hymns for the well-being of a person in the afterlife, and focus on appeasing the god Osiris. The tradition continues until about 2195 BCE.

One of the thirty-two decorated chambers in the mastaba of Mereruka at Saqqara.

2355–43 BCE Reign of Teti, when some of the finest craftsmanship is shown in the *mastaba* of his son-in-law and vizier, Mereruka, at Saqqara.

SAFETY AND SECURITY

There was banditry at certain periods in the countryside. River travel was possibly safer, and certainly cheaper, as the energy was provided by the current of the Nile or else, in the opposite direction, by the prevalent winds from the north.

Occasionally, desert people acted as hunters and trackers for the Egyptian nobility; sometimes small groups of them settled in the valley, and at times desert men fought as mercenaries for Egypt. Invasions from across the deserts were rare, as it was hard for any large army to cross the desert and then attack; small raiding bands were more frequent.

Above: Cats were revered but were also the subject of lighter themes such as this fable drawn on limestone, where a cat with a shepherd's crook and a bag over his shoulder guards geese and their eggs.
Right: A cat coffin; catteries were attached to temples and people paid for their mummification and burial.

CATS

Early in their history, the Egyptians realized that the cat is a useful pet, keeping snakes and the mice that consume food in the house and granary at bay, even if it did hunt wild birds in the reed brakes and marshes. The cat also symbolized a goddess named Bast, originally quite fierce, later like a modern domestic cat. The center of worship of this goddess, with a special temple for her, was the town of Bubastis, which gained in importance around 940 BCE when Sheshonq I was pharaoh. People made annual pilgrimages to the temple.

Egyptians, rich and poor, gave their cats ritual funerals, mummifying their bodies and sometimes also laying rats or mummified rats in their graves. Herodotus wrote in the fifth century BCE that Egyptian people mourned their household cats as they did their family members. In the first century BCE, it was recorded that when a Roman soldier accidentally ran over a cat, a local mob attacked and killed him. Near Beni Hasan was a site for the ritual interment of thousands of mummified cats.

Needless to say, many amulets shaped like cats were worn on the person by women desiring children—as many as the cat's kittens! (See also timeline page 155)

Metalworkers used blowpipes to cast copper.

2355–2200 BCE Metallurgical technology comprises the melting of copper for casting (with the use of the blowpipe).

2350–2190 BCE A temple at Abydos is divided into chambers by walls of brick. The rooms have doorways strengthened with stone. There is also an early temple at Hierakonpolis, on a more complex plan.

2350 BCE (onward) The text of the prayers and of autobiographies becomes lengthy and loquacious, but the autobiography remains an epitaph describing service to the pharaoh rather than the account of a person's life.

2350 BCE A high priest of Memphis claims his rituals protected Teti when he entered his ritual bark. Gone is the single-minded worship of Re and the power of Heliopolis.

2350–2195 BCE Dynasty VI appears to exercise direct control over Lower Egypt, while a governor takes charge of law and order and tribute collection in the valley further upstream.

2350 BCE (onward) There are improvements in copper tools; for example, the axe is given two projections at its base for a firm fastening to its grooved handle (with leather thongs).

RELIGION: CREATION MYTHS, BELIEFS, AND CUSTOMS

As in most ancient religions, Egyptian belief had a number of creation myths. Papyri and references in inscriptions tell us how complex the concepts were. Re, Ptah, Khnum, Aten, or Amun—each was considered central to cosmogony at different times and under different political regimes.

Amun-Re was the supreme god in the New Kingdom to whom pharaohs and members of their family paid homage. Here, Ramesses II is seen kneeling before a deity, while his father Seti I and other gods surround him.

PRIMORDIAL BEGINNINGS

Only on the subject of the emergence of life was there agreement between the various priesthoods in Egypt: in the beginning was the primordial water, Nu; from this emerged the mound. It is on this primordial mound that each temple claims it was built. At Memphis it was believed that the world was a manifestation of Ptah. The god of Elephantine, Khnum (who came into existence by uttering his own name), created man on the potter's wheel—New Kingdom reliefs show him shaping a royal child and his ka on the wheel. In Thebes of the New Kingdom, Amun (the air) was the supreme, invisible creator who had no mother or father, and who was born in secret.

- The equal-arm balance is in use for weighing small items such as gold. The pivot of the balance is suspended from a string held in the hand, and amounts are carefully noted down.

2350–2040 BCE Some temples have secret chambers. At Elephantine Island at the First Cataract, a rectangular temple built against the boulders has an inner area for the hidden images and a pedestal in the courtyard for portable images.

2350–2295 BCE Weni, a high official, commands an army sent to fight the Asiatic Sand Dwellers: the army ravages the land (thought to be south Palestine), destroys the trees and houses, and takes thousands captive.

2350–2200 BCE Many Egyptian aristocrats and officials leave their inscriptions at the First Cataract. Harkhuf, who goes on to explore Nubia, a source of valued products, becomes governor of Upper Egypt.

2343–2297 BCE Reign of Pepy I. He leaves no imposing monument, but many inscriptions across Egypt.

- He marries two daughters of the powerful nomarch of Abydos; two of his successors are children by those marriages.

2343–2297 BCE Pepy I is portrayed in a wooden statue covered with a copper sheath, the eyes inlaid.

2343–2297 BCE Pepy I organizes an expedition to the alabaster quarry at Hatnub on the Wadi Hammamat in the Eastern Desert.

2300 BCE One limestone statue is a self-portrait of the sculptor as an emaciated rustic: his ribs show, and his legs are very thin.

2300–2190 BCE Statues placed in funerary monuments are not just works of art; the sculptor, on finishing the work, recites a spell, such as, "I open your mouth so that you can speak, your eyes that you can see the sun."

2297–90 BCE Reign of Nemtyemsaf I (Merenre). He is served by two officials, Weni and Harkhuf, who leave behind accounts of their activities.

2295–2196 BCE The land of Yam is organized into chiefdoms and some chiefs supply facilities to Egyptian officials on expeditions.

- Officer Harkhuf returns from Nubia with 300 donkeys loaded with incense, ebony, leopard skins, ivory, and throwing sticks.

2290 BCE Harkhuf receives from the boy-king Pepy II a letter saying he is eager to see the dancing pygmy whom Harkhuf has captured and is bringing to the capital.

A relief from Elephantine Island, which was the main center of worship for Khnum, the ram-headed creator god responsible for the inundation of the Nile.

MYTH OF OSIRIS

In the only complete narrative of the Osiris myth, given to us by Plutarch (c. 100 CE), Re, the sun god, dispelled the darkness of Nu, and then he created Shu (air) and Tefnut (moisture). These twins in turn gave birth to Geb (the earth) and Nut (the sky), parents of the third-generation pairs of gods, Osiris-Isis and Seth-Nephthys. Horus, the deity most closely associated with kingship, was the son of Osiris and Isis.

Osiris, who was the first pharaoh, was murdered by his brother—the energetic, radical, and troublesome Seth—put in a coffin, and thrown into the Nile. A grieving Isis went in search of Osiris and found the coffin lodged in the sands at Byblos. She reawakened him and Osiris impregnated her. Their child, Horus, was born and nurtured in secret until he could challenge Seth and take the throne for himself.

By the laws of nature, Osiris could not be allowed to resume his life in this world, and was made ruler of the netherworld, where he judged the souls of the dead. Horus, the distant one, god of the sky, often portrayed as the falcon or hawk, guided the living pharaoh. Osiris, believed to have been buried at Abydos, is often depicted wrapped in mummy bandages, wearing the White Crown of Upper Egypt.

Osiris was the king of the dead, and he, Isis, Nephthys, and Seth were the children of Nut and Geb, part of a group of nine gods worshipped at Heliopolis, while other centers had their own favorite deities; Heliopolis was also the center of the cult of the sun god Re.

2290–2196 BCE Reign of Pepy II, half-brother of Merenre. He builds the last great monument of the pyramid age. (Two sources say his reign endured ninety years!)

2290–2196 BCE Pepy II's pyramid at Saqqara has reliefs that are exact copies of those in the monument of Sahure of the previous dynasty.

2200 BCE The "Instructions of the Vizier Ptah-hotep" contains thirty-seven maxims (such as "The limits of art are never reached; no artist's skills are perfect"), but none of these are related to the conduct of state business.

2200 BCE The number and variety of stone containers declines.

2196–95 BCE Reign of Nemtyemsaf II. He is unable to hold on to power, as in many ways decadence has already set in.

2195–2040 BCE The First Intermediate Period. Nile floods are low because of a fall in the annual rainfall in northeastern Africa. Food shortages occur.

- No ruler can establish his authority over the whole land and although the entire period is not one of unrelenting chaos, there is evidence (such as a mass grave of sixty warriors at Thebes) of frequent disturbances.

Warriors at Thebes.

2195 BCE (onward) The multichambered *mastaba* is reduced to a simple form, with reliefs on the burial chamber, some statues of servants, and Pyramid Texts written on the coffin itself. Some tombs are built of brick.

2195–2040 BCE In the First Intermediate Period, most tombs are small and in the provincial style.

PANTHEON OF GODS

Among other gods are Hathor, with her cattle horns and sun disk, worshipped in the Thebes area and also in Sinai and southern Palestine; Ptah, the fashioner or craftsman of Memphis; Amun, the hidden one of Thebes; Aten, the sun disk; and Khepri, the dung beetle, one who is coming into being. There is no "Great Mother" among these deities, and they could take either human or animal form, or even be composite in form. None of them had attributes that were exclusive, so that syncretism (e.g., Amun-Re or Re-Harakhty) was possible.

Once made for a temple's inner sanctum, an image of a deity was consecrated at a ceremony called the "Opening of the Mouth," during which the deity was induced to inhabit it by priests who had to cleanse and purify themselves for the ceremony. Images in temples were carefully tended. They were bathed, dressed in fresh clothes, anointed, and fed by the temple priests.

Animals were an important part of the pantheon and of ritual practice. There was the Mnevis bull at Heliopolis, a manifestation of Re, and the Apis bull of Memphis, who was a herald of Ptah. Large numbers of these animals were kept in temple complexes. Many animal mummies, a means to gaining a god's favor and acquiring merit, have also been found.

Complex myths and legends abound. In one legend, Nut, the sky goddess, is seen being separated from her lover, Geb, the earth god, by Shu, the air.

GOD'S WIFE

Often a king's daughter destined to be a queen took the rank of "God's Wife." During the New Kingdom, the title sometimes went from mother to daughter. When the high priests of Amun in Thebes assumed political power, it was their women who took the title. In the eleventh century BCE, the rulers of Tanis gave their daughters in marriage to the high priests of Thebes. Royal women were priestesses of Hathor, some of them even managing the estate of a temple of this goddess. Three generations of a provincial aristocratic family are known to have held this office.

2195–2040 BCE Much relief sculpture becomes rough, because many ordinary people—not just the pharaoh and his officials—make funerary monuments for themselves, engaging less-skilled craftsmen.

2195 BCE (onward) The stela becomes the form of the memorial to an individual's life. Inscribed with a prayer, it depicts in relief the act of making offerings for well-being in the afterlife.

2195–1650 BCE The Pyramid Text is transformed into the Coffin Text: ordinary people and petty chieftains have brief spells written in cursive letters on their coffins, many of which are made of wood rather than stone.

2190 BCE (onward) In Upper Egypt, funerary monuments are cut out of the faces of cliffs at the edge of the desert. The practice begins at Meir, Asyut, and other places.

2160–2040 BCE Chiefs of Heracleopolis take control of Lower Egypt, expelling Asiatic incursions and reestablishing the importance of Memphis. At the end of this period, they lose out to their rivals in Thebes.

2160–2066 BCE Rule of Dynasty XI-A in Thebes (Middle Egypt) overlaps with the rule of Dynasties IX and X at Heracleopolis (Lower Egypt). The two centers contest for dominance over Egypt.

2160 BCE (onward) Thebes or Waset at modern Luxor becomes an important political center. Its local god was the falcon-headed warrior god Mont, or Montju.

2160–23 BCE After Mentuhotep I comes Inyotef I, called the "Pacifier of the Two Lands," or one who has some success with political unification.

2160–1781 BCE Middle Kingdom monuments occur all over Egypt, including the Faiyum, in Syria, Palestine, Sinai, northern Nubia, and on the Red Sea coast. Middle Kingdom pyramids are not as grand as those of Dynasty IV; mostly they consist of brick enclosed by a casing of stone slabs.

2160–2000 BCE The tombs of the pharaohs of Dynasty XI in northwestern Thebes have huge sunken courtyards, pillared porticoes, and small pyramids over the actual burials.

2123–2074 BCE Inyotef II takes the title "King of Upper and Lower Egypt," but rules perhaps over only some provinces in the south.

2100–1990 BCE Stone for large buildings and for statuary is obtained from Aswan, Wadi Hammamat, Hetnub, Gebel el-Silsila, and limestone quarries above the First Cataract.

DIVINE POWERS OF THE PHARAOH

The pharaoh was the only one on earth who was a recipient of divine power, validated by the myth of Osiris and Isis and the birth of Horus, both guide and symbol of the presence of the pharaoh. On account of this power he was expected to maintain maat, the balance and harmony of the cosmos: more literally, order and justice in the land. If this was not done, calamity would follow: the Nile would not flood, children would abandon their parents.

Being at least in part divine, the pharaoh was the only person who could offer food and drink to the gods. In reality, because he could not be present in every temple, it was the high priest who officiated in his name, stating at the outset, "It is the pharaoh who sends me." Statues of rulers were set up in temples so that they would pass on the prayers and chants of the priests to the deity. Private offerings outside the temple were also made in the name of the ruler and were called "offerings which the pharaoh gives."

This was why reliefs and paintings represented set themes such as victory in war, foreign people paying homage to the pharaoh, or his coronation. Reports of royal achievements were deposited in the temple, carved, and inscribed on ceremonial mace heads, palettes, and stelae.

The king, being the only legitimate person who could make temple offerings (unless represented by a priest) presents the *udjat* eye as a symbol of protection and continuity of the law of the land.

2074–66 BCE Inyotef III, father of Mentuhotep II, is the last ruler of the transitional dynasty, which chooses the western desert opposite Karnak (Thebes) for its large courtyard tombs.

2070–1780 BCE The royal inscription continues to be composed, giving the several titles of a ruler, his powers and military feats, and telling future rulers to follow in his footsteps. Meanwhile, there is a rise in literary production.

• People write wills bequeathing their houses, slaves, and other belongings to their wives or children, or to those outside the family.

2066–1780 BCE All people owe labor to the state, or service in the army. Prison records show that women can be incarcerated for avoiding state duty. During compulsory labor service people are given bread, together with other necessities such as salt, meat, vegetables, dates, clothing, and sandals.

Ancient art embraced humble workers such as this baker shaping his cakes, as in this statuette, as well as the pharaohs.

2066–14 BCE An important relief in a temple at Tod shows the pharaoh making an offering to Mont (Montju). Three royal predecessors are depicted behind him.

2066–1994 BCE Dynasty XI-B is represented by three pharaohs called Mentuhotep ("Mont Is Content"). Mentuhotep II (Nebhepetre), who is the chief minister of Inyotef III, inaugurates the Middle Kingdom (Dynasty XI-B) after an offensive against local chieftains and their Nubian, Libyan, and Asiatic troops. The Middle Kingdom's center is Thebes, and its chief officials are also Thebans.

2066–14 BCE Mentuhotep II rules for a long time, assuming many grand titles and celebrating his jubilee in his thirty-ninth year, when he takes the double crown and calls himself "Uniter of the Two Lands."

2066 BCE Massive sandstone portraits of Mentuhotep (Nebhepetre) are made at Deir el-Bahri. These are precursors of the school of royal portraiture of Dynasty XII.

2066 BCE (onward) There is an upsurge in the production of faience, with a new technique of glazing that gives brighter colors. Among animal figurines, the hedgehog and hippo are popular.

A faience hippopotamus, the only animal that was strong enough to kill a crocodile.

2066–14 BC E Housing is largely of brick, with rafters and thatch roofs; doorways are sometimes arched; houses of the poor often have four small rooms, those of the rich, dozens of rooms.

Painted relief on the temple wall of Mentuhotep II.

COMMUNICATING WITH THE DEAD

At Tell el-Amarna in the workmen's area were shrines of the dead who had excelled in life. People visited them in family groups to commune with the dead. At Deir el-Medina, artisans would halt at shrines on the wayside to ask questions of the deities. For instance, a man whose garments were stolen had a list of possible suspects read out at the shrine. The god gave a sign, visible to all present, when the culprit's name was spoken.

The gods could be asked many kinds of questions, usually requiring a yes or no in reply. Since ordinary folk did not enter the temples, this only happened when the god was taken out on procession and the public was allowed to accompany the priests and acclaim the god. (There were many such occasions in the year.) The answer to a question would, presumably, have had to be interpreted, and possibly came from involuntary movements of those who were carrying the god in his bark (boat).

SPELLS AND PROTECTIVE DEVICES

Protection against evil was attempted in several ways. Protective amulets worn as rings or pendants were popular, and several have been excavated in the houses of artisans and stonemasons. A deity's name could be written on a piece of papyrus, rolled up tightly and worn suspended from the neck as protection. The *udjat* or *wadjet* eye refers to the myth in which Seth injured Horus's eye, which was then healed by Thoth. This popular symbol represented the deity Horus, the good and the holy. Words and names had special powers. There were good words and the names of good forces that could protect a person against accident and illness. The image of an enemy in wax or wood or drawn on papyrus and ritually "beheaded" removed all danger from him. The largest number of spells, not surprisingly, were against snakes and crocodiles.

The *udjat (wadjet)* eye figures prominently in funeral iconography and in amulets and jewelry; it bestowed protection and healing on the wearer.

2066–1780 BCE During the Middle Kingdom several new settlements are created, some of them military garrisons. Other communities are set up specifically to conduct the mortuary cult of a dead pharaoh.

- An important innovation in technology is the use of tin-bronze, imported from Syria, in place of unalloyed copper and arsenic-bronze; actual alloying in Egypt occurs in later centuries.
- All craftsmen remain dependent on the royal household, temple, or nomarch's estate for their livelihood, receiving rations in return for their work.

2066–14 BCE Nubian influence in the court of Mentuhotep II is apparent from the depiction of his women, who are shown to be dark, with tattooed bodies; there are also Nubian auxiliaries in his army.

- At Serabit el-Khadim in Sinai, a temple of the Egyptian goddess Hathor is built; statuary includes a portrait of the pharaoh Mentuhotep II.

2014–01 BCE Mentuhotep III (S'ankhkare) is probably the

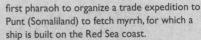

Mentuhotep II

first pharaoh to organize a trade expedition to Punt (Somaliland) to fetch myrrh, for which a ship is built on the Red Sea coast.

2006 BCE Pharaoh Mentuhotep III (S'ankhkare) sends a battalion from Coptos to the Wadi Hammamat to quarry stone for statuary. The officer in charge of the mission digs wells along the route to the Red Sea, and founds a coastal station near the Wadi el-Gasus.

2001–1994 BCE Mentuhotep IV sends an expeditionary force of 10,000 men under the governor of Upper Egypt to the Wadi el-Hudi, southeast of Aswan, to quarry stone slabs for sarcophagi.

2000–1800 BCE The cult of the dead means that regular offerings must be made to statues of the dead ruler and of his family. This involves agreements with local priests about ritual duties, with land, cattle, and personnel allotted to temples.

2000 BCE Metallurgists learn to make bellows of skin for use at the kiln.

2000 BCE (onward) Temples dedicated to gods gradually take precedence over royal mortuary temples, even though fairly large royal pyramids are constructed at el Lisht and Dahshur.

2000–780 BCE Hieroglyphic and hieratic scripts are both in use. The latter is a much simplified script for speedy writing or administrative purposes, but is also written, from right to left, on monument walls. Papyri are written in black (lamp black) ink with red for headings or the first words of sections. Often red dots mark the ends of phrases.

2000–1975 BCE A literary papyrus indicates the low social status of the metallurgist—he stinks and has skin as wrinkled as a crocodile's.

CODE OF MORALITY

Briefly, the sacred was the realization of maat—divine order and harmony. At the existential level it required certain virtues. A message inscribed on a temple wall says, "Do not come in sin, do not enter impure; do not speak falsehood in this house; do not covet things; do not accept bribes; do not add to your weights or tamper with the corn measure." There is the standard tomb autobiography of a priest or official that declares that he has never committed the act of sowing discord or causing a commotion, or kicking up a row. A section of the Book of the Dead contains a declaration by a dead person (seeking bliss in the afterlife) that he has not slain another, or caused another to weep, that he has not had intercourse with a married woman, or entered into a dispute with the king. The fact that a dead person was believed, at least from the second millennium BCE onward, to be accountable for his conduct in life, reveals not only that there was a code of morality, but also that the individual was believed to be responsible for his or her own conduct.

The ordinary Egyptian did not worship just one god, except in the time of Akhenaten. Moreover, gods were not beings encountered in everyday life. Their manifestations resided in remote recesses of temples accessed only by certain priests, until such time as they were brought out in procession. How, then, did an individual establish communication with a god? Sacrifices could be initiated, oracles could be consulted. At Thebes a huge obelisk was set up by a pharaoh against a back wall of the main temple. It was the "Place of the Ear" of Amun, where he would hear the prayers of ordinary people.

The act of worship involved sacrifice to honor and please the god, and requests for protection and favors. There were healing statues and stelae: the child Horus was depicted in relief subduing scorpions, snakes, and crocodiles. Someone who had been stung would touch the stela or pour water on it and then bathe the afflicted area with that water, or have recited one of the spells inscribed on the stela. So, a great deal of religious practice was what is considered to be magic, with worshippers expecting to get results from carrying out rituals or uttering spells.

At home a peasant would have a space for revering ancestors, and for images of the goddess Tawaret and the dwarf god Bes to protect mother and child during birth. It was believed that demons inhabited lonely cemeteries or recently flooded tracts; people prayed to the great gods to control such demons and "protectors," or magicians, would accompany expeditions. The dead could also be jealous or vengeful and cause harm or illness to their kin. Some women, called "red of eye," were associated with Seth and considered witches; there were also wise women who could give advice regarding demons, dead relatives, or an enemy responsible for one's affliction.

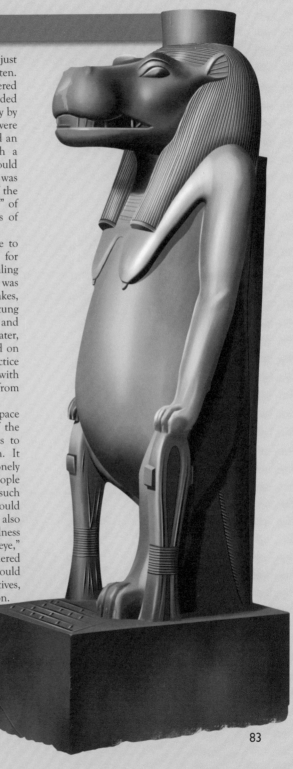

Right: Tawaret, in the shape of a pregnant hippopotamus with lion's paws and hanging breasts.
Left: Bes, her consort, the dwarf god. They were household deities who looked after pregnant women and other family matters.

Amun (Amun-Re):
Principal god of Thebes, later merged with Re. Associated with a ram with downturned horns but usually shown in human form wearing a twin-plumed crown with a solar disk.

Anubis:
Jackal-headed god who presided over funerary rituals: weighing of the heart and mummification.

Aten:
Solar deity represented by the sun disk. Favored by New Kingdom ruler Amenohotep IV (Akhenaten) in a move to curb the priesthood and establish monotheism. On his death, primacy of Amun is restored.

Amun-Re

Atum:
Primordial solar deity of Heliopolis associated with the creation myth. Symbolized by the setting sun, and represented as a man wearing the crowns of Upper and Lower Egypt.

Bastet:
Feline goddess originally shown as a lion, later as a cat-headed woman. Both protective and ferocious, her cult center was at Bubastis (under Greek influence).

Hathor:
Depicted as a cow or a woman with cow's ears. Associated with fertility, motherhood, earthly pleasures.

Horus:
Falcon god, son of Osiris and Isis, associated with kingship.

Isis:
Daughter of Geb (earth) and Nut (sky), sister-wife of Osiris. Archetypal wife and mother, popular in Roman times.

Khnum:
Ram-headed creator god who molded all life on his potter's wheel. Cult center on island of Elephantine.

Maat:
Goddess of justice, harmony, and order in the land.

Mut:
Wife of Amun, probably original Theban deity, depicted as a woman with vulture's head. Temple dedicated to her at Karnak.

Khnum

Neith:
A creator goddess with cult center at Sais. Usually shown wearing the Red Crown of Lower Egypt.

Nekhbet:
Vulture goddess of Upper Egypt, counterpart to cobra goddess Wadjet. Depicted as a woman with the White Crown of Lower Egypt.

Nephthys:
Sister and wife of Seth, she helped Isis collect the dismembered body of Osiris. Responsible for the canopic jar that contained the lungs.

Horus   Isis   Osiris

Osiris:

Son of Nut and Geb, brother-husband of Isis. Became king of Egypt. Killed by his jealous brother Seth. Worshipped as king of the dead. Cult center at Abydos. Represented as a mummy with a white crown with two ostrich plumes.

Ptah:

Patron deity of Memphis, protector of craftsmen. Lost importance on decline of Memphis. Depicted as a mummy; in animal form worshipped as a bull.

Re (Ra):

Preeminent sun god with cult center at Heliopolis. Depicted as a man with the head of a falcon crowned with the solar disk.

Re-Harakhty:

Deity formed by merger of Re and Harakhty ("Horus of the Horizons").

Re-Harakhty

Selket:

Scorpion goddess, shown as a woman with a scorpion on her head. Protector of kings.

Sobek:

Crocodile god of Upper Egypt but worshipped throughout the land.

Tawaret:

Deity protecting childbirth and babies. Shown as a pregnant woman with mouth, ears, tail, and paws of different animals.

Thoth:

Scribe of the gods, a lunar deity, god of wisdom. Depicted as an ibis or a baboon.

Wadjet:

Cobra goddess of Lower Egypt, usually seen wearing the Red Crown and the uraeus, part of the royal headdress.

2000–1750 BCE All kinds of boats—all with spoon-shaped profiles—sail down the Nile: passenger boats, cargo boats, and fishing craft. The sails are made of linen, furled for the upstream journey before the wind.

All kinds of boats were in use, with or without sails; these are made of papyrus.

2000 BCE (onward) Large portraits of upper-class women begin to be made in stone.

c. 2000–1500 BCE The classical "Middle Egyptian" language flowers, concise and elegant. Its literature becomes a model for trainee scribes for centuries to come. While spoken Egyptian evolves, written forms change slowly, resisting everyday expressions in favor of a degree of formality.

2000 BCE By now there are scribal schools in the royal capitals; royal children and the sons of a chosen few, including the sons of vassal chiefs, are taught out of standard books.

2000–1994 BCE Nubia now becomes the producer of gold for the pharaohs.

1994–1781 BCE Dynasty XII rules for two centuries. It leaves behind many memorials along the length of the land, representing the

Sphinx of the pharaoh Amenemhet III.

85

Temple of Amun at Karnak.

The temple as an establishment with a shrine, courtyards, residences, stores, workshops, and officiating and support personnel was known as a *pr*, or "house." Not only were there temples of the major deities of Egypt, but also mortuary temples of the rulers, which ensured their welfare in the afterlife. A king would make a contractual land endowment for his mortuary temple, such as would yield an adequate income to support the priests (men and women) who would make regular offerings of food and libations, and chant appropriate spells tending his ka, or soul, in perpetuity. Such temples were at the pyramid sites in the Old and Middle Kingdom periods and at a distance from the burial in later periods.

(Itj-tawi, or "Seizer of the Two Lands") near Memphis, where the tombs and memorials of the rulers and their high-ranking courtiers lie.

Secular Literature

2000–780 BCE This is the golden age of Egyptian secular literature, with genres such as the adventure narrative, didactic works, and pseudo prophecies written on dozens of papyri found across the country. Many show the influence of the Old Kingdom tomb autobiography.

- The famous romance of Sinuhe is written in about 1964 BCE. He is an official who accidentally hears about a palace coup and, fearing that civil war will break out, flees abroad to face many adventures, but is happy to ultimately return to Egypt with his Asiatic wife.

- Tracts are written on medical problems. One treatise records "muscular complaints, rheumatic troubles, and stiffness in general." One remedy for a gynecological condition states how much stock of Cyperus root, valerian, and cow's milk each are to be cooled and mixed and administered over four mornings.

- Mathematical papyri examine subjects such as the addition of fractions, the calculation of the volume of a truncated pyramid, and two-term quadratic equations.

1994–964 BCE Ammenemes (Amenemhat) I, nonroyal founder of the line from Elephantine, and previously a high-ranking minister, is described in literature as one who brings salvation after a period of disaster. He reorganizes the nome boundaries, and fixes the responsibilities and dues of each provincial administration.

1994–1860 BCE Not only the pharaohs but nomarchs also build many monuments across the land (such as at Beni Hasan, where the nomarch of the Oryx nome leaves rock tombs with wall paintings).

1994–1781 BCE Private monuments and stelae carry somewhat formulaic inscriptions with names and titles, asking for "all things good and pure."

power of its kings, whose deity is Amun-Re. The pharaohs are called either Ammenemes (or Amenemhat, which means "Amun Is Foremost") or Sesostris (Senwosret). They take on their successors as coregents during the latter part of their reign when they find themselves aging.

1994–1780 BCE Although Thebes continues to be important, the capital is now el Lisht

THE PRIESTHOOD

Temple reliefs and paintings show only the king performing rituals in the temple— even if the king never came to that temple. So priests were representatives of the king. But ordinary people were not allowed into the inner enclosure of the temples of deities, so these were, in effect, the realm of a diverse priesthood.

No large city temple of a god dating to the Old Kingdom or Middle Kingdom has been excavated. But we know that the number of priests of the gods' temples varied in number according to the size of the temple and its establishment. Some priests served full-time, others for a month in every four.

There were priests who were "servants of god," which the Greeks translated as "prophets"–high up in the hierarchy. There were also priests who, like the prophets, came from families of the elite of the locality. The lector priest was the one who carried the ritual book, and could recite its verses from memory to accompany the different rituals. He was responsible for the preservation of the texts on papyrus and also had to document the oracles that were announced.

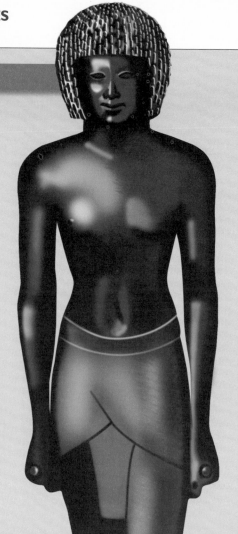

A priest of the god Amun, probably of Dynasty XXX; functions of the priesthood continued until the end of the pharaonic period.

DUTIES OF THE PRIEST

A priest in the temple of Horus in the ninth century BCE says about his initiation: "I was introduced into the horizon of heaven [the temple] to sanctify the mysterious image of the god, and satisfy him with offerings." Put through various rituals, he then entered into the presence of Horus in the holy place, "afraid and in awe of the god."

The daily rituals that were the priest's main responsibility were directed toward keeping the idol sanctified and the deity satisfied. Each day before dawn, a cleansed and appropriately dressed priest would open the door of the dark and secluded sanctum housing the idol, and prostrate himself before the god. The idol was then washed, dressed, given kohl for the eyes, anointed, and bedecked with jewelry. Incense was lit and the god was, with songs and spells, invited to eat a consecrated meal offered in the name of the pharaoh. Chanting spells and singing songs, accompanied by clapping and the rattling of the sistrum and dancing, were integral parts of most rituals. Lustrations or libations were acts of cleansing and purification, but were also life-giving, which is why representations show not water but lots of ankh signs (for "life") flowing out of libation jars.

1994–1781 BCE Execration Texts scribbled on potsherds or on clay figurines become more common.

1994–781 BCE The warrior falcon god Mont of Thebes is upstaged by the human-headed Amun, the "Hidden One," sometimes shown ithyphallic, with two tall feathers in his hair, and holding a flail. Amun is assimilated to Re. The national god is now "Amun-Re, King of the Gods" and his main temple is at Karnak (Thebes).

- The pharaohs of Dynasty XII tend to honor past kings. For example, Ammenemes I takes the epithet "Repeater of Births" and Sesostris I dedicates a statue to Inyotef and an altar for Mentuhotep III.

- Abydos becomes a place of pilgrimage (replacing Heliopolis), as it is believed to be the birthplace of Osiris—the dying and the dead "become" Osiris. Many private memorial stelae are set up here on behalf of those who cannot actually be buried here. The tradition of the ritual pilgrimage to Abydos by boat begins: a dead person is taken there on a boat with furled sails; the return was made with sails unfurled.

1974–29 BCE Reign of Sesostris (Senwosret) I. He organizes the improvement of agriculture in the Faiyum by land reclamation and control of the annual overflow of the Nile into the basin.

1974–29 BCE Monuments of Sesostris I are at more than thirty-five sites in Egypt, from the Mediterranean to the First Cataract (Aswan).

- Sesostris I sets up a huge obelisk (more than 49 feet high) in the Faiyum depression.

Birds, found in large numbers in the vegetation surrounding the Nile, were popular food items.

1974–29 BCE Ten nearly identical and larger-than-life limestone statues of Sesostris I show him seated on his throne.

1950 BCE The geographic name for Nubia—Kush—appears for the first time in Egyptian records.

1932–896 BCE Ammenemes II reigns.

1932–880 BCE Egyptian domination of trade and politics in western Asia.

1902 BCE Ammenemes II leaves a commemorative stela on the Red Sea coast after a successful naval expedition to Punt.

1900–1880 BCE Sesostris II reigns. During his time, royalty and nobles hunt fowl and fish in the Faiyum. His pyramid lies on the route to the Faiyum.

PURE AND GODLY

A priest had to enter the temple in a pure state. Before each of the three daily services, he had to wash in the temple tank or basin, rinsing his mouth with natron in water. Priests were circumcised, and had to remove all body hair and abstain from sex while in the temple. They dressed in wool, leopard skins—at Heliopolis, a fabric covered with stars—and white sandals. As proxy servants of particular gods, they could claim the qualities of those gods. Thus, a servant of Re was "great at seeing," while his counterpart in the temple of Ptah was "great at directing the crafts." A priest would even wear the mask of the deity during certain rituals.

PRIESTLY HIERARCHY

Though differing titles existed during the Old Kingdom, it was in the New Kingdom that the priesthood became a specialized vocation. The first servant of Amun, established as the supreme deity of Egypt, was still the reigning pharaoh but there was now an office of the highest-ranking priest in the realm, the overseer of all prophets of Upper and Lower Egypt. There was a first prophet at Thebes, below him the second to fourth prophets, in descending order of importance. From the ninth century BCE the office of first prophet of Amun at Thebes was taken over by powerful men and the Thebaid became semiautonomous.

Priests could be scholars who constituted the intelligentsia of ancient Egypt. As far as the propagation of the literary and scholarly tradition by priests is concerned, the temple contained the House of God, where divine statues were made and consecrated; a House of Books, where the papyri on sacred literature (spells, the names and lists of deities, manuals for rituals) were written and copied; and the House of Life, in which were texts about the coronation of the king, mummification, and allied rituals that brought kingship and priesthood together.

Women were also associated with the temples. Royal women were priestesses of Hathor, there were female priests and singers, and women were also involved in temple administration.

Lector priests were high in the priestly hierarchy.

TEMPLE OFFERINGS

Because daily offerings at major temples could be on occasion 5,000 loaves of bread and 204 jars of beer, temples needed a constant flow of resources from land endowments. Temples like that of Aten at Tell el-Amarna had hundreds of stone altars and brick tables for such offerings to be laid out. Amulets, labels, and shards of storage jars have also been found. Other temple compounds contain traces of dozens of ovens and broken bread molds, areas for animal sacrifice, and extensive storage facilities. The temple received gifts from the pharaoh and also from state expeditions sent abroad—gold from Kush, for example. A papyrus listing all the benefactions of Ramesses III on various temples includes buildings, people, livestock, ships, and sacks of grain by the hundreds. In addition, mines and quarries were assigned to certain temples from time to time. Administratively, the temple was a state institution in every sense and priests were state functionaries rather than leaders of parishes.

1900 BCE (onward) The economic importance of the Faiyum grows and with it, the importance of its crocodile god Sobek and his consort Renenutet, the cobra goddess.

1900–1880 BCE The pyramid of Sesostris II is built at el Lahun, on the route to the Faiyum. Two other Dynasty XII pyramids are also built here.

1900–1550 BCE Tomb reliefs and paintings often show how bricks are made: earth is dug out with a hoe, mixed with water, straw, and sand, and kneaded with the feet. It is then placed in wooden molds. Bricks are dried in the sun for about ten days.

1900 BCE The Tod treasure is possibly a gift from Byblos to Ammenemes II.

1881–40 BCE Rule of Sesostris III. He travels north to overthrow the Asiatics in southern Palestine, but also builds several brick forts between the First and Second Cataracts.

1880–40 BCE Sesostris III has many brick forts built along the Upper Nile. Nubia is now a province of Egypt and Sesostris III invades southern Palestine. At the port of Byblos, there is Egyptian influence on the material culture, and hieroglyphic writing is used.

1880–00 BCE Stone sculptors show the aging, haggard faces of pharaohs Sesostris III and Ammenemes III. These are the most expressive (and hence, considered the best) statues hitherto sculpted of Egyptian kings, as facial types were not given as much importance as posture (standing, seated, moving) or gesture, and were, by and large, portrayed in a fixed manner.

These two gigantic seated statues of Ammenemes III, known as the Colossi of Memnon, are at Thebes, on the Nile's west bank.

1880–1794 BCE Sesostris III and Ammenemes III commission large sets (exceeding 100) of giant stone statues of themselves; one is 39 feet high.

1875–40 BCE Two rulers of Byblos (on the coast of Lebanon) receive valuable gifts from Ammenemes III and Ammenemes IV.

1850 BCE (onward) The practice begins of interring an anthropomorphic *ushabti* figurine with the dead. Carved from the wood of the *shawab* tree, it represents a substitute who will carry out the compulsory labor everyone has to perform in the afterlife on the estates of Osiris.

Ushabtis, inscribed with spells, were placed in the coffin or tomb of the dead.

1842–1794 BCE Ammenemes III builds a temple complex in the Faiyum on a truly gigantic scale.

1800 BCE The rectangular wooden coffin that has replaced the stone slab sarcophagus is now human-shaped, depicting a masked and mummified Osiris. Spells are written on the inner lid of the coffin to protect the deceased in the afterlife. These Coffin Texts now completely replace the earlier stone Pyramid Texts.

• From now on, texts express a new idea, that of the deceased as a spirit.

1800 BCE The custom begins of drawing up onomastica, or lists of physical phenomena—e.g., settlements, parts of the body, plants, fish, animals, and liquids—arranged according to the contemporary system of classification.

1800 BCE A sphinx figure from this era was found in Ugarit, Syria, and another at Tell Atchana even further north, both near the Mediterranean coast.

1800–1550 BCE The cultures of Lower Nubia (above Aswan and the First Cataract) and Kerma (near the Third Cataract) gradually diverge and develop their own characteristics.

TEMPLE AT ABU SIMBEL

In Nubia, south of the First Cataract, Ramesses II (1279-1212 BCE), taking advantage of a soft sandstone cliff facing the Nile, built a temple of truly stupendous proportions, dedicated to the gods Amun, Ptah, Re-Harakhty, and Ramesses himself. Four gigantic figures of the seated king more than 66 feet high were carved out of the cliff face in front of a flat facade. At ground level, a doorway led into the cliff, which was carved out to make an immense hall. An inner chamber was, in turn, connected to three others, so that the temple as a whole pierced almost 180 feet into the rock. Yet, on two days of the year, the rays of the rising sun could illuminate the figures in the innermost sanctum.

TEMPLE AT DEIR EL-BAHRI

The semicircular cliff on the edge of the Western Desert, facing the Nile opposite Thebes, was sculpted by many pharaohs and nobles. Mentuhotep Nebhepetre (2066-2014 BCE), the founder of Dynasty XI, constructed the first temple here. Though it is not completely rock-cut, its columned courtyard and raised hall were most likely a model for the temple of Queen Hatshepsut (1472-1457 BCE). Mentuhotep's temple was terraced and it was also his tomb. At its far end, inside the cliff, was a mortuary temple, and even further in, the burial place of the pharaoh.

Hatshepsut's spectacular funerary temple was cut into the face of the high cliff at Deir el-Bahri and has a superb natural setting. The first fully developed mortuary temple of the New Kingdom known to us, it lies near Mentuhotep's Middle Kingdom temple, from which it takes certain elements. Hatshepsut's temple also copied features from other tombs, such as the rows of pillars which were seen in the tombs of Inyotef I, Inyotef II, and Inyotef III of Dynasty XI-A (2140-2066 BCE). The tomb facades of those pharaohs had single or double rows of 20 to 24 pillars, and are referred to as *saff* tombs (*saff* means "row" in Arabic).

Hatshepsut's temple at Deir el-Bahri is cut into the cliff side.

The exceptional qualities of Hatshepsut's temple derive partly from the gleaming white limestone of which it is built, partly from the various elevations, and partly from the vivid reliefs.

The temple featured a causeway, a huge open courtyard, and a series of three porticoes or courts, tiered on top of each other. Each portico was fronted by a colonnade, and was approached by a central ramp.

Exotic trees and shrubs from Punt were planted in the lowest courtyard. A shrine to Hathor is located at one end of the second colonnade and, at the uppermost level, in front of each column stood a statue of Hatshepsut with the attributes of Osiris.

Reliefs on the lowest portico show ships transporting two obelisks of red granite from Elephantine. On the portico above are shown Hatshepsut's miraculous divine birth and the trade expedition to Pwene or Punt, in Year 9 of her reign. Her ships are shown arriving at their destination and returning home. Punt's bearded chief and his hideous wife greet the ambassadors of mighty Egypt. Their faces and dress, the thatch-domed huts, the palm vegetation, and fauna are carved with vigor and an eye to detail, and exhibit a surprising interest in a foreign culture for that time. Hatshepsut's gifts of beer, meat, and fruit are presented. (See also page 190)

Tuthmosis II defaced many of these scenes once he had assumed total power from Hatshepsut. (See also timeline page 113 and 172)

Queen Hatshepsut and her teaple, showing a reconstruction of the three terraces.

FORM AND PLAN OF TEMPLES

In general, Egyptian temples were complex buildings with pylons, porticoes, open courtyards with trees and pools, and hypostyle (multicolumned) halls. Within a brick wall enclosure, a temple complex could have individual structures surrounded by stone walls. Roofs were flat, with beams made of stone. Temples of the sun god Aten, however, had no roofs because the rays of the sun were crucial to activity within. Akhenaten built four temples for Aten at Karnak. Because there were no roofs, the foundations did not go deep and the building blocks were light and easy to handle. The unroofed walls were covered with scenes of nature and daily life.

FOUNDATIONS
Many temple foundations were laid on strata of clean sand, symbolic of the mound of creation, perhaps, or else as it ensured a virgin site for building.

PYLONS
One characteristic of Egyptian temples was the construction of pylons, or two towers, at their entrances. Rectangular in plan, the flanking towers were surmounted by cornices with sloping sides, often covered with low reliefs.

SANCTUM SANCTORUM
The portico or vestibule was entered through the pylon entrance, and led to chambers, one of which would house the main deity. It was often laid out so that early morning sunbeams would touch its figure.

COLUMNS
Egyptian architecture pioneered the use of stone columns with carved or decorated capitals to support horizontal beams, which the Greeks later made more slender, at the same time improving the relative dimensions of halls and columns.

STATUES, RELIEFS, AND OBELISKS
Temple complexes were replete with two-dimensional reliefs, paintings, and hieroglyphic

Left: A column at Edfu with a leaf-designed capital.
Overleaf: Pillars and statues at the temple at Abu Simbel.

1800–1600 BCE People are buried with models of hearts (amulets) of green stone with their names inscribed on them, together with spells that will ensure a favorable judgment in the afterlife.

1798–85 BCE The reign of Ammenemes IV is relatively short, but is still acknowledged as far away as Sinai.

c. 1794 BCE Statuettes of Ammenemes III represent rare examples of arsenic-bronze casting in the lost wax method: on one of these the head cloth has been cast separately.

1794 BCE Ammenemes III's buildings are on the grandest scale of all raised by Dynasty XII. The funerary monument at Hawara, with its great number of courtyards, impresses Herodotus more than the pyramids.

1785–81 BCE Sobekneferu, the sister of Ammenemes IV, occupies the throne briefly, assuming several royal titles. She is the last of the line.

1781–1650 BCE Dynasties XIII and XIV. They comprise seventy mainly insignificant rulers. The capital remains Itj tawi near Memphis.

1781–1650 BCE The level of the Nile appears to have been generally low during this period.

- Dynasty XIII is unsuccessful in defending the borders of the country from Asiatic incursions; its seventeenth ruler, Khendjer, bears a foreign name even though his pyramid at Saqqara is Egyptian in style.
- Seven kings of Dynasty XIII take the name Sobekhotep, "Sobek [the Crocodile God of the Faiyum] Is Satisfied."
- There is an increase in the number of military titles, which indicates military insecurity.

1780 BCE From now until 550 BCE, the scarab, shaped like the dung beetle (*Scarabaeus sacer*), which has symbolic meaning for the Egyptians, is popularly used as an amulet worn on the person.

Human-headed green jasper scarab set in gold and mounted with a spell.

texts; there were also stelae, obelisks, statues, the god's bark, and papyri for the lector priest. The Old Kingdom introduced the custom of installing immense statues, often of the sphinx, at approaches to temples. Somewhat surprisingly, even when temples were carved out of hillsides, neither construction techniques nor form and dimension were changed.

TEMPLE STRUCTURES

From late predynastic times, Egyptian architecture began to rely on mud bricks. These included a sand and straw component and were sun-dried in frames to form rectangular bricks. Regular niches (buttresses and recesses) in the outer walls imparted additional strength. Some temple enclosure walls were laid as much as 36 feet thick—in alternating courses of headers and stretchers, with matting spread between courses now and again. At Hierakonpolis and Abydos, early mortuary temples of pharaohs had niched enclosure walls coated with white plaster. The facades of some nonroyal tombs and palaces of the late fourth- and early third-millennium delta also had such niches, probably influenced by Mesopotamia. Another sign of Mesopotamian architectural influence is the use of decorative cone mosaic designs on outer walls at early Buto in the delta.

Pictures drawn on early wooden labels indicate that some shrines were low domed huts, surrounded by reed enclosures, with posts and flags at the entrance. Located at a crevice between two granite boulders in the bed of the Nile is a sanctuary at Elephantine: on the far side was a sanctuary and image, in front an open-air table for the image. The idea was the emanation of the divine through the gap in the rocks. This shrine was visited by Egyptians from the Naqada to the Roman period, and acquired a mud-brick construction during the Old Kingdom.

Stone blocks, pillars, and statues were on a gigantic scale, while relief carvings could be delicate and detailed.

USE OF STONE

Building entirely in stone goes back to Dynasty III. At first, the stones were of brick size, as in the Step Pyramid, which also has a stone enclosure wall. In fact, stone constructions often show imitations of the paneled recesses of brick buildings, or logs of wood on ceilings, or ribbed columns that evoke bundled reed posts.

When stone slabs were used for construction, they were laid with thin mortar between two courses, which were secured by clamps. These were removed once the mortar had dried. The surface was then dressed smooth with hammer and chisel, given a thin plaster wash, and covered with a grid to guide the artists who would carve or paint the surface. Large stone buildings would not have been possible without appropriate sophisticated instruments for measuring dimensions and angles.

Scarabs of Hyksos kings.

1780–1650 BCE Sculpture after the Middle Kingdom sees a formalism verging on rigidity. The realistic treatment of the faces of Dynasty XII statues gives way to a hardening of facial features.

1780–1700 BCE Several papyri from el Lahun, a settlement near the pyramids of Dynasties XII and XIII, are found to be official records, letters about administration, and sacred texts for funerary ritual.

- A house census from el Lahun documents the fluctuating number of personnel—from three to eight—in one soldier's household.

1780–1650 BCE Written records mention men of Asiatic origin working as trusted family servants. So common is this that *amu*, meaning "Asiatic," also comes to mean "slave."

1780–1650 BCE An administrative roll from the tomb of a woman is a register of eighty fugitives from compulsory labor service for the state. If caught, they will be condemned to labor for life.

1770 BCE Scribes are writing down mathematical problems and tests. One papyrus contains the question "If ten gallons of fat are issued in a year, what is the daily share of it?"

1750 BCE (onward) Fairy tales are written. A famous one recounts a shipwrecked sailor who comes upon a huge snake who has lost all his kin. Ultimately the snake gives him a cargo of myrrh, incense lumps, giraffes' tails, and other goods to load on a ship that arrives to take him back to Egypt.

1750–1550 BCE As state institutions collapse, cultural standards decline: in sculpture, there is little attention to style, and faces become rigid and devoid of expression.

1750 BCE By now there are huge numbers of Asiatic migrants in the lower and upper Nile Valley.

- Many Nubians migrate into Egypt as prisoners of war and mercenaries, leaving behind shallow graves with leather clothes and simple ornaments.

1725 BCE Pharaoh Neferhotep visits the House of Writings to examine old texts to find out the correct form of a statue of the god Osiris that he wishes to commission—this probably represents a degree of cultural continuity with the Middle Kingdom.

Before 1650 BCE Semitic people from southern Palestine regularly migrate into Egypt to graze their flocks, trade, or work as domestic servants, brewers, or tailors. The second generation of immigrants often took Egyptian names.

1650–1550 BCE Dynasty XVII rules in Thebes and ultimately establishes sovereignty over all of Egypt.

1650–1535 BCE Dynasty XV rules in the delta. They are known in Egyptian as the six "Chieftains of Desert Uplands," the Hyksos of modern history. The Hyksos' political center is Avaris (Tell al-Dab'a) in the eastern delta, a town with a perimeter wall and small houses settled in the Middle Kingdom as a frontier post. Hyksos rule is loose, but they still assert political supremacy over regional chiefs in Upper Egypt.

1650–1550 BCE Coffins are usually of ordinary wood and painted with the image of the sky goddess Nut, who is asked to take the deceased in her winged arms to the deceased's eternal place among the stars.

1650–600 BCE A text on surgery (the Edwin Smith surgical papyrus, reported to be the oldest such text in the world) deals with injuries to the head, chest, and spine. It is remarkable because each case is dealt with methodically: it suggests careful examination, then the diagnosis, and then the cure.

1650–1550 BCE A Theban scribe named Ahmose makes a copy of an earlier mathematical text that sets several problems in arithmetics and geometry. His copy survives as a complete roll: the Rhind Mathematical Papyrus.

Section of a mathematical papyrus.

1650–1550 BCE The Hyksos bring many elements of eastern Mediterranean culture to Egypt: Minoan fresco painting, the horse-drawn

RELIGION: THE AFTERLIFE

From late prehistoric times, affluent Egyptians were sent to their fate generously equipped with ornaments, pottery, food, and other necessities and luxuries. Not only did images of the afterlife change over time; there is in the same period an ambivalence in the texts, and contradictions in the practices relevant to this theme. However, so much of Egyptian civilization—monumental architecture, science, sculpture, literary creativity, and craftsmanship—developed in the very context of preparation for the afterlife, that this was a central pivot of ancient ideology, directly impacting everyday life.

chariot for use in war (and the use of Canaanite terminology for the chariot and its wooden parts), and new weapon forms such as the composite bow and the scale armor. The Thebans gradually adopt these new instruments of war.

- The title *mr* appears, written as a sign of a man on a horse, meaning "commander of horsemen."

Anubis weighs the heart of the deceased against a feather while Thoth, the scribe, records the result that should qualify the deceased for the afterlife.

KA AND BA

There was a conviction that while life on earth is limited, individuals who prepare can prolong its joys into the infinite existence hereafter. A person would put his or her energy and resources into this preparation by planning a tomb and accumulating the various goods with which to equip it: furniture, food, cosmetics, and other objects of comfort and luxury.

Each individual had a ka, or double; a ba, or soul, that left the body at death; and an ankh, or spirit, which symbolized bliss in the afterlife, sometimes depicted as a bird. The body was not discarded at death; it had to survive so that the ba could recognize it and home in on it in the afterlife. Hence, a person with resources would make arrangements not only for the tomb but also for mummification and for the performance of rituals and regular offerings to ensure well-being in the hereafter.

THE TRANSITION

Heaven was called the Beautiful West, the region beyond the desert cliffs where the sun set. It was also Starry; in some genres it was the Field of Reeds. The transition from this life to that was difficult, even for a pharaoh, as the Pyramid Texts reveal. The dead pharaoh required nurture from goddesses in a kind of rejuvenation process. He was awakened from the sleep of death for his journey to "heaven," his body intact and kept pure, and given his insignia for the journey—the myth of Osiris is relevant here.

Another image was the ferrying of the dead pharaoh to the realm of Re in a boat. The papyrus-shaped cedar boat, buried carefully in a pit near the Great Pyramid, was one of five. Some texts indicate that the ruler arrived in heaven with a crash and a bang: the rumble of thunder and the necessity to vanquish the lesser gods who stood in his way, with all the magical devices at his disposal. Once he arrived, the pharaoh became a star in the sky or, in a solar metaphor, one who lived with and journeyed with the sun. Clearly, he was now divine and his pyramid and the cult of the dead king blessed the country.

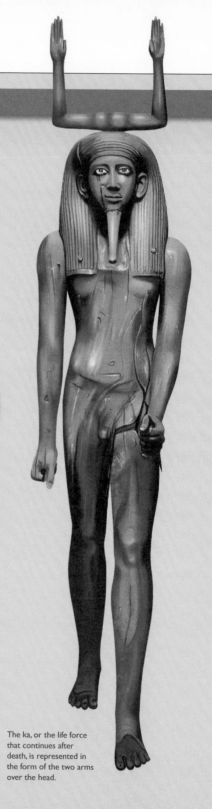

The ka, or the life force that continues after death, is represented in the form of the two arms over the head.

- There is a greater use of tin-bronze in daily life. Silver, smelted from *argentiferous galena*, is imported from the Mediterranean. Earrings, made of twisted or plain silver or copper wire, are of a form only suitable for pierced ears.

1650 BCE Humped Asiatic cattle are introduced into Egypt.

1650–1535 BCE At Avaris the Hyksos people worship Seth, an animal god, perhaps an adaptation of the West Semitic Baal.

Sobek, the crocodile god, with the king.

- Among papyri of the Hyksos period are hymns to the crowns of Upper and Lower Egypt—which refer to the crocodile god Sobek as a manifestation of Horus, the deity associated with Egyptian kings.

1650–1550 BCE In impoverished Thebes there is no good wood for rectangular coffins; these are now abandoned for anthropoid coffins roughly cut from local wood and painted.

1650–1525 BCE Hundreds of scarabs are found in Palestine, not all of them actual Egyptian imports.

1650 BCE After this time the forts erected by the Middle Kingdom along the First and Second Cataracts are abandoned by the Egyptians and occupied by the local herders. Both the Egyptians and the Nubian kingdom at Kerma recruit mercenaries from the Eastern Desert.

- The kingdom of Kush is independent. Egyptian goods are used in Nubian graves, however, and there is much Egyptian influence in metallurgy and faience.

1600 BCE Fifty years after settling at Avaris, the Hyksos take on the rest of Egypt, contesting against the rulers of Thebes and later receiving tribute from the latter and marrying their women. They adopt the Egyptian system of writing, the royal titulary, the worship of Re at Heliopolis, and other practices.

1600 BCE The weaving loom is now upright, an improvement on the earlier loom.

- There is a preference for painted pottery, with red, black, yellow, and blue pigments depicting people, birds, river life, and geometric motifs.

c. 1600 BCE By this time, because pharaonic rule has weakened, Nubians, like the Hyksos, become prominent in Egypt. Nubia's first royal graves are made; the largest at Kerma has more than 300 retainers.

Manetho

According to the chronicles of Manetho, the priest of the late fourth century BCE, there was no Dynasty XVI. Manetho's "thirty-one dynasties" of Egypt, up to the invasion of Alexander, form a useful chronological framework that historians are loath to discard.

1565–58 BCE According to legend, the Hyksos ruler of Avaris complains that the hippos of the Theban ruler Taa I (Senakhtenre) disturb his sleep at night. This complaint probably leads to an armed confrontation.

1565–24 BCE The wives and mothers of the last three kings of Dynasty XVII and the first king of Dynasty XVIII are women of exceptional influence. Both brother-sister and uncle-niece marriages take place during this period.

1565 BCE (onward) Tetisheri is the queen of Taa I (Senakhtenre) and the mother of Taa II (Seqenenre). Her mummy at Deir el-Bahri shows she died an old woman with scant white hair. Her grandson commemorates her in a stela and states that he will create a monument for her.

1558 BCE Taa I dies in agony at a young age (his corpse is twisted).

1558–54 BCE Reign of Seqenenre (Taa II), whose queen, Ahhotpe ("The Moon Is Content"), is the mother of Kamose and Ahmose (Amosis), both of whom will rule in Thebes.

- A stela of Ahmose exhorts people to revere Ahhotpe, for she "cast the rebels out of Upper Egypt" (probably at the death of Taa II). She is active during the reigns of both her sons.

The stela of Ahmose.

PROTECTIVE SPELLS

PYRAMID TEXTS

Inscribed in hieroglyphs on the walls of royal burials of the Old Kingdom, on the sarcophagi of nobles in the First Intermediate Period, and on a royal tomb of the Middle Kingdom, these were rituals and utterances to protect the person in death or for recitation during rituals carried out after death.

COFFIN TEXTS

These appeared during Middle Kingdom times as more and more people sought the protection of words in death. They are derived from the Pyramid Texts, but are brief and inscribed in hieratic on coffins of royals and nonroyals alike. Osiris is now more important than Re. It is he who will judge the dead.

BOOK OF GOING FORTH BY DAY (BOOK OF THE DEAD)

These were inscribed in both writing and imagery on tomb walls and on papyri buried with the dead. This tradition, which also originated in the Pyramid Texts, appears to have begun in New Kingdom times. Written in a special form of hieroglyphic, this book contains spells to enable the dead to overcome threats from malign forces in the afterlife. Sections have been found in the tombs of a wide range of people—a royal scribe, an offerer of incense, a chantress of Amun, a soldier, and a priest. If written on papyrus, it was rolled up tight, tied with a strip of linen, sealed with clay, and placed in the coffin (perhaps tucked into the mummy bandaging), or outside the coffin in a wooden figurine. The paintings are among the best the Egyptians produced. One of the themes is a weighing balance with the dead person's heart in one pan, an act that will decide whether the person deserves admission to the kingdom of Osiris.

By the beginning of the second millennium, the realm of the dead was so much an extension of life that, somewhat paradoxically, people had to show up for compulsory labor there. *Ushabti* figures were buried with the dead, holding agricultural tools in their hands.

Above: A scene from the *Book of the Dead* in which the supplicant prays before the goddess Hathor; words and images were always combined.
Right: Detail from the Coffin Text of General Sepy (c.1850 BCE) shows the nine elliptical roads that the deceased had to cross in order to reach the sun god Re.

1554 BCE Kamose of Thebes begins a war of liberation soon after this date. He regrets the fact that with a chief in Avaris and another in Kush, "I sit in league with an Asiatic and a Nubian, each in possession of his slice and I cannot get past him to Memphis." He sails down the Nile with Medjay and Nubian mercenaries, and attacks some Hyksos settlements.

1554–50 BCE As Kamose sets out to unify Egypt he intercepts a letter from the Hyksos chief of Avaris to the chief of Kush, asking, "Have you not beheld what Egypt has done against me?"

1550–24 BCE Amosis (Ahmose) of Thebes gains control of the entire land, and brings Hyksos rule to an end in the delta after a long siege of Avaris and a fort in southwestern Palestine.

• Pharaoh Amosis marries Ahmose-Nofreteroi, the most celebrated of the queens of this royal line. Possibly a daughter of his brother Kamose, she holds a high post in the Amun temple. (At Deir el-Medina, some centuries later, she is shown with a dark complexion, although she had no African blood.)

1550 BCE (onward) Egyptian culture develops a greater openness and pluralism; non-Egyptians are no longer considered to be outside the pale; literature opens to the influence of folklore.

1550–1500 A biography is written of an intellectual who claims to have devised a way to measure time.

1550–1500 BCE Middle Bronze Age Jericho in Palestine is destroyed by fire; some scarabs (in levels associated with the destruction) bear names of the Second Intermediate period: This event might be connected with the expulsion of the Hyksos from Egypt.

1550 BCE Stone statuary is prolific and colossal statues are built, with high standards of masonry.

1550–1355 BCE Thebes is the preeminent city of Egypt, with many pharaohs contributing to the temples of Karnak and Luxor in its vicinity. (Sculptures and inscriptions from the Theban settlement and necropolis are the main sources of history.)

1550–1298 BCE The monologue of a town official voices a longing for the countryside, the papyrus clumps and meadows, and activities such as snaring waterfowl.

1550–1150 BCE During this entire period the nomarchs, chiefs of the individual nomes or

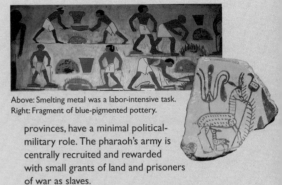

Above: Smelting metal was a labor-intensive task.
Right: Fragment of blue-pigmented pottery.

provinces, have a minimal political-military role. The pharaoh's army is centrally recruited and rewarded with small grants of land and prisoners of war as slaves.

1540 BCE The Papyrus Ebers, a reference work on medicine, is written.

1524–1150 BCE Pharaohs carve their "tombs" in the Valley of the Kings, and build their funerary temples on the adjacent Nile plain. A workmen's village is inhabited for generations at Deir el-Bahri for the making of these monuments.

1524 BCE A huge number of inscriptions and reliefs at Karnak give rich information on the deeds of the pharaohs of Dynasty XVIII.

1524–03 BCE Amenophis I follows Amosis on the throne at Thebes. Amun-Re is the state deity at Karnak-Thebes.

1524 BCE (onward) Amenophis I abandons the pyramid in favor of a rock-cut sepulchre on the edge of the Western Desert near Thebes.

1510 BCE Amenophis I starts a new practice: a mortuary temple built at a distance from the actual tomb. The latter is in a remote wadi of the Western Desert, at the edge of the plain of the Nile, and hence no longer surrounded by the tombs of courtiers. This temple of the pharaoh is built for regular commemorative rituals.

A gold and silver statue of Amun-Re.

1503–1491 BCE Reign of the third pharaoh of Dynasty XVIII, Tuthmosis I. In his first year he announces his full royal titulary—to be used during offerings to deities and when oaths are taken.

1500 BCE Dynasty XVIII inaugurates the New Kingdom. A long period of exceptional prosperity and pharaohs with strong personalities follows. A period of imperialism and the expansion of the pharaohs' territories begins, especially in Nubia (for its gold). This land, along with some western Asiatic city-states and chiefships, becomes a tributary of Egypt.

EARLY BURIAL COMPLEXES AND THE PYRAMID

While previous generations interred the dead in chambered tombs, the people of Dynasties I and II began constructing brick buildings above these chambers. These buildings had flat roofs and sloping sides, and outer facades with shallow niches or paneling. In due course, a false door on one exterior wall was carved out, where the dead person would receive offerings. Called mastabas because they resemble benches, these were the tombs of the elite.

As the institution of kingship took shape, intellectuals such as Imhotep (Dynasty III) experimented with upper stories on the flat topped mastaba. The Step Pyramid of Djoser at Saqqara had five of these, built of small stones, each being progressively smaller in area. The "true" pyramid with sloping sides evolved after two other stepped pyramids of Dynasty III at and near Saqqara.

The pyramid was the burial complex of a reigning monarch, square at the base, four-sided, with each side the shape of a high triangle. The Egyptian word for this structure came from a root meaning "to ascend." The pyramid complex comprised the pyramid, built over a set of royal burial chambers; a mortuary temple on its eastern side; a causeway joining this temple with the valley temple on the riverbank; the burial of boats in pits; and a wall enclosing not only these but also small pyramids for queens and mastabas for the court. The complex was constructed on the west bank of the Nile, in the direction of the setting sun.

Above: The reconstructed funerary boat of King Cheops.
Overleaf: The pyramids at Giza.

Pyramid Construction

Pyramids—there are ninety-eight in all—were built by pharaohs of Dynasties III–VI, XII, XVIII, and the Late Period, at Saqqara, Meidum, Dahshur, the Faiyum, Giza, and Abusir. They are mostly stone constructions, beginning with limestone and moving on to harder granites. These monuments were not, however, solidly packed with large stone blocks: there were often chambers filled in with sand or, in the smaller pyramids, a limestone center and radiating walls with brick packing around. The largest pyramids were some of the earliest.

At a height of about 480 feet, the Great Pyramid at Giza of Khufu of Dynasty IV is so huge that it could engulf several of the greatest cathedrals of Europe. It was constructed of about two million limestone blocks, each weighing roughly 2.5 tons. Such a heavy structure had to be erected on the bedrock, which had to be leveled. Earth ramps enabled builders to climb with the structure as it went up. These may have been straight with a gradual slope, or spiraling around the monument. When complete, the pyramid was encased in thin slabs of limestone, which were most often stolen in ancient and medieval times.

Pyramid construction was a matter of managing and coordinating 15,000 to 20,000 skilled and unskilled workers at any one time. Excavations at Giza reveal facilities for the mass production of bread as well as a copper-smelting facility, evidence of a resident workforce.

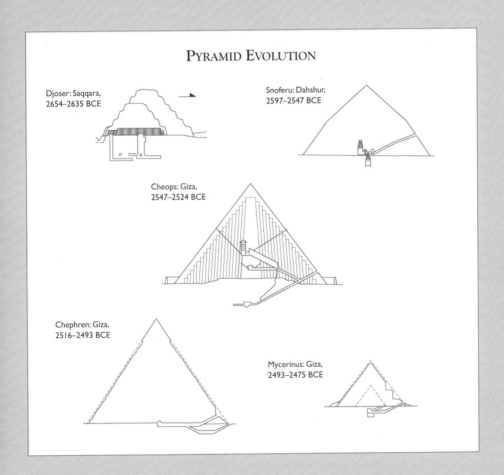

Pyramid Evolution

Djoser: Saqqara, 2654–2635 BCE

Snoferu: Dahshur, 2597–2547 BCE

Cheops: Giza, 2547–2524 BCE

Chephren: Giza, 2516–2493 BCE

Mycerinus: Giza, 2493–2475 BCE

MUMMIES AND MUMMIFICATION

Beginning with the conservation of the bodies of pharaohs around 2600 BCE, mummification was eventually extended to the elite and to a few ordinary people, and even to domestic cats, sacred bulls, baboons, and crocodiles. As a practice it survived until Christianity came to prevail in the second century CE. The science of mummification reached its peak during the New Kingdom.

The body was washed on the banks of the river. Embalming and wrapping was specialized work, accompanied by words and ritual. Internal organs had to be removed quickly to prevent decomposition. Clearly, knowledge of anatomy was essential. The roof of the nasal cavity was perforated and fine hooked instruments were inserted to remove the brain in bits and pieces. The inner skull was then flushed clean with liquids. The liver, lungs, stomach, and intestines were removed and embalmed separately for storage in individual containers, called canopic jars, protected by images of deities on them. The heart, as it was the essence of a person, was never removed.

What remained of the body was thickly covered with natron and other salts to dry it out, and the body turned into a thin, wrinkled skin lying on the skeleton. Some remodeling was done, using sand, mud, linen, or resin to fill out the face and other features. Aromatic

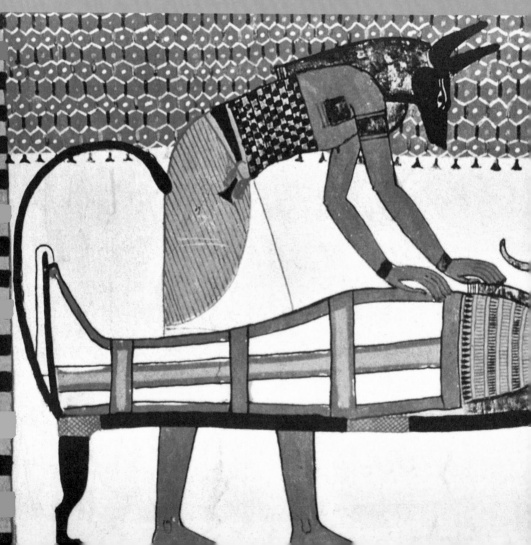

oils, unguents, and perfumes were applied to strengthen the skin and remaining body. The hair was arranged, the eyes replaced with glass. The body was wrapped in linen strips impregnated with resin, beeswax, and other preservatives. Yards and yards of linen were required. Amulets were tied and sometimes protective spells were painted onto the linen itself.

Finally, the Opening of the Mouth ritual was performed—the opening of those parts of the body that would enable the dead person to speak, hear, and eat in the afterlife.

The god Anubis anoints the mummy in preparation for the journey to the afterlife.

1500 BCE After a war in Nubia, Tuthmosis I makes a daring expedition to Syria against the kingdom of Mitanni, where he kills many people and takes others prisoner. The victory is then celebrated with an elephant hunt. No pharaoh has come so far into Asia.

1500–1150 BCE Artisans of the New Kingdom make the extremely thin gold leaf, having acquired the skills to refine gold to an exceptional degree.

1500 BCE (onward) Small amounts of iron are imported from Greece or Anatolia for use in tools in Egypt.

1495 BCE Founding of the workmen's village of Deir el-Medina in the Theban necropolis. (Ostraca—waste stone chips from tomb cutting—found here by the thousands, testify to the use of written records of attendance at work, handouts, the hire of donkeys, exchanges between individuals, and letters.) The settlement is surrounded by a mud-brick wall and comprises two blocks of back-to-back houses with a street between them. The settlement has its own adjoining cemetery and sanctuaries for Hathor and other popular deities.

1491–79 BCE The reign of Tuthmosis II begins with an expedition to punish Nubian rebels who, in league with tribes from the desert, have carried off cattle from Egyptian forts above the First Cataract. The son of a Nubian chief is brought hostage to Thebes.

1480 BCE Glass now becomes an important craft in Egypt, the technology arriving from eastern Mediterranean lands. (It is possible that Tuthmosis III brings captive glassmakers back from his military campaigns.)

1479 BCE An official writes that at the death of Tuthmosis II, his son "ruled on the throne" while his wife Hatshepsut "governed the land"

and the "two lands were under her control." (See also pages 92–94)
• Tuthmosis III is young, but a powerful party supports his claim to the throne, even though his stepmother keeps him in the background for years.

Image of Amun, from a temle of Tuthmosis III.

1479–24 BCE Tuthmosis III, after a military victory against Nubia near the Fourth Cataract, hunts a rhinoceros, a rare feat. At least three of his wives are foreign women.

WORKMEN'S SETTLEMENT, DEIR EL-MEDINA

Founded probably between 1524 and 1503 BCE, this settlement for the artisans and unskilled workers who made the tombs and sepulchres for the pharaohs was given a perimeter wall after 1500 BCE. Among the residents were officials, scribes, and workers such as stonemasons, builders, smiths, carpenters, potters, and basket makers. In their spare time these artisans made artifacts for the residents of Thebes. Occasionally they married residents of Thebes town. About sixty men would work as a team on a particular (living) pharaoh's tomb.

Remains of the workmen's settlement at Deir el-Medina.

Painting of a cow emerging from a papyrus thicket.

1475 BCE A long inscription is carved on the walls of the temple of Amun at Karnak, narrating in great detail the events of the first campaign of Tuthmosis III to western Asia, culminating in the battle of Megiddo.

1475–24 BCE Rekhmire, a senior official of Tuthmosis III, has left behind a tomb with graphic reliefs depicting many aspects of artisanship and technology. These include the depiction of a ship that displays a developed rigging and yet can take a number of rowers, showing that for a northward journey on the Mediterranean the sails cannot be adjusted to the winds that always blow from north to south.

1475–24 BCE Two long inscriptions in the tomb of Rekhmire are later copied verbatim by other senior ministers.

1472–57 BCE Six stone statues show the high official Senenmut with Hatshepsut's infant daughter, Ra'nofru, in his arms.

1472–24 BCE Sometime during this period, Tuthmosis III takes power in his own hands, and then systematically erases Hatshepsut's cartouches from monuments, replacing them with those of Tuthmosis I or II, to vindicate his own claim to legitimate rule.

1470 BCE Tuthmosis III sets out on a campaign in Palestine and Syria. The chief enemy is the kingdom of Mitanni on the upper Euphrates, but en route many chiefs are defeated (there is a fierce battle at Qadesh on the Orontes), and Egyptian garrisons are established at key places.

1470–50 BCE A period of enormous output in stone statuary: 38 statues of Hatshepsut from Deir el-Bahri, engaged with walls or pillars or free standing, are thrown away by Tuthmosis III, one of them being almost 20 feet high.

1470 BCE Megiddo appears to have been laid

Workers were closely supervised. Attendance lists were kept and when metal tools were handed out, a record was kept on a piece of stone exactly the same weight as the copper tool. Even wicks for lamps, needed to light the rock tunnels, were recorded. Sometimes the men spent nights at the work site, returning only after ten days to the village. All workers were given rations from the state store, mainly wheat for bread and barley for beer. Arrangements were also made for local people to supply them with water, fish, vegetables, and wood for fuel.

A surprisingly large number of papyri and ostraca have been unearthed in this small township and we come across events such as marriages, divorces, disputes, and inheritance matters. From carvings on stelae, we find that women made offerings to family ancestors; they also willed property to their heirs.

On one occasion a strike occurred after a formal complaint about short rations was lodged with the local temple administration, after which there was a sit-in at one of the mortuary temples. Ultimately a written petition had to be sent across the Nile to Thebes, and only then did the delayed rations for the inhabitants arrive.

The community had its own dispute settlement procedures. For instance, if an exchange of fat for grain was agreed and one of the parties reneged, warnings were handed out to the wrongdoer, who was threatened with physical punishment.

In the time of Ramesses IX (1123–1104 BCE), organized gangs looted various tombs in the Valleys of the Kings and Queens. Charges and countercharges about responsibility were made, and workmen were implicated. Then, at the end of the rule of Dynasty XX, another spate of looting occurred. Thereafter, the high priest of Amun ordered the inhabitants of Deir el-Medina to collect the surviving royal mummies and secrete them away. A result of this act of salvage is the "Deir el-Bahri cache."

Carpenter on scaffolding working with an adze.

waste by Tuthmosis III. (There is a destruction level at the excavated site.)

1463 BCE Hatshepsut sends an expedition to Punt, on the Red Sea coast of the Horn of Africa.

1460–49 BCE Some Syrian chiefs' sons are taken hostage to Egypt, but there is rebellion and repeated campaigns are necessary to subdue them.

1457 BCE (onward) Tuthmosis III contributes to the extension of Amun-Re's temple at Karnak: the existing one was too modest, so he adds a hall, a pylon, and doorways, all with reliefs. He also builds a temple at Napata near the Fourth Cataract.

Temple of Karnak, dedicated to Amun-Re.

1450 BCE The first record of the Egyptian use of four-wheeled ox carts; this is mentioned in a stela inscription describing Tuthmosis III's campaign in the Levant.

1450 BCE A rare white marble is used to portray Tuthmosis III.

1450–1300 BCE Raw glass is probably imported from the eastern Mediterranean, by sea.

1424 BCE The tomb of Hatshepsut is placed high on a cliff near Deir el-Bahri but does not escape vandalism. Her funerary temple, below an imposing cliff opposite Thebes, is an architectural masterpiece, combining some elements of pillared tombs with some elements of Mentuhotep's tomb nearby.

1424–1398 BCE Amenophis II fights battles in northern Syria and is able to take back to Egypt many Maryannu families (Maryannu are expert charioteers living in Syria). He also captures horses and chariots.

1424 BCE (onward) The nobility build their gallery tombs at Qurna (Theban necropolis area), with splendid wall paintings on a variety of themes.

1400–1348 BCE Pharaohs Tuthmosis IV, Amenophis III, and Amenophis IV (Akhenaten) fight practically no wars except to crush the occasional Nubian rebellion.

The glass goblet of Tuthmosis III.

1400 BCE (onward) Glass is very expensive, as is evident from the tombs of even rich men who have wooden vessels in imitations of glass originals. A few glass workshops exist near palaces, containing crucibles and fritting pans, and glass rods indented by tongs. After this time experiments are made with the coloring of faience with cobalt, antimony, and tin.

1390 BCE On a large scarab, an inscription by Tuthmosis IV refers to "Aten the Sun Disk." This is the solar disk whose rays terminate in hands that hold the hieroglyphic signs for "life" and "power."

1390 BCE A huge obelisk lying unattended at Karnak is reerected by Tuthmosis IV. (More than 90 feet high, it is now in Rome.)

1388–78 BCE Five inscriptions on large scarabs, each with multiple copies, commemorate important events in the reign of Amenophis III, including the arrival of a Mitannian princess. These are sent around the kingdom.

1388–48 BCE Under Amenophis III and his chief queen Tiy, Egypt is at the zenith of its prosperity and power. His inscriptions tell of the wealth that he bestows on temples in Thebes.

Queen Tiy, wife of Amenophis III and mother of Akhenaten.

THE CULT OF ATEN

The reasons behind Amenophis IV/Akhenaten's new cult of Aten have long been debated. The Aten, or luminous disk of the sun, was not a new symbol of divinity: it was venerated as early as the Old Kingdom.

Perhaps the new cult was a move against the priests of Amun who were amassing huge revenues from the temple estates and becoming powerful. There are signs that Akhenaten's predecessors were feeling the pressure.

Akhenaten confiscated some temple estates in Memphis, Thebes, and elsewhere. It is also significant that Aten was accessible only to Akhenaten, with no mediation required from priests.

One theory claims Akhenaten's wife, Nefertiti, was a foreigner who wanted to introduce her own monotheistic religion into Egypt, and inspired the religious revolution. It is true that some portrayals of her are unusual, such as depicting her as a military figure smiting an enemy, but there is no substantiating evidence for this theory.

The ordinary people living at Akhetaten, the new capital, continued to practice their old superstitions, as indicated by small finds and short inscriptions.

King Akhenaten, his wife Nefertiti, and their children worshipping the sun disk Aten.

1388–48 BCE The brick palace of Amenophis III at Thebes has superb wall paintings of birds and plants.

1388–48 BCE Colossal (over 65 feet high) statues of Amenophis III are placed on the route to the Western Desert cliffs opposite Luxor. The sandstone is transported from Lower Egypt.

1388–48 BCE In temples built by Amenophis III near the Third Cataract (Nubia), his and his wife's statues are worshipped.

• Amenophis has several wives. He marries a Mitannian princess from Anatolia; she brings a bevy of Anatolian girls with her, and prize gifts. There is also a matrimonial alliance with Babylon's ruling house.

1388–43 BCE Pharaohs Amenophis III and Akhenaten are engaged in hectic diplomatic activity, writing and receiving letters from many rulers and chiefs.

1380 BCE (onward) Large scarabs are made to commemorate events such as a king capturing wild bulls or an artificial lake being made for a queen.

1370 BCE Tjaununy, Scribe of the Recruits, is entrusted with a census of Egypt—he is shown on the walls of his tomb as a scribe enlisting soldiers. Scribes are also entrusted with recruiting people for labor on building projects.

1360 BCE Amenophis III makes several references to Aten in different inscriptions.

1360–43 BCE Amenophis IV is crowned at Karnak in the Amun temple, but in his sixth year he changes his name from "Amun Is Content" to Akhenaten, "Of Service to Aten."

1355 BCE (or earlier) Akhenaten imposes the cult of Aten on the Egyptian state, closing the Amun temples. He is directly in contact with Aten: "There is none who knows Aten save his son Akhenaten."

1350 BCE The capital is shifted from Thebes to an uninhabited site today called Tell el-Amarna, and the new city built there is named Akhetaten, or "Horizon of Aten." It is north of Thebes, south of Memphis, on the east bank of the Nile.

1350 BCE Akhenaten brings about a revolutionary change in the portrayal of royal people in stone statuary: he, his women, and an occasional high official are shown with their physical defects; in his case, a long chin and a protruding abdomen.

Colossal statue of King Akhenaten at Karnak.

1350 BCE (onward) Many pharaohs' tombs are located in the Biban el-Moluk, known as the Valley of the Kings, opposite the city of Thebes in the Western Desert. None, except that of Tutankhamun, escape the depredations of vandals. Only a few sarcophagi, mummies, and wall reliefs survive.

1350–43 BCE Mycenaean pottery is found at Amarna.

1348 BCE At Karnak, statues of the scribe Amenhotep, son of Hapu, are thought to intercede between the gods and illiterate worshippers. In later centuries he is deified.

1345–30 BCE The successor of Akhenaten, Smenkhkare (Neferneferuaten), abandons the

THE TOMB OF TUTANKHAMUN

AS DISCOVERED BY HOWARD CARTER

If Tutankhamun is the most famous pharaoh of all, known throughout the world, the reason is that his is the only intact tomb of the ruler of an important dynasty to be excavated in modern times. Tutankhamun was the last ruler of the "Amarna Age," an age of radical new thinking on religion and much innovation in art, that was introduced by Akhenaten and his beautiful wife Nefertiti. Tutankhamun succeeded to the throne at the age of nine, four years after Akhenaten's death, and is thought to be the son of Akhenaten and a lesser wife, Kiya. His original name, Tutankhaten, was changed to Tutankhamun, reflecting the return to favor of the god Amun in place of Aten. Known as the "Living Image of Amun," the young Tutankhamun ruled for ten years, between 1343 and 1333 BCE, before he suddenly died at the age of nineteen. The tomb had four chambers packed with choice furniture and artifacts of the highest standards of craftsmanship in gold and precious stones.

Some of the objects found in the tomb were associated with the pharaoh in his daily routine; others with the funerary ritual; and yet others were to sustain him in the afterlife in the style to which he was accustomed. There were four coffins, one inside the other, the innermost entirely of gold. The alabaster canopic chest with the embalmed internal organs was enclosed within a shrine made of wood plated with gold and enamel, with four exquisite statues of goddesses attached to it.

heretical religion. (So did Tutankhamun, as his name indicates.) Smenkhkare moves the capital back to Thebes and also replaces some of Akhenaten's cartouches with his own.

1343–33 BCE The short reign of Tutankhamun, who ascends the throne as a young boy. Thebes is his capital; he makes offerings there to Amun and Mut and restores neglected sanctuaries.

1343–33 BCE The finely painted tomb of Huy, the chief official of Tutankhamun in charge of Nubia, is evidence of the importance of that province for the gold that is used in such huge quantities by the rulers.

1343–33 BCE Military expeditions, if any, are left to the nonroyal minister Ay during the pharaoh's reign.

1333–28 BCE The reign of Ay, who has overseen the burial rites of Tutankhamun. His sepulchre in the Biban el-Moluk is noticeably small.

1328–1298 BCE The nonroyal Horemheb is the last ruler of Dynasty XVIII. He comes from a small town in Lower Egypt and rises in the administration to gain command of the army. He makes Memphis his headquarters.

1300 BCE Exceptionally fine reliefs are carved in the tomb of Horemheb.

1300–1150 BCE Workers in Deir el-Medina use

Above: Howard Carter.
Above left: Unquestionably the most famous of Tutankhamun's treasures, the solid gold mask, found placed over the mummy's head and shoulders, is evidently molded to mirror the pharaoh's facial characteristics. The vulture and cobra heads over the brow symbolize sovereignty over Upper and Lower Egypt.
Left: Ensconced on the west bank of the Nile, at the base of Al-Qurn mountain, the Valley of the Kings, or Biban el-Moluk, was the New Kingdom's royal necropolis. Part of Thebes, the capital of the empire at the zenith of its power, it is 435 miles south of Cairo. Among the numerous tombs built for pharaohs and nobles of the New Kingdom is Tutankhamun's— its entrance is at the center of the picture.

King Horemheb kneels before the god Atum.

Top: Breaching the doorway of the sepulcher wall.
Above: Carter and Carnarvon beside the broken-down wall of the burial chamber's outermost shrine.
Right: The linen-swathed body of the pharaoh lay within the third (innermost) coffin of solid gold.

THE TOMB OF TUTANKHAMUN

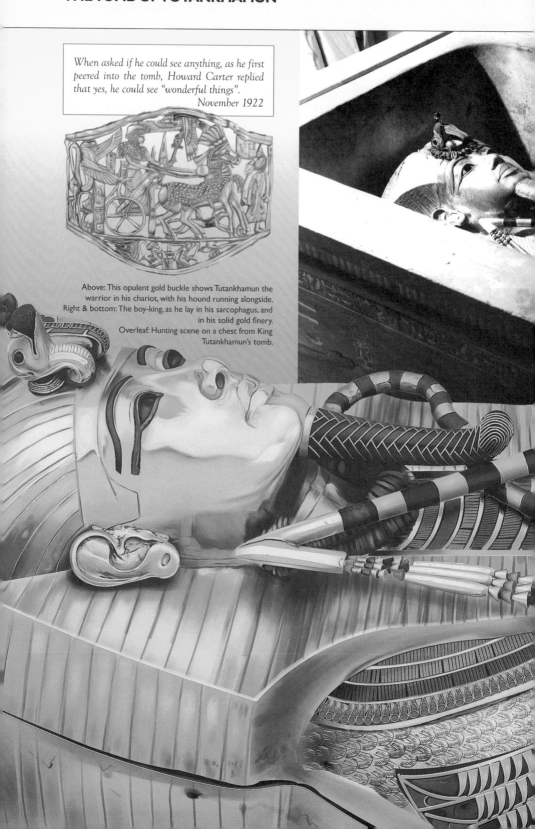

When asked if he could see anything, as he first peered into the tomb, Howard Carter replied that yes, he could see "wonderful things".

November 1922

Above: This opulent gold buckle shows Tutankhamun the warrior in his chariot, with his hound running alongside.
Right & bottom: The boy-king, as he lay in his sarcophagus, and in his solid gold finery.
Overleaf: Hunting scene on a chest from King Tutankhamun's tomb.

THE TREASURES WITHIN THE TOMB

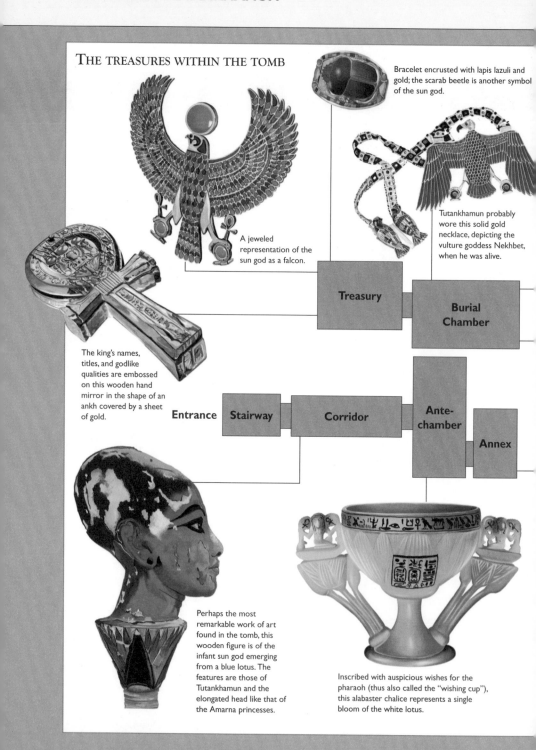

Bracelet encrusted with lapis lazuli and gold; the scarab beetle is another symbol of the sun god.

A jeweled representation of the sun god as a falcon.

Tutankhamun probably wore this solid gold necklace, depicting the vulture goddess Nekhbet, when he was alive.

The king's names, titles, and godlike qualities are embossed on this wooden hand mirror in the shape of an ankh covered by a sheet of gold.

Treasury

Burial Chamber

Entrance **Stairway** **Corridor** **Ante-chamber** **Annex**

Perhaps the most remarkable work of art found in the tomb, this wooden figure is of the infant sun god emerging from a blue lotus. The features are those of Tutankhamun and the elongated head like that of the Amarna princesses.

Inscribed with auspicious wishes for the pharaoh (thus also called the "wishing cup"), this alabaster chalice represents a single bloom of the white lotus.

Gold case with two figures of Tutankhamun, one fair and the other dark.

This gold figure of the pharaoh forms the top of a staff, possibly held by him at his coronation.

This ivory-carved panel from the painted wooden chest, one of the most outstanding works of art among the treasures, shows Tutankhamun being handed two bouquets by his graceful wife.

a variety of wooden furniture, complemented by leather and rush: beds, leather-seated chairs, rush seats, low stools, and three-legged stools.

1300 BCE (onward) Written Egyptian approximates to the spoken language and incorporates many foreign words. Fiction books include historical romances, but errors in the manuscripts indicate that scribal standards have deteriorated.

1300–1150 BCE People now use razors, scissors, blunt-ended tweezers, and hair-cutters of bronze regularly in their day-to-day lives. Everyday objects such as mirror handles and small statuettes are made in bronze in the lost-wax technique. Faience jewelry and decorative objects are made in pieces and then luted together. Gold and silver wire, and granulation, are in use and the *wesekh*, made of tubular faience beads, with variations, becomes popular. Faience vessels are abundantly made; interestingly, as the tin content of bronze falls, so does the use of tin as an element in the manufacture of faience.

1300–1100 BCE Several papyri dealing with medicine are buried in tombs. They discuss burns, pregnancy, tumors, bad breath, worms, and other ailments.

1298–1187 BCE Dynasty XIX rules. Ramesses I ("Re Has Fashioned"), a man of northeastern Egypt who has been the chief minister of Horemheb (early statues portray him as a scribe), is appointed pharaoh by the latter and founds the dynasty. He rules for two years.

- The state god is Amun, the administrative and religious capital Thebes, but the preferred residence is at Memphis or Per-Ra'messe, the latter in or near the delta (its exact location is unknown). Dynasty XIX needs the support of the priests of Thebes, whose power has grown; yet, trouble with pirates and migrants off the coast and military preoccupations in western Asia make residence in the north more practical. Ramesses probably takes a military expedition into Palestine.

1298–1064 BCE The power of the priesthood of Amun at Karnak grows inexorably; they succeed in making the office hereditary, and documents show the huge land properties owned by the temple.

1298–79 BCE Ramesses I begins and Sethos I completes a temple (which still stands) at Abydos, with shrines for Osiris and his family, as well as other deities. These probably win the

SCULPTURE AND PAINTING

Sculpture and painting in Egypt was not art for art's sake. A statue buried in a tomb was not just the likeness of the owner, but contained the deceased's spirit and was essential for his or her continued existence in the afterlife. Reliefs and paintings in the tomb also enabled the deceased to live a life of contentment in the other world.

The art that is described below was for a sophisticated elite, an expression of noble values with its own canons and aesthetic codes. Only a few persons at court were given permission to have statues carved of themselves. Only a few could have their tombs built and decorated with relief and painting. Yet sculptors, masons, and painters were not members of the ruling class, and a relief or statue was often the output of several men working at different stages of the preparation—preliminary chiseling, then the execution, polish, and finish.

Temple reliefs depicted real historical events that took place during a king's reign, and always showed him in a superior position, unless he was in front of a god.

RELIEFS AND PAINTINGS

A painting of dancers and musicians.

Reliefs could be low or else carved deeply, above the background surface of the wall, or sunk into it. At the outset, hieroglyphic signs and images were given bold outlines so that the colors could be filled in without smudging.

The main colors used by Egyptian painters were white (the pigment was made from chalk or gypsum), green (malachite), black (charcoal), and red (red ocher), but shades of yellow (yellow ocher or orpiment), blue (azurite), and brown (ocher) were also used in painting (on a ground of gesso on wall plaster). Especially in the New Kingdom, the paintings on tomb walls, coffins, and papyri had bright hues. In the Amarna Age (c. 1370–1340 BCE), a crowd of men would be painted with their skins in different shades: a dark blue would be next to a lighter shade of the same color, and so on.

new "outsider" pharaohs popular acclaim and priestly support. The seventh chapel at Abydos is for Sethos.

1298–01 BCE Stelae of Sethos I and Ramesses II at Serabit el-Khadim in Sinai attest to continued quarrying there of turquoise, which carries on into the reign of Merenptah.

1296 BCE The tomb of Ramesses I is hewn out of the cliff in the Biban el-Moluk (the Valley of the Kings); its halls are coated with plaster and painted, and the inscriptions on the sarcophagus are also painted, instead of carved; however, the tomb is unfinished.

1296–79 BCE Sethos (Sety) I, the son of

Reliefs on the temple at Karnak.

Ramesses, begins his reign with a military expedition to Syria. In the Lebanon range he has tall trees felled and also takes back prisoners of war and booty. In further expeditions he takes on the army of the Hittites under Mursilis II.

1296–79 BCE Reliefs on hypostyles at Karnak narrate Sethos I's military exploits in Palestine, Lebanon, and Syria.

1296–79 BCE Sethos I's land charter to the new religious establishment at Abydos is inscribed 560 miles in the south, near the Third Cataract,

131

THE HUMAN FORM

Several stylistic conventions were used when depicting the human form. A walking king would be shown with one foot behind the other, but both feet would be flat on the ground. In two-dimensional depiction—that is, in painting and relief—a person would invariably be shown with the head in profile but the visible eye in full form facing the viewer, as also the shoulders and torso, though the legs and feet would be in profile. The proportions of the human figure were standardized on a grid of equal squares. From the soles of the feet to the knees were six squares, to the hairline (not to the top of the head, which could take a wig or a crown or headdress) was a height of eighteen squares, and in later periods, twenty or twenty-one squares. In three-dimensional statuary the same rules applied and a grid was made. The width of the shoulders, for instance, was a third of the height of the figure until the New Kingdom.

When a man and a woman were depicted together, seated or standing side by side, they were usually of the same size, the woman on the man's left, with her right arm reaching out to his shoulder or waist. Complexions were also regularly distinguished, and men were portrayed much darker than women.

Left King Sesostris I: the human form in profile is always shown with one foot in front of the other.
Right: One of the earliest such sculptures shows the sculptor himself and his wife.

and has a poetic preamble describing the beauty of the temple. At Abydos, he sets up a list of great kings in Egypt in the past, which provides a source for later compilers such as Manetho.

1296–79 BCE Where Akhenaten has had the name of the god Amun hacked out, Sethos has it restored and also gives more importance to Osiris by constructing his temple at Abydos.

1296–79 BCE With its brilliantly painted reliefs, Sethos's sepulchre is perhaps the last that we can call work of the highest quality. The funerary temple of Sethos is perhaps the most imposing sepulchre in the Biban el-Moluk. Exceptionally beautiful are the burial chamber with a painted ceiling, and his huge alabaster sarcophagus—only 2 inches thick and

Egyptians at war with Libyans.

translucent.

1290 BCE The judgment of Osiris and the night journey through the netherworld are now favored themes in tombs.

1290 BCE (onward) Many wars are fought against the peoples of the Libyan desert who encroach into the western delta. The Egyptian army expands with Libyan, Nubian, and Sherden men who are taken prisoners of war.

1290–75 BCE Egypt enjoys its maximum territories in western Asia although the actual administration is left to local potentates, and the Egyptians only act as the pharaoh's ambassadors. In contrast, Nubia is directly governed.

1289 BCE Sethos I has nine wells dug along the route across Sinai to the Jordan valley and Syria, protecting each with a fort.

1280–1064 BCE Most images are stereotypes of scenes of war or religious offerings; the architecture of the period is impressive rather than beautiful; hieroglyphs are carved in the wrong proportions.

1279–12 BCE Rule of Ramesses II, the great builder, grandson of Ramesses I, who was sent to war with his father Sethos I in western Asia. Ramesses II is preoccupied with wars abroad, battering the frontiers of the Hittite empire, keeping down minor princes of Palestine, Lebanon, and Syria, and ultimately signing a peace treaty with Hattusilis, the Hittite king. He constructs a line of forts as defenses along the west coast road against the incursions of the Libu, Meshwesh, Tjemhu, and Tjehenyu of the Western (Libyan) Desert.

1279–12 BCE Ramesses II's reign is marked by the great length of his inscriptions on monuments that describe his victorious military campaigns.

1279–12 BCE Ramesses II adds a shrine to his predecessor's complex at Abydos, but its reliefs and hieroglyphs are not of good workmanship. At Karnak he completes the hypostyle hall begun by Horemheb (1328–1298 BCE) and continued by Sethos (1296–1279 BCE). His own funerary temple in Thebes, called the Ramesseum, has an immense pylon standing at the entrance to two colonnaded courtyards; a statue of the seated pharaoh is made of one totally unblemished block of black stone, but this is less well preserved than another statue (now in the British Museum).

- Ramesses II also installs multiple stelae in different places.

1279–12 BCE A damaged stela of Ramesses II has been found near Beirut; much Egyptian

Hypostyle hall at Karnak.

PERSPECTIVE

Hieroglyphic writing and painting were closely allied. Just as the written sign in the shape of a bird could be of the same size or larger than the open rectangle for house, so also in painting and relief, realistic scale was not essential. It was the importance of a person or thing in the particular context that determined relative size. If something was an important feature of a figure, it would be shown even if it would not have been visible from the angle of the viewer. (Thus, invariably, the arches under the soles of both feet, and all the fingers of both hands, were shown with a person in profile.) Similarly, one breast on the far side of a woman in profile was almost invariably shown. (This had nothing to do with how women actually dressed, because in statuary both breasts are shown covered.)

One frame might show the same person in sequential events. Also, a rectangular pond was depicted as a rectangle, without foreshortening; the trees growing at the edges of the pond would be shown growing outward: upright at

the far end, horizontal on each side, and upside down along the near edge. For a long time, two boats on the Nile would be shown one above the other, each on wavy lines depicting water, without one partially hiding the other behind it, and of the same size. In other words, there was no perspective. As one modern historian has put it, perspective is an illusion: Egyptians depicted nature not as they saw it but as they understood it. Yet some three-dimensional tomb models, carved in wood, prove a charming exception to the rule. A row of three porters on a wooden base may show them progressively larger the closer they are to the viewer, as if they (or one porter) were actually nearing the viewer. And in a few reliefs of the Amarna Age, when groups were the theme, one person would be partly hidden by the other.

Trees growing around a garden pond; here a Dynasty XVIII scribe and his wife are shown standing in judgment before Osiris (unseen).

SCULPTURE IN THE ROUND

For stone statuary a sculptor must chip away from a stone mass. In the process, any outstretched arm or foot might break off the parent block, and so the human form was never completely detached—a pillar would remain along the back, or a bridge between an arm and the chest and between the feet. As art historians have put it, the Egyptian sculptor "struggled to free" his figure from the block. (Sculptors may have traveled to the stone quarries because in one period it is possible to detect stylistic differences according to the stone and where it was found.) Occasionally, a great sculptor was honored by the pharaoh and given the title "Provided with Gifts." Technically, the handling of stone advanced so far that by the time of Dynasty XXVII, hard stones such as basalt and schist were polished to a sheen.

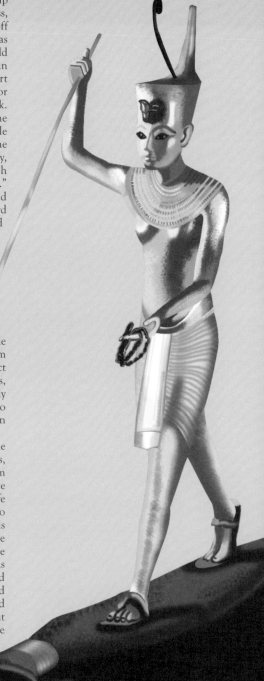

The hieroglyph for "statue" is a standing man in profile holding a long staff and a scepter. In the Egyptian sculptural canon certain forms were produced: the seated or standing pharaoh, the seated and standing god, the seated high official, the striding pharaoh, and so on. From the Middle Kingdom to the end of the first millennium BCE, "block statues" were produced: compact figures of nonroyal men seated on pedestals, the outline of the whole remaining basically geometric. The Middle Kingdom is also important for the beginnings of the depiction of old age in nonroyal portraiture.

But it is the Amarna Age that saw the greatest subtlety and innovation. Before this, the statues of buried kings had to show him in his youth and health, for that was the condition of this enjoyment of the afterlife (so much so that labels were necessary to distinguish the pharaoh's mother from his wife). But around 1400 BCE, much more realism was introduced in the portrait of the pharaoh, even unflattering features such as excess fat around the middle, an elongated face, or a long nose. Another unusual and effective innovation was to bypass rigid frontality, where the characters face straight ahead, and instead give a figure—such as the goddess —a turned head and an open-

influence must have been felt in the Levant, with the Egyptian garrisons scattered between Sinai and the Orontes River.

1279–12 BCE The Sherden (probably Sardinians) attack Egypt in warships, fighting with peculiar helmets, round shields, and strong swords, but later are mentioned as the pharaohs' bodyguards, and still later, as cultivating small plots of land.

• Ramesses II has wells dug for the workmen who convey gold from the Wadi el-Allaqi (Nubia). Only one minor war is fought in Nubia, a de facto province of Egypt at this time.

1245 BCE Ramesses II marries the eldest daughter of Hattusilis, the Hittite king.

1244 BCE Ramesses' masterpiece is a temple carved into the sandstone cliffs at Abu Simbel (Nubia) for Amun, Ptah, Re-Harakhty, and himself. This monument contains four massive

Four colossal statues of Ramesses II at the Abu Simbel temple.

armed posture. These poses were easier to create when, instead of stone, the statue was made of wood overlaid with gesso and then gilded. The tension and movement in the wood-and-gold statue of Tutankhamun harpooning a hippo is also remarkable. Little details also delight: it was in the Amarna Age that all five toes and toenails were shown on statues.

A technological artistic breakthrough was achieved in Dynasty XXV (752–656 BCE), when objects were modeled in clay, but then cast in bronze.

statues of Ramesses II wearing the double crown of Upper and Lower Egypt. Each is more than 65 feet high, carved out of the rock face. Between the feet and along the sides each has portraits of his wives or children. Beyond the entrance courtyard are sculptures of the gods and himself. Near this stupendous temple he builds a less imposing one to honor his wife, Nefertari.

King Merenptah, successor of Ramesses II.

Above: The goddess Selket is depicted in an unusual stance, with head turned and open arms.
Facing page: The famous image of Tutankhamun as the harpooner on a raft is one of the few depictions of the human figure that conveys a lively sense of movement, unlike most sculptural or pictorial representations.

As early as the Badarian period (5000 BCE), Egyptians decorated their bodies with beads of copper, glazed steatite, and other colorful stones. In the Naqada period, faience beads were added to these. Malachite and galena were used as eye makeup, and the palettes for grinding these were elaborately carved.

In the time of Dynasty I, we see that the wife of a pharaoh was buried with an armlet containing gold, turquoise, and amethyst. During the Old Kingdom, amethyst, crystal, agate-carnelian (all from the Eastern Desert), turquoise and malachite from Sinai, and lapis lazuli originating in eastern Afghanistan were in use for ornaments. Gold and electrum added to the glamour. As for techniques, gold leaf and cloisonné, or the making of rounded circles in which colored stones could be inlaid, were introduced. Statuary indicates that pectorals were worn. In time these became large and rectangular in outline.

During the time of the Middle Kingdom, red and green jasper (called *khenmet*, meaning "to delight") were imported from the Eastern Desert. The cloisonné technique was perfected. A stunning gold pectoral was placed in a tomb in El Lahun.

To the list of colorful substances was added, in the time of Dynasty XVIII, glass in many colors, set in cloisonné. Later there was coral (seventh century BCE) and, under the Ptolemies, beryl/emerald and pearls. Pearls were probably acquired after the

Musicians dressed in pleated gowns and wore scented cones on their heads, and had a great deal of jewelry.

A collar in the form of a vulture.
A bracelet inlaid with lapis lazuli
showing the *wedjat* eye.

early Roman trade with peninsular India had begun, and these, from the waters off southern India and Sri Lanka, began to flow into the Mediterranean.

The poor were content with headbands of green grass and fresh flowers—ironically, these were imitated in expensive materials for the rich! Egyptians also wore girdles of beads, pendants, and amulets at the throat (including scarabs and the *wedjat* eye); pectorals and earrings from the time of the Middle Kingdom; finger rings; and the *wesekh*, a broad collar of long beads strung in five to seven rows, which was first made in the time of Dynasty I but was especially fashionable for the elite of the New Kingdom, when much faience was used. Hoops or elaborate earrings with filigree (from the time of the Middle Kingdom) and granulation were worn in the New Kingdom. As for finger rings, King Tutankhamun wore one with a bezel cast as one piece in metal. Under Dynasty XX there was the gold signet ring, the name of its owner chased into the surface.

Certain colors carried symbolic value. Yellow (the color of gold), with which mummy masks were colored, stood for what endures. Green (malachite, the Eye of Horus

1244 BCE The Abu Simbel temple is so cut that for two days in the year, in spring and autumn, the rays of the rising sun penetrate through all the halls and light up the statues of Amun-Re, Ptah, and Re-Harakhty (and one of Ramesses himself) in the sanctuary.

1212–01 BCE Merenptah comes to the throne at the age of fifty; he is the thirteenth son of Ramesses II.

1207 BCE The Libyan incursions come to a head; the Libu with other groups, "Peoples of the Sea," lead a huge migration into the delta from Palestine. The Egyptians mutilate the bodies of the Sea Peoples they kill in battle; if uncircumcised, the corpses are castrated, otherwise their hands are cut off. Merenptah's victory over the Sea Peoples is narrated on the wall of the Karnak temple—he has repulsed a horde of migrants who arrive with their women and children to "seek food" and settle in Egypt.

1205 BCE Merenptah mentions Israel in an inscription—he desolated the land and it was left with no seed. Israel is listed along with other states of Canaan that have been defeated by Egypt.

1201–1187 BCE The reign of three rulers, each for short spells, one a child and the last of them (also the last ruler of Dynasty XIX) being Tawosret, the principal wife of the previous ruler. (Her funerary jewelry and vandalized mummy have been found.)

• There are law-and-order problems in Thebes: bribery, theft, snatching property, and physical violence (mentioned in various papyri). Few monuments are raised in the last decade or so of the rule of Dynasty XIX.

1200 BCE By now, as testified to by the important Papyrus Harris, temples enjoy huge incomes from their estates, and the wealthiest of these is the temple of Amun at Thebes. The later pharaohs of Dynasty XX will have to face the consequences of the great power of the priesthood.

1200 BCE (onward) Scribes who are sent abroad on errands show their familiarity with places such as Byblos, Tyre, and Qadesh in western Asia.

1187–85 BCE Rule of Dynasty XX.

1187–1064 BCE All Dynasty XX pharaohs, apart from the founder (Sethnakhte), are called Ramesses (Ramesses III to XI). Only Ramesses III has any claim to greatness.

1185–53 BCE Ramesses III is the last pharaoh

who can claim to be a great warrior. Up to about 1174 BCE he fights three major wars, twice against the Libyan confederation, once in

The Ramesseum

western Asia (narrated on his funerary temple at Medinet Habu and on the Papyrus Harris). His second campaign (c. 1177 BCE) is a naval battle against a huge horde of Sea Peoples—including women and children—from groups such as the Peleset, Tjekker, Sherden, and Weshwesh, who have ravaged the Hittite capital and are advancing on Egypt after creating turmoil in Syria and Palestine.

1185–53 BCE The palace (its brick foundations remain) and funerary temple of Ramesses III adjoin each other at Medinet Habu. The temple copies many features from the Ramesseum, including some reliefs depicting fighting in Syria, which this ruler never actually did! His tomb is now in the Biban el-Moluk, and his mummy in the Cairo Museum.

1185–53 BCE Interesting events such as a naval battle are depicted on the walls of the less-preserved palace of Ramesses III.

1185–53 BCE Ramesses III's funerary temple is one of the best-preserved sanctuaries in the

Ramesses III's name on his temple at Medinet Habu.

Theban necropolis; it has giant pylons, columnar courts, a roof that is still in place, and dozens of dwellings for the staff; its eastern gate is inspired by Syrian fortification architecture.

A headdress in the shape of a wig of a lady from the court of Tuthmosis III.

A pendant from Tutankhamun's tomb.

amulet) meant vegetation, new life, that which is life-producing. Red (carnelian, for instance) stood for life and victory, but also for fire and anger. As for blue (lapis lazuli), it stood for water, the Nile, the flood, and also the sky.

Amulets give us an insight into not just Egyptian aesthetics but also ideology and iconography, and the everyday problems and anxieties that Egyptians faced. They were ornaments that protected the wearer against injury or evil; their power was intrinsic in the creature or god that they represented, perhaps also in the material and color of the amulet. Not only were they worn in everyday life—as pendants, nail caps, on necklaces, and attached to clothes—they were also laid on mummies or mummy bandages. More than 300 types of amulets have been documented in pharaonic Egypt, and they were particularly plentiful after about 150 BCE. There were amulets in the shape of royal crowns or the *djed*-pillar (the hieroglyph for "endurance"); there were amulets representing Thoth, Hathor, Ba the bird, child gods, hybrid animals, and pregnant hippos. The *wedjat* eye was the lunar eye of Re, and was associated with Thoth; it was considered the best protection against jealousy, curses, or misfortune.

1185–53 BCE Faience tiles are made for Ramesses III's funerary temple at Medinet Habu depicting non-Egyptians with their own features and dress; they indicate an interest in other cultures.

1180–1064 BCE Papyri of this period indicate the range of "crimes" that people could commit, such as bribing henchmen of officials to have their accuser arrested, joining in the carrying of a god's statue when a punishment was yet to be determined, and helping oneself to garments from a temple store.

1174 BCE Ramesses III restores peace: he claims, "I planted the whole land with trees and verdure and let the people sit in their shade," and also claims that the women of Egypt can now travel freely.

1170–1064 BCE People begin to have very personal relationships with certain deities: it is held that Amun listens to humble entreaties, stretching out his hand to the weary, and whoever goes to him with a troubled heart comes away rejoicing.

1165–1065 BCE There are more written sources for this period—monumental, on ostraca, and on papyrus—than for any other in Egyptian history.

1160–55 BCE The Turin Papyrus is written in hieratic letters at Medinet Habu. It describes a palace conspiracy that began when a major-domo attached himself to the king's chief wife and then, in the harem, proceeded to foment resentment and rebellion—several officials and six wives were charged.

1160 BCE Minor papyri show that people were

A wall painting in the tomb of foreman Inerkha at Deir el-Medina depicts him with his family.

FAIENCE

The ancient Egyptians made beads, pendants, inlays, amulets, votive offerings, dishes, goblets, and other objects of faience. More than a hundred faience objects have been recovered from King Tutankhamun's tomb. In Egypt, as in Mesopotamia and South Asia, faience was, in practical terms, a substitute for semiprecious stones such as lapis lazuli and turquoise (although it was later made in other colors as well). Perhaps more accurately, it was a synthetic gem.

The word faience comes from Faenze, a town in Italy, where a glazed earthenware was made in late medieval times. Tjehenet, the Egyptian for faience, also means "shining"—faience is a material with a glaze. It is a sintered material because when it is fired only some of the ingredients melt and hold the whole together. The body was made of crushed quartz mixed with the right proportions of lime and natron

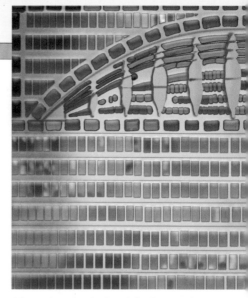

A faience tile panel used in Djoser's Step Pyramid at Saqqara.

or plant ash and the coat was a bright green-blue glaze that derived its color from powdered copper ore together with lime, silica, soda, and other minerals. The Egyptians had learned, in prehistoric times, to glaze steatite, but a glaze on stone is generally less bright than a glaze on frit, which is the irregular core of a faience artifact.

The faience of early Egypt was self-glazing: certain powders were mixed into the body of the artifact and then moved to the surface as the object dried, to form a crust. Later, the cementation technique caught on: the body of the artifact was given a coat that would partially melt and glaze it a pleasing color. Not only the aesthetic but also the practical value of this substance, soft enough to shape as desired, made it valuable.

In the Early Dynastic and Old Kingdom periods faience was largely glazed with the efflorescence technique, and shaped by pressing it into a mold or by flowing the mixture around a rod. Djoser's Step Pyramid was decorated with about 36,000 tiles, approximately 2 inches by 1.5 inches, of green-blue faience (the color probably carried a particular significance in Egyptian culture). When these were shaped in the mold, the reverse surface was

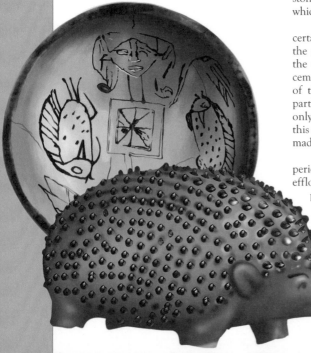

Above left: A bowl made from faience.
Left: Small statuettes, such as this faience hedgehog, were made around a straw core.

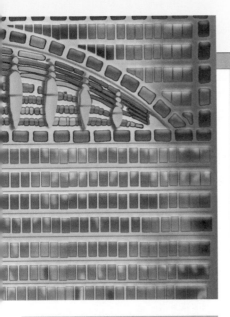

persuaded to write spells and make wax images to be smuggled into the women's quarters in the palace, but they were unsuccessful.

1160 BCE Up to this time Egypt retains its hold over lower Nubia and over Kush, further upstream.

1156 BCE A strike occurs in the workmen's village of Deir el-Medina when the monthly rations of the workers are not allotted.

1153–1064 BCE Ramesses IV to Ramesses XI. All have short reigns, and all begin their tomb construction in the Biban el-Moluk; their residences are increasingly confined to the delta and simultaneously the wealth of the Theban priests grows. There is much crime in the Theban area (evidenced from papyri)—where the priests grow exceptionally powerful as the pharaohs limit their interests to the north.

1150 BCE Ramesses IV leaves a record in the

The Great Harris Papyrus, written in hieratic.

Wadi Hammamat about the quarrying of graywacke for his huge stelae.

1150 BCE Papyrus Harris, written in beautiful hieratic letters for the state archive at Medinet Habu, with a colored picture of the gods and Ramesses III, describes all the latter's endowments to Thebes, Heliopolis, and Memphis: buildings, temple equipment, land, and what was earned through taxation.

1142 BCE The Wilbour Papyrus, 328 feet long and written in 5,200 lines, refers to the taxes on the lands of temples in Thebes, Heliopolis, and Memphis; whole families are liable to pay the taxes.

1141 BCE Ramesses V (as his mummy shows) dies of smallpox.

1100–700 BCE There is little archaeological information because of poor soil conditions at the delta sites; therefore, everyday life, house forms, and furniture are not well known.

NATRON

Natron was an easily available salt, a carbonate, the prime material used for mummification. Among its many other uses were: faience production, helping get rid of vermin in the house, and cleaning the teeth and other parts of the body. A circle of strewn natron powder constituted a simple spell against an unwanted influence or presence.

---

given a boss. The boss was later perforated and rows of tiles were threaded with copper wire, and then placed on the plastered wall surface. An early faience production center has been discovered at Abydos.

During the Middle Kingdom, production expanded, cementation was common, glazes were bright and adhered well to the body, and many new kinds of objects were made in faience. In the time of the New Kingdom, there was faience production at Tell el-Amarna, where hundreds of terra-cotta molds (for open casting) were found. The mold technique meant that identical items, such as faience rings, could be made by the dozen for the pharaoh to bestow as gifts on his subjects during festivities.

Writing, painting, and relief were used for communication in early Egypt: there was true writing with miniature image-signs standing for phonetic values (for spoken words, personal names, and also for concepts), interspersed with pure pictures. Unlike cuneiform writing, in which one sign stood for one syllable, in Egyptian hieroglyphic writing a sign generally stood for an entire word.

1141–33 BCE Ramesses V leaves the last record of pharaonic activity at the turquoise quarries of Serabit el-Khadim, Sinai.

1113 BCE The high priest of Amun has by now arrogated to himself a status no subject of a pharaoh had ever pretended to: he is shown on reliefs in the same height as the pharaoh, petitioning Amun-Re for long life, as does the pharaoh.

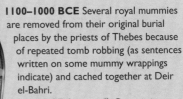

Canopic jars stored the internal organs (liver, lungs, stomach, and intestines) of the deceased during the process of mummification.

1100–1000 BCE Several royal mummies are removed from their original burial places by the priests of Thebes because of repeated tomb robbing (as sentences written on some mummy wrappings indicate) and cached together at Deir el-Bahri.

1100 BCE (onward) Canopic jars are popular recipients for mortal remains—the liver, lungs, stomach, and intestines—their lids are shaped and painted in the form of human or animal heads. All four are placed in the tomb.

1100–900 BCE Faience workers acquire the technique of making open-work

Left: Thoth, the ibis-headed god of writing, was the official recorder of the Weighing of the Heart ceremony before the journey to the afterlife.
Facing page: Seshat was the female version of Thoth, the goddess of writing and keeper of chronicles.

147

SCRIPTS

HIEROGLYPHS

The system of hieroglyphic writing that was also, with its picture signs, a kind of art, flourished from at least 3000 BCE to 394 CE. The word hieroglyph in Greek means "sacred carving." In this writing, pictures of men, vessels, stars, plants, and animals were carved and painted, or just painted, on votive objects such as large cosmetic palettes, and on temple and burial chamber walls, pyramid causeways, altar plinths, stelae, and statues. These signs conveyed the words and sounds of the spoken Egyptian language and were called mdw-ntr, or "god's words."

Writing began as a way to keep administrative memos or accounts, and for use as labels and captions (e.g., a personal name or a subject) on ceremonial mace heads and cosmetic palettes, burial chambers, or temple pillars that were decorated with scenes of ritual and worship. Thus, from the start, Egyptian writing was both utilitarian and linked with monumental display. In the beginning it did not necessarily give complete sentences. It was only around 2600–2500 BCE that continuous texts or complete sentences were written (lists and monumental captions continued), and the expressive potential of writing was realized. Even then, and even as signs that depicted an object came to have secondary associated meanings—for example, the picture of a scribe's palette also stood for "scribe," and the image of the sun conveyed not only "sun" but also "day" or "hour"—an artistic canon remained for drawing the signs; the orthography (how signs were to be written) was standardized by about 2600 BCE. Moreover, each sign had to have a particular color: the sun was red, the moon yellow. There were neither spaces nor marks between words.

Not only could one sign convey associated meanings, it could also have meanings unconnected with the picture: words with the same consonants (similar sounds) but quite different meanings. To make meanings clear, determinatives were used: the personal name of a man was written with the abbreviated picture of a seated man, a collective noun was accompanied by three short strokes, and so on.

In the Egyptian language—as in Semitic Hebrew and Arabic—the roots of words were

Hieroglyphs were miniature images that played an explanatory role side by side with sculptural reliefs or paintings; in later times they were almost exclusively used on temple walls.

mostly of three consonants and a hieroglyph stood for one such tri-consonantal root; vowels that had to be added in order to give the verbal form, case ending, and number were not written. So no one can read aloud the writing of ancient Egypt. In course of time, syllabic signs did, however, come into use; for example, the sign of the vulture conveyed the vowel "a" in the time of the New Kingdom.

This elegant script was used for three millennia with very few changes. There were about 750 hieroglyphic signs—used not only for monumental purposes (including legal and historical texts in temples) but also for ritual texts and high literature.

Above: The three main kinds of script: hieroglyphics (top), hieratic (center), demotic (bottom).
Above right: Thoth, the god of writing, could be depicted as a baboon.

HIERATIC

Sometime after 2600 BCE, the quicker, cursive writing system known as hieratic developed. This involved joining up signs in set ways, and this became a more practical script than hieroglyphics. Theoretically, hieratic conveyed the spoken form of Egyptian, which had been developing through the centuries apart from the written hieroglyphic form. From about 2000 BCE, hieratic was taught to trainee scribes. In this script were written administrative documents, personal letters, religious and magical papyri for the everyday use of priests and magicians, and graffiti on wadi rocks and terra-cottas. This "script of the priests" was simplified for everyday writing on papyrus in the later second millennium BCE, and further simplified in the Late Period (seventh century BCE).

COPTIC

Around 300 CE, with the advent of Christianity, the Egyptian language was written in Greek alphabets (with the addition of seven signs of the demotic script for sounds not found in Greek), and this script was known as Coptic. The Egyptian language, now incorporating many Greek words, was used as the language of biblical and ecclesiastical texts until about 1300 CE. It is still used in the Coptic church, though it ceased to be a spoken language after about 600 CE.

DEMOTIC

Herodotus used the term demotic ("of the people"—as distinct from "sacred" writing) for the script that developed in the delta around 700 BCE for everyday use. It was a very rapid form of writing, cursive, with ligatures, and its development from hieratic is known but not easy to demonstrate. Between 700 BCE and 450 CE, demotic was the standard script for vernacular use, on papyrus, wooden tablets, and pots. The Egyptians called it "letter writing."

However, even as late as the Saite Period (664–525 BCE), the hieratic script as developed during the New Kingdom was still in use, at the same time as the late hieratic script of Thebes, as well as the new demotic. Hieroglyphics were still being written on monuments.

When the Macedonian Greeks conquered Egypt, demotic writing was mainly in use. Greek was the language of the pharaohs during the three long centuries of Ptolemaic rule, when the status of the Egyptian language declined. Though Egyptian and Greek borrowed from each other, the period of bilingualism spelled the beginning of the end of Egyptian writing and literature. Native Egyptian ceased to be spoken and written for everyday purposes after about 400 CE.

WRITING TOOLS

Papyrus: Egyptian scribes used brushes of sedge (Juncus maritimus) with uneven—often chewed—tips, cakes of black and red pigment, and rolls of papyrus. The stalks of the tall papyrus plant of the delta, a sedge (Cyperus papyrus) that grows along the edge of sweet-water marsh, were peeled and then cut into long and narrow strips. While damp, these were placed lengthwise over other such strips, and pounded so that the strong but soft pith fibers adhered together—without a glue—into a sheet. Ivory-colored and much more durable than paper, papyrus was kept in large rolls of about twenty sheets tied with a string.

It has been calculated that the cost of a roll of papyrus was as much as a skilled artisan's salary for six days' work, and, at least in Ptolemaic times, papyrus was a royal monopoly. Most scholars believe that the word papyrus (Greek papuros) could have come from the word pa-per-aa, meaning "that of pharaoh," but this term was not actually used for writing material by the ancient Egyptians. In pharaonic times, papyrus fiber was also used for rope, basketry, and sandals. Papyrus went from Egypt to all parts of the Roman Empire, and was last used in Rome in the eleventh century. The papyrus plant was nearly extinct in the time of Napoléon, growing only in the Sudan and Sicily at that time, but it has now been reintroduced in Egypt.

Ostraca: Besides papyrus and votive objects and the doors, pillars, and walls of monuments, much use was also made of ostraca—potsherds and flakes of flint—for a variety of texts in the townships of workmen and artisans near tomb sites. For student scribes, there were also wooden writing boards.

The scribe would keep several brushes handy, dipping them in water and using black or red ink to write with. The red ink was only for highlighting words such as subheadings or totals. After 300 CE, the papyrus scroll was replaced by the codex, a book of sheets of paper.

Left: A woman holds stalks of the papyrus plant that would be painstakingly prepared before it could be used for writing.
Overleaf: The scribe was a highly respected official.

containers (e.g., for jewelry) in bright colors.

1100–700 BCE Medical papyri deal with snakebites, skin infections, and how to defeat malevolent spirits.

1094–64 BCE In the time of Ramesses XI there is a revolt in Thebes against the high priest Amenhotep; he is held captive by ruffians for six months. Marauders harm life in the towns.

• Herihor, earlier a military officer, becomes high priest of Amun; he is enormously wealthy and is depicted in reliefs with the pharaoh's double crown on his head, and bears all the names that pharaohs traditionally bore.

1075 BCE (onward) When asked to settle legal questions, the high priests of Thebes consult the oracle before making their decisions. The statue of Amun-Re, in his bark, nods when the name of a winning claimant or defendant is uttered.

1070 BCE A fictional narrative is written about the adventures of Wenamun in coastal Palestine. His dealings with the local people there reflect the low esteem that Egypt now holds in the world, in the time between Dynasties XX and XXI.

1064–656 BCE The Third Intermediate Period, rule of Dynasties XXI to XXV. There are mostly two centers of power—Tanis in the northeastern delta, and Thebes—they coexist without constant warfare. At Thebes, power is exercised by the high priests of Amun.

1064 BCE As Dynasty XXI comes to power in Tanis, the narrative of Wenamun states explicitly that the pharaoh is mortal and that the true overlord is the god Amun.

1064–38 BCE The first ruler of Dynasty XXI is Smendes, a man of the delta region who is

The solar bark crosses the heavens, containing the sun disk inscribed with an image of Amun carrying an ankh symbol.

possibly a son-in-law of Ramesses XI, the last king of the previous dynasty.

1064–940 BCE Royal sepulchres are insignificant compared with those of the New Kingdom.

- At Deir el-Bahri, underground galleries lead to more than a hundred coffins, as well as many *ushabti* figurines and statuettes buried with the mummified priests of Amun-Re.

1064–750 BCE This is considered a period of artistic decline where stone sculpture is concerned; rulers of Dynasty XXII appropriate older statues.

1064–656 BCE The importance of Amun, his priests, and his temple is acknowledged in Tanis, whereas the Theban priests accept the pharaohs of the delta as legitimate rulers.

1064–940 BCE The deity Amun-Re is transformed into the primordial god and source of all the other deities: his solar aspect is now played down except for his role of tirelessly crossing the heavens.

1060 BCE (onward) There is a large-scale reuse of stone from existing royal buildings, mainly at Tanis, but also in Thebes.

1050 BCE (onward) The *Book of Amduat* (or *What There Is in the Netherworld*) accompanies the dead in burials: in pictures and hieroglyphs it describes four regions of the netherworld corresponding to the twelve hours of the night.

The gold funerary mask of King Psusennes I, which shows the royal headcloth with the ureaus (cobra).

1049–26 BCE Pinudjem I is high priest of Amun and is also titled army commander. His sons succeed him to this position in Thebes.

1038–34 BCE Amenemnesu rules for only four years.

1034–981 BCE Psusennes I occupies the throne at Tanis and is buried there. His father is high priest of Amun at Thebes.

1000 BCE A long inscription engraved on a wall at Karnak describes how a high officer is tried for dishonesty. The matter is serious enough for an annual procession of the deity to Luxor to be postponed until he has chosen between one of two tablets about possible guilt.

1000 BCE (onward) Several small forts are built in Middle Egypt, in which the rural population takes refuge because of perennial skirmishes.

- Cartonnage is a much-used medium: it consists of layers of papyrus or of linen, stiffened with plaster of paris (gypsum). It is used for cases for mummified burials. The final gypsum layer is then painted.

1000–650 BCE Bronze casting becomes a major industry in Dynasty XXV Egypt, perhaps because of renewed imports of metal from Nubia. Earlier, under Dynasty XXI, *ushabti*

A princess dressed in the panther skin garb of a priestess is seated before a table covered with offerings.

figures were made of bronze.

- Protective spells written on small bits of papyrus have the same function as magical

LITERACY

The craftsman or stonecutter who carved hieroglyphs on tomb walls probably could not read them. As few ancient Egyptians were literate, written passages would have been read aloud. In one instance, the statue of an intellectual (c. 1820 BCE) was inscribed, "O people of Upper and Lower Egypt who come to pray, I will relay your words to Amun." Also, the spells inscribed in tombs were considered effective only when uttered. In Egyptian, "to read" also means "to recite" so that a pharaoh would "chant the writings."

Literacy and knowledge of the power of the written word did spread throughout the country. A middle-rank priest could write a series of letters to his family about quite ordinary things—telling them not to let the fields get flooded, or let a maid continue to give trouble when he was away on work. At Deir el-Medina, thousands of excavated ostraca prove that many people were reading and writing. Another indication of the spread of literacy and the power of the written word is the large scarabs of Amenophis III (1388–1348 BCE) of Dynasty XVIII. These contain between them five messages about hunts and about queens.

A papyrus detail shows the combined use of script and images containing spells from the *Book of the Dead* (c. 1032 BCE).

LITERATURE

Written material in ancient Egypt comprised many genres. For mundane purposes there were terse lists and accounts. Surviving records include annals that list years according to a significant event in a king's reign; legal texts, which are basically contracts or court decisions; and royal decrees, which were usually inscribed on stelae. Private letters on papyrus were folded up, tied with string, and sealed with clay. Tracts on medicine, mathematics, and astronomy have also been found on scrolls of papyrus.

In the category of religious literature were ritual recitations and procedures (lector priests carried rolls of papyrus and recited the texts in them during temple and funeral rites), pyramid spells often written on tomb walls, the Coffin Texts, and myths.

Besides royal decrees there were hymns, or eulogies, of some pharaohs and, after 1500 BCE, long texts commemorating victories in war. Long autobiographies (epitaphs) of the nobility—but not of kings—were inscribed in hieroglyphics on the walls of tombs.

There is also wisdom literature, didactic texts or teachings, laments, onomastica (lexicons), and narrative fiction. There are relatively few texts that one can classify as "popular" literature.

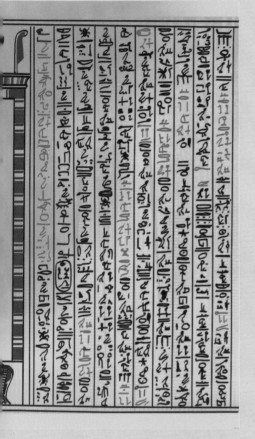

been settled in the delta. Their names reveal their foreign origins.

961–22 BCE The Israelite kingdom of Solomon flourishes in Jerusalem: there is an Old Testament verse (1 Kings 3:1) that states Solomon was married to a daughter of the Egyptian pharaoh, but no extant Egyptian source refers to this.

950 BCE (onward) Royal construction mainly takes place at Thebes, Tanis, Bubastis, Memphis (priests' tombs), and Giza (a small temple).

950–750 BCE Paintings of hieroglyphs and images on wooden coffins and mummy cartonnages almost become an art form by themselves. Several figurines of gold in the royal tombs at Tanis are made in the ninth century BCE.

Gold sandals on the mummified body of Shoshenq II ensured that he would be clad like the gods in the afterlife.

950 BCE (onward) There is a marked increase in the worship of animal gods. The bull cult, banned by Akhenaten, is revived. Meanwhile, the cult of the cat deity, Bast, gains in importance.

948–743 BCE Dynasty XXII, based in the delta, at Tanis. Its first ruler, Sheshonq I or Shoshenk, raids

Cats were highly revered and associated with the goddess Bast.

amulets and call on Amun for his continuous support.

1000 BCE (onward) Many unmarried royal women are given positions of ritual importance as "God's Wife" or "God's Wife of Amun."

984–74 BCE Amenemopet succeeds his father Psusennes I but after him there is a break in the line of succession.

981 BCE Psusennes I is buried in his tomb at Tanis with a gold mask on his face and in a gold coffin, but the outer sarcophagus is that of an earlier pharaoh.

968–48 BCE Rule of Siamun, a pharaoh with a purely Egyptian name, but possibly also of Libyan ancestry. He has the Deir el-Bahri cache with its New Kingdom mummies sealed up.

964–68 BCE Rule of Osokhor. He is the son of Meshwesh, chief of Libya, whose ancestors had

Palestine, probably sacking Jerusalem during this attack. His statue at Byblos indicates there was a political alliance there.

945–40 BCE Psusennes II is probably a high priest of Amun, who then seizes power in the delta.

940 BCE (onward) Sheshonq I develops the town of Bubastis in the eastern delta region as a cult center. From now on, thousands of commoners make pilgrimages there to the large temple of its local deity, the cat goddess,

155

THE SCRIBE IN SOCIETY

Palettes, water pots, brushes, pens, and papyrus rolls were part of the equipment required to write; here a scribe reads out an inventory prepared by other scribes.

A New Kingdom scribe was buried about 1550 BCE in a tomb on the west bank opposite Thebes, with his pens, ink pellets, palette, and a miniature terra-cotta of a baboon. This was an image of Thoth, the god of writing and the patron of scribes. In Giza, at least fourteen tombs that were built for high-ranking scribes have been found.

At Deir el-Medina, an ordinary, low-ranking scribe earned about a third more in grain allotment from the royal granary than did an artisan. Many tombs of the nobility at Saqqara and Giza had statues buried in them that showed a cross-legged man with papyrus on his knee, perhaps to convey the idea that the tomb owner was literate. This in turn shows that literacy carried status value. (Incidentally, model palettes of alabaster and ivory that had

never been used were found in the tomb of Tutankhamun.)

While literacy carried prestige, however, no king was ever depicted actually in the act of writing, nor was any high official. More befitting royal activity was hunting and fowling, or warring on the battlefield. It was the lower-level scribe who did the actual writing, recording the work at gold workshops, measuring fields, and estimating their revenue.

In the early periods, boys learned to read and write from their fathers, if they happened to be scribes; in the Middle Kingdom there was a scribal school (a "House of Life") near the palace, where boys began at the age of seven, practicing on ostraca and wooden boards, and later becoming apprentices to ritual specialists or medical men, or else entering state service as clerks.

Bast. Cats are so loved and revered hereafter that even workmen embalm their pets before burial. *(See also page 71)*

927–892 BCE Rule of Osorkon I. He is honored by a statue, with a Phoenician inscription at Byblos.

c. 917 BCE "And it came to pass that in the fifth year of king Rehoboam [the successor of Solomon] that Shishak the king of Egypt came up against Jerusalem and he took away the treasures." (I Kings 14:25–26).

900–800 BCE At the entrance to the Karnak temple precinct, pharaohs of Dynasty XXII raise the "Bubastite Portal," which depicts, among other events, war in western Asia.

877–38 BCE Osorkon II has a long reign and his reliefs at Bubastis depict the celebration of his Sed festival. He replaces the hereditary priest at Memphis with a member of his own family.

867–724 BCE The Theban Dynasty XXIII. It coexists somewhat with Dynasty XXII at Tanis. The first ruler is Harsiese, who began his career as a high priest.

850 BCE At Bubastis, Osorkon II constructs his Jubilee Hall.

877–38 BCE The priests of Thebes are exempted from a number of dues and state inspections.

877–38 BCE At Karnak, Osorkon II sets up an autobiographical inscription in seventy-seven columns of hieroglyphs. Shiploads of donations for Karnak and his regular visits to the sanctuary

Basically, writing was the repository of literature and "organized knowledge" in ancient Egypt. It was used for recording and accounting; it had, like painting and relief, a display function; and in its ritual function the written word was secreted away in tombs.

Writing was important for the temple and the pyramid complex. It was essential to draw the signs accurately because the written word had such power. If a particular sign that was to be written in a mortuary temple for a pharaoh took the form of a creature known to be dangerous, a scribe would distort the sign or mutilate it by omitting a limb, or he would substitute an inanimate object for the creature. In other contexts, a statue could be inscribed and then libations would be poured over it in order to effect a remedy.

are some of his activities that are mentioned.

850 BCE It becomes the custom at Thebes for oil lamps to burn in the sanctuary of Amun-Re and for geese to be sacrificed daily for subsidiary deities at Karnak.

853 BCE Egypt joins the "coalition of Qarqar," comprised of several Palestinian polities as a defense against the encroachments of the Assyrian king, Shalmaneser III.

838–743 BCE While the pharaohs of Dynasty XXII are generally acknowledged as legitimate, in reality there are numerous polities enjoying various degrees of autonomy during this period.

752–656 BCE The Nubian kings of Dynasty XXV rule over Egypt.

752–656 BCE Nubian rule does not bring about any religious transformation— the god Amun had been worshipped at Napata for centuries.

752–17 BCE The Nubian Piya (Pi'ankhi), whose center of power lies at Napata near the Fourth Cataract, goes north and brings the rulers of the delta under his control, and then withdraws to Napata, where the event is narrated on a stela.

750–650 BCE Under Dynasty XXV, old art standards are revived; much sculpture is done under the old classical canon of Egypt, but it depicts African people. In Nubia, meanwhile, stone carvers from Memphis depict Pharaoh Taharqa as a man-lion in the style of the New Kingdom.

743–15 BCE The Tanite Dynasty XXIII. There are few records of their rule.

731–17 BCE Dynasty XXIV rules from Sais in the western delta. Only the pharaonic titles of two rulers are known.

700 BCE (onward) The demotic script comes into use.

690–64 BCE Taharqa, the fourth ruler of Dynasty XXV, faces the Assyrian army of Esarhaddon.

674 & 671 BCE Esarhaddon the Assyrian, having taken his army to the Phoenician coast and consolidated his hold on Tyre, makes two attempts to take Memphis.

670 BCE Esarhaddon of Assyria writes about his battles with Taharqa: "Five times I hit him with the point of my arrows . . . and then I laid siege to Memphis, his royal residence; I destroyed it, tore down its walls, and burned it down."

666–62 BCE The last great Assyrian conqueror, Assurbanipal, conquers Thebes and divides Egypt among several vassal kings despite the efforts of the Nubian pharaoh Tanutamun to halt his advance. Assurbanipal strips the old

PHARAONIC INSCRIPTIONS

Ramesses II's description of his heroism in the Battle of Qadesh in Syria

"His Majesty started at a gallop and entered amid the host of the fallen ones of Khatti (the Hittites) being alone by himself, none other with him. His Majesty went to look about him, and found surrounding him 2,500 pairs of horses . . . There was no captain with me, no charioteer, no soldier of the army, no shield bearer; my infantry and chariotry melted away before the enemy, not one of them stood firm to fight . . . Then said His Majesty, 'What ails thee, father Amun? . . . Have I done anything without thee, do I not walk and halt at thy bidding? . . . What will men say if even a little thing befall him who bends himself to thy counsel?' "

Finally, Amun saves Ramesses by sending troops, who had been stationed nearby, in the nick of time.

Sethos I's inscription at Nauri near the Third Cataract concerning his new sanctuary at Abydos

The pharaoh wished to make conditions marginally less awful for the gold-washers in the Eastern Desert, who were to be dependents of the new temple. This is a charter for the new foundation. The pharaoh says:

"How miserable is a road without water! How shall travelers fare? Surely their throats will be parched. What will slake their thirst? The homeland is far away, the desert wide . . . Come now, I will make for them the means of preserving them alive, so that they may bless my name in years to come, and that future generations may boast of me for my energy, inasmuch as I am one compassionate and regardful of travelers."

Ramesses II attacks the Hittite fortress of Dapur in Syria.

temple of Karnak of its treasures.

664–525 BCE The Saite rulers of Dynasty XXVI have their tombs constructed in the precincts

A wooden coffin decorated with inscriptions; at the head are two eyes that enabled the mummy to look out from behind a painted door through which the spirit could pass.

of their temples in the delta, but are highly aware of their ancient heritage, the pyramids; some of them wish to be buried in the old pyramid cemeteries.

664–550 BCE The elite in the delta revere Menkaure, the Dynasty IV pharaoh, and dedicate a wooden coffin at his pyramid in Giza. Its inscription reads, "O King of Upper and Lower Egypt, Menkaure, live forever!"

664–525 BCE Dynasty XXVI rules. They are "northern merchant princes" with their center of administration and power in the delta. They institute a century of law and order by bringing Greek mercenaries into their armies.

660–50 BCE There are many immigrants living in Egypt during this period, and in statuary and relief carving, older styles are consciously emulated, especially Old Kingdom styles. (Some scholars feel this art is therefore stilted.)

656 BCE Tanutamun, the last Nubian pharaoh of Dynasty XXV, withdraws to Napata and his line dominates Nubia for decades.

653 BCE Lower Egypt, under the leadership of Psamtik (Psammetikhos I), ruler of Sais, revolts against Assyria, and finally expels the Assyrian forces. He founds Dynasty XXVI.

610–595 BCE Nekho II begins digging a canal from the Lower Nile to the Red Sea; according to the Greek historian Herodotus, he commissions a Phoenician fleet to sail around Africa.

610 BCE A relief depicting women in agitated mourning is stylized but there is also a rhythm about the upraised hands.

159

Having taken a literary form under Dynasty VI, the long autobiography was to remain an important literary genre for centuries to come. Autobiographical narratives are not simple self-praise. Instead, they are to be understood as epitaphs in the quest for immortality—as such, the narratives are stripped of the subject's errors and faults, and of inessential details.

THE AUTOBIOGRAPHY OF HARKHUF

This is carved in fifty-eight lines on the facade of a stone tomb at Aswan. The stone facade is soft, and the inscription is in a poor condition. The son of a lector-priest, Harkhuf began his career under Merenre and then was appointed governor of Upper Egypt for Pepy II, who sent him on four expeditions to Yam (Nubia) to prospect for stones, wood, and other valuable materials. He returned from the expeditions with 300 donkeys laden with incense, ebony, animal skins, and other goods, having accepted tribute or submission from local chiefs.

When he was returning from his last mission to Yam, writes Harkhuf, he received a letter from the pharaoh, telling him to hurry and bring to the palace the "Deng of the God's dances" (thought to be a dancing pigmy) from the "land of the horizon dwellers" (i.e., from the ends of the earth) whom he had captured, and to make sure no mishap occurred to the man, to guard him and make sure he did not fall off the boat. Harkhuf could look forward to the rarest of honors should he accomplish this task. "My Majesty desires to see this Deng more than all the tribute of the Mine Land and of Pwene."

There was a profusion of hieroglyphics and images on the walls of royal tombs In the New Kingdom.

THE AUTOBIOGRAPHY OF WENI

The shrine of Weni's tomb at Abydos was inscribed in hieroglyphs in fifty-one vertical columns preceded by a single line praying for offerings.

Weni had a long and adventurous career in public life from the reign of Teti through that of Pepy I, into the beginning of the reign of Merenre (c. 2345 to 2290 BCE). He began as a nobody ("a filet-wearing youth"). His first responsible task was to guard and escort the king, whom he obviously pleased, for when there was a conflict in the king's harem that had to be kept confidential, he was chosen to investigate. He was sent to the palace to make an inquiry and submit a written report to the pharaoh. "No official was there, only I alone."

There followed a war against the "Sand-dwellers" of Asia and a huge army had to be recruited; Weni distinguished himself as the commander of the army, and perhaps was so grateful to have completed the war unscathed that he offers up a poem:

"This army returned in safety;
It ravaged the Sand-dwellers' land.
This army returned in safety;
It flattened the Sand-dwellers' land.
This army returned in safety;
It cut down its figs and vines."

Later, as governor of Upper Egypt, Weni headed expeditions to bring stone for various tombs and buildings of the king. It is clear that ancient Egypt had no bureaucracy in the true sense of the word, for there was no specialization of tasks in the administration. One man could be deputed to different tasks, and could be granted various titles.

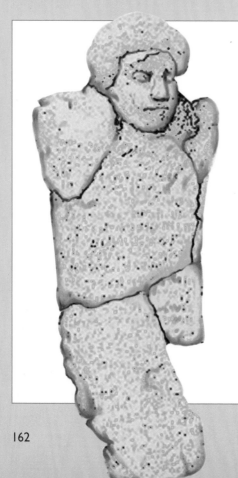

THE EXECRATION TEXTS

Since the time of the Old Kingdom, but especially from the reign of Sesostris III (1880–1840 BCE) onward, scrawled messages in the hieratic script could be found on potsherds, small bowls, and small figurines of men with their arms bound behind their backs, in clay or stone. These were deliberately broken and buried near tombs in Thebes and Saqqara and in a few places in Nubia.

The content of the inscriptions shows us that this was nothing but a magical practice. The texts were lists of people or things that were regarded as dangerous to the pharaoh and the tomb owner. Dead Egyptians (whose malevolent spirits might be on the prowl) and foreign princes (of Nubia, Libya, and Palestine) were among those named. The foreigners are described as those who might rebel or weave intrigue–they were all feared. The magical theory behind this practice was that by breaking the statuettes and the texts, known as Execration Texts, the person referred to would also be ritually destroyed.

A statue inscribed with an Execration Text.

600–500 BCE Regular contact of the Greeks with Egypt has its effect on the techniques, proportions, and classical lines of Greek statuary, according to some art historians.

600 BCE Naucratis no longer dominates the trade with the Mediterranean.

- The kick wheel is now used in Egyptian pottery.
- Knowledge of the medicinal properties of plants and seeds begins to spread to Greece.

595–89 BCE Psammetikhos II sets up several monuments and narrates facts about his expedition to Nubia in Greek, on the colossus of Ramesses II at Abu Simbel, at Tanis, and at Karnak.

Migration into Egypt

For decades Greeks had been migrating into Egypt in small groups, often marrying Egyptians, sometimes gravitating to their cult centers. The fifth century BCE is a century of massive immigration—of Greeks, Persians, and Jews—into Egypt. The major impact was felt on language (Greek and Aramaic came into Egypt) and the literary medium. Legal documents of the Jewish settlers in Aswan translate several clauses found in standard Egyptian contracts into Aramaic. These immigrants followed their own customs regarding marriage and dowries, but according to the laws of Egypt. In the late fourth century BCE, as Alexander's successors struggled for the domination of Palestine, more Jewish people were taken to, or encouraged to migrate to, Egypt, so that a large Jewish community began to form there. Documents of the fifth century BCE attest to slavery among the Jewish settlers, and to slaves being branded with the name of their owner on the right hand, being given to others in lieu of a debt, bearing the owner's children, and being freed.

589–70 BCE Apries rules. He is probably Hophra in the Old Testament (Jeremiah 44:30).

589–70 BCE The palace of Apries is the last surviving pharaonic palace. It is built in Memphis on a 43-foot-high platform.

588–87 BCE Nebuchadnezzar of Babylon has Jewish people of Jerusalem deported to Babylon; many of those left behind choose sanctuary in Egypt.

570–26 BCE Amasis rules. He loses allies in the eastern Mediterranean and is defeated by the Persian emperor Cambyses.

550 BCE (onward) Legal documents, in cursive hieratic or demotic script, take on a set format according to whether they concern sales, leases, divisions of property, or marriage settlements.

550 BCE (onward) Votive and *ushabti* faience figurines are mass-produced in molds; inscriptions are carved on them.

525 BCE Egypt finally surrenders to Cambyses at Memphis, and becomes a province of the Persian empire.

525–405 BCE Conventionally known as the period of Dynasty XXVII. Egypt is now under the administration of a Persian satrap and lower-level Persian officials from whom Egyptian functionaries take orders. The new rulers do not adopt any aspects of Egyptian culture.

525–400 BCE The goddess Neith, whose sanctuary is at Sais, becomes important.

525–22 BCE Though remembered by Greeks and Jews as a cruel ruler who destroyed Egyptian temples, Cambyses is recorded by an Egyptian priest as having cleared the important temple of Neith of foreign squatters after hearing a petition, and restoring it and its revenues to its priesthood. The inscription commemorating this is made in hieroglyphics

Darius I, Emperor of Persia.

on the statue of the priest Udjerharresne.

521–486 BCE Darius I, Emperor of Persia, orders the completion of a canal (about 47 miles west to east) along the Wadi Tumilat, through the Eastern Desert between the Nile near Bubastis and the northern end of the Red Sea. Twenty-four ships sail down this canal, taking the tribute of Egypt to Persia. The course of the canal through the Eastern Desert to the Red Sea is marked by a series of stelae inscribed in hieroglyphs and cuneiform.

- Darius I also has a temple to Amun built in the Kharga Oasis in the desert, far west of Abydos.

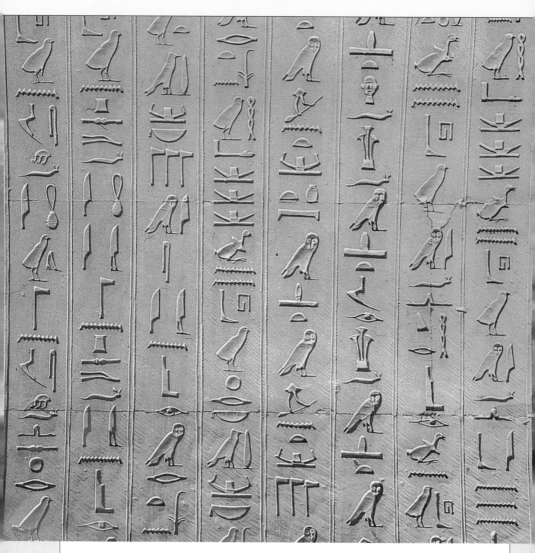

Pyramid Texts

Pyramid Texts were also inscribed on pyramid chambers of the same period, incantations to ensure the well-being of the tomb owner after death. In the royal pyramids, the texts describe how the pharaoh becomes identified with certain stars:

> "Make your seat in heaven,
> Among the stars of heaven,
> For you are the Lone Star . . .
> You shall look down on Osiris
> [who rules the dead in the Netherworld]."

The ferryman is then woken in the morning to ferry the dead across the waters that separate the sky from the earth.

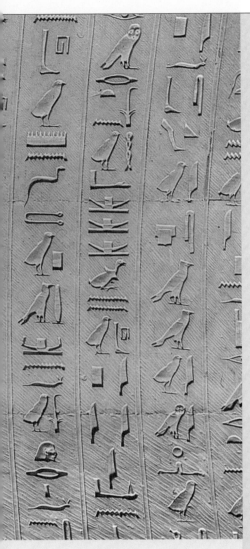

A detail from the Pyramid Text of a Dynasty XXVI official.

- Respecting the civilization of Egypt, he gives an order that its laws should be codified.

521–486 BCE At Susa (southern Persia), a large statue of Darius I in gray limestone that comes from the Wadi Hammamat, intended for a temple in Heliopolis, bears inscriptions not only in the three languages in cuneiform, but also in Egyptian hieroglyphs.

512 BCE In the famous "great demotic papyrus" found at el Hiba, an elderly man complains at length about the wrongs done to him, depriving him of his ancestral rights to property.

500 BCE (onward) Jewish settlers at Elephantine have built their own temple and the Persian emperors show interest in protecting their religious rights here as in Palestine.

500 BCE The stela of a priest-healer of Upper Egypt, which thanks the ram-headed Arsaphes for protecting him on his foreign travels, shows that Egyptian healers are in demand abroad.

500 BCE A few surviving pieces of red glass attest to the continuity of specialized glass workshops into the final decades of the pharaonic period.

Molded red glass figures considered to be Amarna princesses.

- Coinage, hitherto unknown, is introduced in Egypt. Mainly Persian and Greek issues, it is often valued for its metal rather than for its exchange function.

500 BCE Naucratis and Defenna have iron-smelters' workshops.

- By now the technology of faience production has improved: an apple-green color is achieved with the use of copper ore or antimony, and the glaze is

Block statue of an official and sage covered in incantations; water was poured over these, then collected in a basin at the feet of the statue and used for healing.

IRON AGE IN EGYPT

Egyptologists and archaeologists are not only concerned with monumental buildings and great art, but also with technology and the materials used for common tools or weapons. Iron came to Egypt relatively late: around 650 BCE, although it was being smelted in Anatolia before 2000 BCE. Elsewhere, bronze industries were still flourishing. Iron-smelting probably developed in northern Anatolia because of favorable natural conditions—iron-rich sands along the Black Sea coast contain impurities suitable for fusing.

There are some early exceptions in Egypt: King Tutankhamun (1343–1333 BCE) was buried with an iron-bladed dagger—still completely rust-free when it was found—which had a hilt and sheath of gold, and there were also sixteen small iron chisels in his tomb. But Egypt lacks plentiful iron ore. Perhaps Egyptian iron technology developed at the copper- smelting stations in Sinai, where iron ores may have been used as a flux for copper smelting. However, the regular use of iron in Egypt only came with Assyrian domination, around 650 BCE (the Assyrian army was equipped with iron weapons by 800 BCE, if not earlier). Rich iron ores are found near Meroe, and the hematite of the Eastern Desert was also a source of iron.

Stages in craft production with workers using blowpipes and other instruments.

HEALING STELAE

Egyptology can also unveil the practices and beliefs of ordinary people, such as statues and stelae that were used for healing.

On one gray schist stela, made about 350 BCE, there is a relief of the young god Horus surrounded by writing and images. The god subordinates the snake, scorpion, crocodile, and oryx. The function of the piece was to work healing magic, especially for body injuries.

People would go up to a stela such as this, touching it or pouring water on it that would then be brushed on the wound. The spells inscribed on the stela were then recited; for instance, "Be greeted, Horus! Come quickly to me today to protect me from the lions in the desert, the crocodiles in the river, and the snakes in their holes . . . May I be saved from evil by the power of your words."

more durable.

500 BCE "Healing" statues of child gods are set up to which worshippers can go for healing; some stelae (such as the Metternich Stela, now in the Metropolitan Museum) are specially made for particular individuals.

500–200 BCE Hieroglyphs continue to be used for inscribing spells—or good wishes—to look after the dead.

c. 500–400 BCE Jewish people in Egypt refer all matters of the temple and religious practice to Jerusalem.

485 & 463 BCE Unsuccessful rebellions occur against Persian domination.

459–54 BCE Herodotus travels to Egypt and writes extensively about it in his Historia.

Technology

The body core of the Naucratis faience consisted of an iron-rich clay that gave a black color when fired under reducing conditions; this technology did not reach Upper Egypt, where black continued to come from the addition of manganese. Faience "new year flasks," perhaps containing perfume, were exported all over the Mediterranean, popular for new year festivities. In metallurgy, the use of tin alloy for bronze decreased and this—a probable decline in the supply of tin—was to have a bearing on the advent of iron as the industrial material. Iron ores of the Eastern Desert off Aswan began to be exploited.

450 BCE A bundle of papyri written in Aramaic (one of the languages of the Persian empire and one which replaced Hebrew in Palestine), is deposited on Elephantine Island. These are a source on matters relating to Jewish people in the Persian garrison.

425–04 BCE A highly placed official, probably from Memphis, writes letters on leather in Aramaic.

420 BCE Literacy is still restricted, so the scribe who draws up a legal document would write the names of the witnesses to the contract, instead of the witnesses writing it themselves.

410 BCE At Elephantine there is a clash between Jewish settlers and Egyptian priests, and the Jewish temple is razed to the ground.

405 BCE A rebellion against the Persian satrap

is successful and for five years Egypt is independent, under a ruler from Sais known as Amyrtaios (Dynasty XXVIII).

405 BCE Some oracles are written in demotic on papyrus.

400 BCE–700 CE There is a steady output of Greek literature on papyrus, much of it written in Egypt.

399 BCE Amyrtaios is defeated in battle by Nepherites I, who becomes pharaoh at Mendes, north of Bubastis in the delta. He founds dynasty XXIX.

393 BCE Political divisions occur, especially in the delta, during the time of Dynasty XXIX. The winner of the dynastic dispute reigns for less than a year.

Tiny glass fragments made into a mosaic of the Horus falcon.

393–80 BCE Akhoris, grandson of Nepherites I, with the support of Athens and Cyprus, resists a Persian invasion.

380–42 BCE In the time of Dynasty XXX, Egypt falls intermittently under Persian domination.

The marvelous Avenue of Sphinxes leads to the temple of Luxor from Karnak.

380 BCE The first attested mosaic glass in Egypt is made by fusing together fine rods of different colors in intricate designs.

380–42 BCE Coins are minted in Egypt to pay Greek mercenaries.

380–42 BCE The Sphinx avenue is created for

As in all societies past and present, in ancient Egypt women had the important social role of making the home, giving support to the husband at work on the farm, and, most important of all, bringing up the children. There is much textual and artistic evidence, however, that they also had an important presence in the public realm. This was strange for Greek visitors such as Herodotus, accustomed to a society where women did not enjoy citizenship. Finding the Egyptian world bizarre by his standards, Herodotus wrote that Egyptian women went to the market while their men stayed at home weaving.

MARRIAGE

Ancient Egyptian literature recommends that once a young man prospers, he should found a household and cherish his wife, feed and clothe her well, and remember that "ointment soothes her body." It is good if a man gladdens the heart of his wife and does not confront her in court. A maxim says that if your wife is joyful, do not be indifferent to her.

The words for getting married were the same as "to moor a boat" and "to found a house."

There is no word in Egyptian for marriage as an institution; it was a private arrangement and event, and judging from the fact that there is no written testimony whatever for a marriage ritual, it was not a sacrament. It was not necessary to have a legal contract at marriage until the Late Period, and mostly among the Greek population. There were no public records of marriage. Divorce did not require a legal sanction either, only a disclosure of incompatibility or desire to separate. In addition, it appears that there were no rigid rules about whom one could or could not marry. Yet the institution was important for the socialization of the young, and also because the family was the group that took care of a person in the afterlife.

A couple made an independent home at marriage. A father may state that he has "given" his daughter in marriage to a man, but it appears that the young people had a choice. While parents did give personal goods, clothes, and jewelry to a daughter at her marriage, there was no dowry system as in ancient Greece (until the Greeks settled in the north), and there is sometimes evidence of grooms bringing gifts.

The private tombs of upper-class persons reveal that up to five wives could share the same afterlife as a dead man. We do not know if these are successive marriages or evidence of widespread polygamy. The literature does tell us that, as in so many other cultures, there were occasional stories about wicked stepmothers.

A painting from the tomb of a noble depicts the man and his wife seated at their dining table; though the woman is shown much smaller in size, this was not always the case and women were accorded great respect in ancient Egypt.

the approach to the temple at Luxor. A temple is built at Elephantine for Khnum. The island of Philae near Elephantine has its first buildings.

380–42 BCE Dynasty XXX sees a significant revival of sculpture in the round. In relief, statues reveal a marked tendency to emulate the work of Dynasty XVIII.

342–32 BCE A period of transition from Persian to Macedonian rule in Egypt.

332 BCE As Alexander the Great invades Egypt, the last Persian satrap surrenders without a fight and Alexander proceeds to Memphis to sacrifice a bull in the Egyptian custom. He consults the

oracle of Amun in the Sihwah Oasis, which was very popular with the Greeks, and places the administration in the hands of separate governors of Upper and Lower Egypt, each with his own treasury,

A bust of Alexander the Great.

in place of the satrap of the Persian period. Having appointed a deputy to see to the administration and tax collection, Alexander leaves Egypt. More fighting awaits him in Asia.

331 BCE Alexander the Great lays the foundations for the city of Alexandria near an existing Egyptian village that will be a suburb of that city.

330 BCE Alexander gives the Jews in a special quarter of Alexandria the same rights as the Greek settlers.

323 BCE Alexander dies and Ptolemy I Soter ("the Savior"), a Macedonian and one of Alexander's bodyguards, succeeds him as satrap of Egypt.

323 BCE Ptolemy annexes Syria and Palestine to Egypt.

320 BCE Egypt gains control of Cyrenaica in modern Libya, whose main town is Cyrene.

320 BCE Alexandria replaces Memphis as the capital of Egypt: Egypt has now become a land looking out to the Mediterranean rather than

one bounded by desert on west and east. Memphis retains its eminence and awes the Arabs who invade Egypt three centuries later.

320–30 BCE Demotic is used for temple affairs, marriage contracts, wills, divorce decrees, and tax receipts, and also for private letters.

315 BCE As satrap, Ptolemy makes a treaty and gains the regular use of the island of Rhodes as a trading base for Egypt. (Egypt also has a depot on the island of Delos.)

312 BCE The island of Cyprus becomes a Ptolemaic possession.

311 BCE Ptolemy's "Satrap Stela," written in hieroglyphs, declares that the territory of Patanut (Egypt)—with all its villages and towns, all its inhabitants and fields—that rightfully belong to the temple of Horus have been restored to the god forever.

305 BCE Ptolemy declares himself the king of Egypt, founding a dynasty of pharaohs who are Macedonian by birth, language (Greek), and culture.

305 BCE (onward) The hieratic script is used only for funerary papyri; there is a book for burial written in hieratic, but the owner's name is inscribed in demotic.

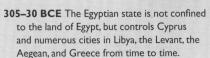

305–282 BCE Ptolemy I chronicles the campaigns of Alexander.

Portrait head of Queen Arsinoe II; she came from the line of Macedonian rulers that reigned in Egypt after the death of Alexander the Great.

305–30 BCE The Egyptian state is not confined to the land of Egypt, but controls Cyprus and numerous cities in Libya, the Levant, the Aegean, and Greece from time to time.

- The Ptolemies portray themselves in reliefs as pharaohs wearing the crowns of Upper and Lower Egypt, with the symbols of Hathor, the *ankh*, or life sign, and other Egyptian symbols. Yet on their coins they are portrayed as Greeks, wearing diadems.

- The administrative capital and the palaces of the rulers are located in Alexandria on the Mediterranean coast, a city founded by Alexander the Great. The Ptolemaic state administration runs on the meticulous keeping of records, especially of the complex system

THE ROYAL ADVANTAGE

Royal couples of the Amarna period are frequently depicted in art; here the queen holds a bunch of flowers while the figures, their movement, and the elaborate style of dress place the couple around the time of Akhenaten and Nefertiti.

Not only the ruling family but others as well are known to have married close family members. There is nothing in the written records to indicate that this was regarded as sinful. Many pharaohs of the New Kingdom are known to have had sister-wives, so too the Nubian pharaohs of the eighth century BCE, and the dynasty best known to have had incestuous marriages were the Macedonian Ptolemies (eight of them married their own sisters).

Where royal brother-sister marriages are concerned, we know that succession required both primogeniture and purity of royal blood from the mother's side. Besides, some ritual duties and privileges came to a royal wife and it may have been preferred to name a daughter of the family as a queen. (Priestesses of Amun were, after the New Kingdom, called "Amun's wife and daughter," even though those women took vows of celibacy.) In periods when the priesthood began to claim special prerogatives and there were crises of authority and legitimacy, it was imperative for a royal family to follow strict endogamy.

During the Ptolemaic period, the cult of the pharaoh and his queen developed into a cult of the ruling family: divine kingship may have been another reason for keeping marriages within its fold.

PRIESTESSES

Since early times, priestesses recited incantations, poured libations, and carried offerings in the temple of Hathor. In the Late Period in Thebes, their importance increased. Women are depicted on New Kingdom stelae making offerings to a god or ancestor. They are mentioned in temple documents as priestesses and chanters. Some women priests of high rank were temple administrators as well. With the advent of a full-time professional priesthood, royal women succeeded one another as the "god's wife." Many lower-ranking women were employed in the temple of Amun as "singers," probably attendants of the "god's wife."

of compulsory labor. Egypt now in many ways (commercially, politically, culturally) belongs to the Mediterranean world.

- The armies that control Egypt are staffed mainly by Greeks (Macedonians in particular), but in 246 and 216 BCE, Egyptian contingents have to be raised.

300 BCE After this date, the Greeks who are settled in Alexandria are governed entirely by Greek law.

300 BCE (onward) The hematite ores of Meroe (Sudan) are smelted for iron.

300 BCE The population and the cultivated area both expand from now on. Egypt is probably the most populous country in north Africa, the Mediterranean, and western Asia. For 200 years, Egypt's is perhaps the wealthiest ruling class in the region. Egypt is the last territory to fall to the Roman Empire.

- Euclid works in Alexandria, consolidating the corpus of Greek mathematics.

300–30 BCE Money is widely used throughout the economy but at the same time debts and payments are often tendered in kind. Egyptians who cannot write or speak Greek do not find employment in the administration. A camel contractor complains of ill treatment because he does not know how to behave like a Greek. Lawyers argue revenue cases against the malpractices and fraudulent exactions of officials.

- The Greek population relies on its own system of medicine rather than adopting the age-old practices of the Egyptians.

300–30 BCE The Ptolemies are mummified and buried

Painted coffin of a Ptolemaic ruler.

in sarcophagi at death in the old Egyptian way. Many Egyptian deities, however, are given Greek names. The worship of various animal deities grows. Crocodiles are mummified and buried by the hundreds, wrapped in papyrus. They are often placed singly or in groups in sarcophagi. So too are the sacred bulls at Memphis.

WOMEN RULERS

Four women were rulers before Cleopatra:

Nemtyemsaf II, or Nicotris (2196–2195 BCE), was described by the historian Manetho as "the noblest and loveliest of the women of her time." She was the last ruler of Dynasty VI and her reign brought the Old Kingdom to an end.

Sobekneferu (1785–1781 BCE) held a similar position at the end of the Middle Kingdom, as the last of the strong rulers of Dynasty XII. She is said to have succeeded her brother, Ammenemes IV, which may point to a dynastic feud.

Hatshepsut (1472–1457 BCE) of the illustrious Dynasty XVIII first seized power as the regent of the young Tuthmosis III, but within a few years assumed the royal titles and both crowns, and began to exercise power unilaterally. She is sometimes portrayed in a man's dress. In a propaganda act designed to strengthen her claim to the throne, she ordered reliefs that depict her birth by divine conception. She enjoyed a successful reign, but after her death, when Tuthmosis III became sole ruler, he had Hatshepsut's name erased from inscriptions and monuments. This may have been because he resented her seizure of power, resented a female ruler, or simply wanted to claim all the achievements of their joint reign for himself. She is not mentioned in any of the king lists. Yet it was she who organized a maritime expedition to the land of Punt, ordering her sculptors to capture for posterity the people, houses, vegetation, and products of that exotic land, and it is her temple at Deir el-Bahri that ranks as one of the finest of pharaonic Egypt. In 2007, her mummy was tentatively identified. (See also page 94)

Tawosret (1189–1187 BCE) was the last monarch of Dynasty XIX. There is very little information on her.

This image of Queen Hatshepsut from her funerary tomb at Deir el-Bahri is a rare one of her looking like a man; she kneels holding a vase with the symbol of stability, most probably before the god Amun.

Image of Cleopatra VII, the most famous of Egyptian queens by that name.

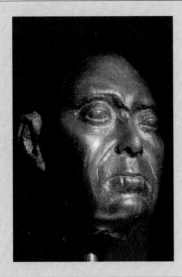

A Roman aristocrat is shown as an Egyptian, carved in Egyptian style.

CLEOPATRA

Cleopatra came to the throne at the age of seventeen to rule jointly with her ten-year-old brother, Ptolemy XIII, in 51 BCE. She married him in 48 BCE and then later married another brother. Julius Caesar's attack on Egypt was soon followed by their love affair, and Caesarion was born to them in 47 BCE. After Caesar's assassination in 44 BCE, Cleopatra once again was in need of support against her enemies at home, and her journey (as described by Plutarch) by boat to meet Mark Antony in a barge with silver oars, purple sails, and other lurid trappings may have been an act of vulgarity, but has inspired some great writing. She was portrayed together with Antony on silver denarii coins. Although she was a Greek pharaoh, Cleopatra knew the Egyptian language, appeared at certain key temple festivals, was portrayed wearing the traditional uraeus headdress, and was interested in the cult of Isis. Rather than face humiliation at the hands of Octavian, who defeated Antony, Cleopatra killed herself in a characteristically Egyptian way, holding a cobra or asp to her breast. *(See also timeline page 183)*

- Hundreds of terra-cotta figures and amulets in various kinds of stone testify to the nature of the popular religion.
- There are several synagogues in the country, especially after 180 BCE, when there is a new spurt in Jewish immigration. (Jews are granted the freedom to practice their own religion.)

300 BCE Philadelphia in the Faiyum depression is now settled. Built on the grid plan, it has good housing: two courtyards give access to two sets of rooms, there are mosaic floors for the bathrooms, and the walls of certain rooms are painted.

300–30 BCE Several superb portrait heads are attributed to Ptolemaic sculptors during this period, when the true portrait is born. Details include lines on the face skillfully rendered. Ptolemaic temple reliefs are often monotonously repetitive. Occasionally, figures are placed to face the viewer.

300–100 BCE An ibis of hollow silver, its eyes of glass with gold rims, is made for a ritual burial in the ibis cemetery at Hermopolis.

300–200 BCE A schoolbook in Greek contains the names of the Macedonian months, the names of numbers, deities, and rivers; there are poems, extracts from Homer, and humorous monologues.

300–30 BCE Greek is used for official documents of the elite, and for everyday communication—more in Alexandria than in the rest of Egypt.

300–100 BCE Although Egyptian exports earn huge revenues, most farmers tend their small plots and herds themselves.

- The main centers of glass production are Alexandria and a few coastal towns in the Levant. For glass vessels, a core is dipped into molten glass or else multicolored rods are fused together in a mosaic.

Sculpted head in the style of Ptolemaic royal portraiture of an unknown woman known as La Dame d'Alexandrie.

300–250 BCE The existence of the Great Library (House of Books) at Alexandria means that an educational institute, the Shrine of Muses or Museon, can be established.

290 BCE Ptolemy I establishes a new cult, the

WOMEN IN ART

Relaxed couples, family tableaux, a pharaoh and his mother were popular subjects in art. The women were shown as either the same size as the men, or smaller—relative size depended on the purpose of the depiction as well as comparative status. If statuary depicted queens and princesses in the funerary monument of a pharaoh, they would be shown on a relatively small scale, sometimes just knee-high to the colossal figure of the latter. At the same time there were many statues portraying the togetherness of a couple, royal or nonroyal, where the figures were on the same scale and the wife had an arm around the waist or the shoulder of the husband. Occasionally the huge figure of a queen mother holds a future king on her knee. Royal and upper-class women are never shown with haggard faces or bulging waists—except in the case of Nefertiti! Only the peasant woman is depicted hard at work, grinding grain, baking bread, or weaving.

A life-size statue in black granite of an aristocratic woman of Middle Kingdom times in her husband's tomb at Kerma, Nubia, is one of the instances of women as the sole subject of monumental art, seated in the same posture as any man for his funerary statue.

King Pepy II is shown on the lap of his mother, in the same way as Horus is shown on the lap of Isis.

Women in a royal harem playing games; retired dowagers also lived in the harem premises, which were strictly monitored for signs of conspiracy or unrest.

174

Royal wives were Hathor incarnate, portrayed with cow horns and the sun disk on their crowns. Chief queens appear to have had certain ritual functions.

Ahmose Nefetari, chief wife of Ahmose, founder of Dynasty XVIII (1550 BCE), had the title "God's Wife of Amun," and with the title gained certain privileges and grants of land.

Tiy, "King's Great Wife" of Amenophis III (1388–1348 BCE) of Dynasty XVIII, is mentioned with unusual frequency in his inscriptions, and her images abound, often alongside the pharaoh.

Nefertiti was the slender and graceful wife of Akhenaten, also known as Amenophis IV (1360–1343 BCE). Images of her show that she adopted completely different styles of clothing, headdresses, and jewelry from earlier fashions. She bore Akhenaten six daughters, and had an important role in the dissemination of his new religion. Then, like her husband, she fell into oblivion. No one knows the whereabouts of her tomb or her mummy.

Nefertari, wife of Ramesses II (1279–1212 BCE), was honored by the construction of a temple exclusively for her.

Nefertiti, commonly understood to be Akhenaten's chief queen, is depicted in sculptures and reliefs that have created the modern stereotype of the seductive Egyptian woman.

RIGHTS OF COMMON WOMEN

Ordinary Egyptian women occupied a more favorable legal position than women of other ancient civilizations. For example, the Greek polity from the sixth through third centuries BCE had an exclusively male citizenry. Greek women were not citizens, only the mothers of citizens; they did not participate in the assembly or the jury courts, and if they happened to own land, were not free to sell it or rent it out. If a marriage failed, the wife's dowry reverted to her father. In large-scale economic transactions, a Greek woman could not act without a male sponsor.

In contrast, Egyptian women were not debarred from owning property, even in early times. Although the husband was the provider and most women were buried in tombs built for their male relatives, women could inherit land. Since Middle Kingdom times, brothers and sisters could inherit equally, and from both parents—the condition being that they took responsibility for their parents' funerary rituals. In a particular case in the twelfth century BCE, a man left his entire estate to his wife rather than his siblings or children, "adopting" her in order to make doubly sure there would be no counterclaims. A woman's marital status made no difference to her right to property. A state record of the New Kingdom of the extent of land rented by different categories of people lists various classifications, including herdsmen, soldiers, priests, and women. Unless an adulterer, a divorced woman was given financial security, with her share of assets owned by her and her husband carefully calculated.

Egyptian women made loans on interest; they also made wills. They could initiate legal proceedings, which had the same weight as a man's. But if an adulterer herself, a woman faced harsh punishment.

Many statues of men with their wives are an indication of the near-equal position given to women; the wife is usually shown on the right of her husband.

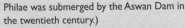

cult of Sarapis. There are shrines to Sarapis in Alexandria and Memphis, but elsewhere this deity is not popular.

284–46 BCE Ptolemy II Philadelphos ("Lover of His Sister/Brother") is less a general (he leaves warfare to his trusted commandants) than an intellectual, interested in zoology and botany, and is the first Ptolemy to marry his sister (Arsinoe II).

• Detailed laws are drawn up about revenues. Gold coins are issued.

280 BCE (onward)

Statue of a woman from the Ptolemaic period.

Elephants are used in the Egyptian army; camels begin to be imported.

280 BCE Ptolemaic sculpture in the round brings a new naturalism to Egypt, with soft curvatures as seen in female statues.

280 BCE (onward) Alexandria is less an Egyptian city than a Greek port on the Mediterranean.

• Ptolemy II sends gifts of silver and wheat to Athens.

275 BCE (onward) Some intellectuals at Alexandria write treatises on anatomy and physiology on the functions of various bodily organs.

275 BCE Manetho, an Egyptian priest, is commissioned to write a history of past pharaohs; he writes it in Greek. It remains a basic source for historians today.

270 BCE The temple of Isis is built soon after this date on the island of Philae. It is the chief sanctuary of Lower Nubia in the Ptolemaic period. (A small island above the First Cataract, Philae was submerged by the Aswan Dam in the twentieth century.)

258 BCE The orders for a census of Egypt are recorded on a demotic papyrus.

250–30 BCE Rural people live in constant fear of bandits on the country roads.

246–22 BCE Ptolemy III is known as Euergetes ("the Benefactor"). He promotes learning and issues an order that all travelers bringing books into Egypt must deposit these in the Library of Alexandria, so that a copy can be made.

246 BCE Ptolemy III invades northern Syria and for some decades Egypt rules the Levant, wrested from the Seleucids.

240 BCE After this date bronze coins begin to circulate in Egypt, issued by Ptolemy III, and in the reign of his successor, bronze totally replaces silver as currency.

• At the Library of Alexandria, Eratosthenes calculates the circumference of the earth by measuring shadows during the summer solstice. He makes the first attempt to draw a map of the world on a grid of longitude and latitude lines.

c. **240 BCE** The "Demotic Chronicle," a collection of tales about past pharaohs, is

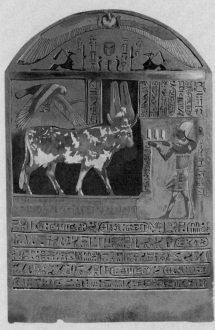

Ptolemy V Epiphanes offers a field to a holy bull in this painted and gilded relief.

The Sinai peninsula, Palestine, and Syria were the sources of valuable materials for Egypt, and contacts with these places are evident from prehistoric times and throughout the pharaonic period. Around 1475 BCE, a policy of military aggression was launched against Palestine and Syria, but after a century such confrontation gave way to a policy of marital alliances and diplomacy. This is known as the "Amarna Age," when a regular correspondence was maintained between the pharaohs and the rulers of Anatolia (the Hittites), Syria (the Mitannians), and Babylon, and also with several client chieftains of Palestine.

Nubians bringing tribute to the pharaoh; this could be in the form of animals, jewels, or any other offering.

SINAI: MINING AND MINERALS

The prehistoric settlement of Maadi near Cairo gives evidence of links with Sinai and south Palestine as early as the late fourth millennium BCE, when land routes were followed, and donkey caravans carried the goods. At Serabit el-Khadim and Maghara in western Sinai, and also at Timna on the eastern frontier of Sinai, the Egyptians mined copper and copper ore (a green stone called malachite also used as a cosmetic for the eyes), and blue turquoise. By Old Kingdom times the Egyptians had reached the Serabit el Khadim–Maghara mines by crossing the Gulf of Suez, as shown by the rock engraving of a ship near one of the mines. Sinai inscriptions, reliefs, and stelae depict the might of various pharaohs, and a temple of Hathor at Serabit el-Khadim built during the Middle Kingdom also indicates that hundreds of Egyptians labored there. (Hathor has been described by modern historians variously as the patron deity of miners, the deity of Sinai and Palestine, and the mistress of turquoise.)

It was the local Canaanite miners working for the Egyptians who invented the first alphabetic writing in the world, between 2000 and 1600 BCE. This alphabet of twenty-seven signs utilized the pictures of the Egyptian hieroglyphic script for short inscriptions that were mainly supplications to various Canaanite gods, and was inscribed on rocks, statues, and votive objects. Although the Sinaitic writing had spread to settlements in southern Palestine by 1600 BCE, the Phoenician alphabet—from which all other alphabets ultimately derive—probably originated as one of several parallel developments.

At Timna, the rock formation is comprised of soft sandstone that is easily cut and is rich in malachite and other oxidic ores of copper. By the time of the New Kingdom, Egyptian copper mining was proceeding on a large scale. This was made possible by technological innovations such as the invention of a slag-tapping device. If slag can be regularly let out of a burning kiln, it does not have to be periodically closed. Continuous smelting, however, meant that the vegetation of the area was badly depleted, and the hillsides were scarred by miners' shafts and galleries. Egyptian mining in this region probably came to an end by 1100 BCE.

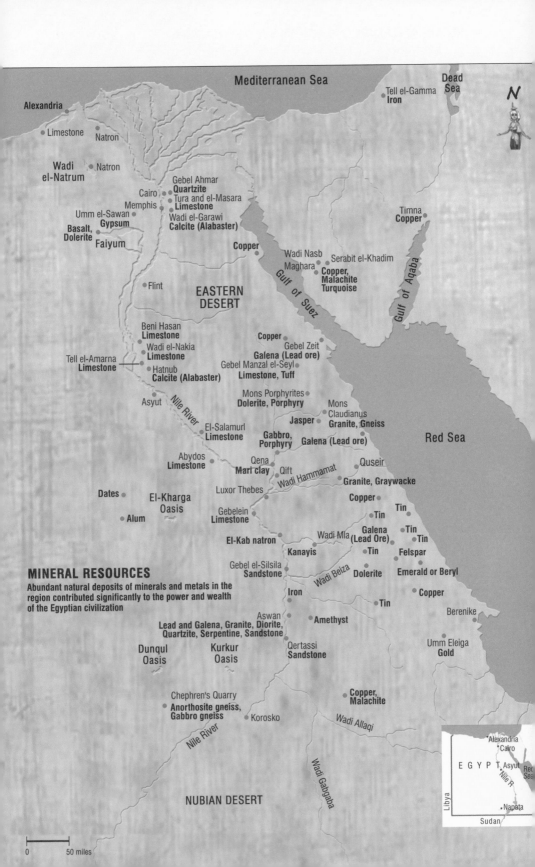

Mediterranean Sea

Dead Sea

Tell el-Gamma
Iron

N

Alexandria

• Limestone
• Natron

Wadi el-Natrum
• Natron

Timna
Copper

Gebel Ahmar
Quartzite
Cairo •
Tura and el-Masara
Limestone
Memphis •
Wadi el-Garawi
Calcite (Alabaster)

Umm el-Sawan
Gypsum
Basalt,
Dolerite
Faiyum

Copper

Wadi Nasb
Maghara
Serabit el-Khadim

Copper,
Malachite
Turquoise

Gulf of Suez

Gulf of Aqaba

• Flint

EASTERN
DESERT

Red Sea

Beni Hasan
Limestone
Wadi el-Nakia
Limestone
Tell el-Amarna
Limestone
• Hatnub
Calcite (Alabaster)

Copper •

Gebel Zeit
Galena (Lead ore)
Gebel Manzal el-Seyl
Limestone, Tuff

Asyut •

Nile River

Mons Porphyrites •
Dolerite, Porphyry

Mons
Claudianus
Granite, Gneiss

El-Salamurl
Limestone

Jasper •

Gabbro,
Porphyry
Galena (Lead ore)

Abydos
Limestone

Qena
Mari clay
Qift
Wadi Hammamat

Quseir

Dates •

El-Kharga
Oasis

Luxor Thebes

Granite, Graywacke

Copper •

• Alum

Gebelein
Limestone

Tin •

Tin •

El-Kab natron

Wadi Mia

Galena
(Lead Ore)
Tin •

• **Tin**
• **Tin**

Felspar

Kanayis

Tin •

MINERAL RESOURCES
Abundant natural deposits of minerals and metals in the
region contributed significantly to the power and wealth
of the Egyptian civilization

Gebel el-Silsila
Sandstone

Wadi Beiza

Dolerite •

Emerald or Beryl

Iron •

Copper •

Tin •

Berenike

Aswan •

Amethyst •

Umm Eleiga
Gold

Lead and Galena, Granite, Diorite,
Quartzite, Serpentine, Sandstone

Dunqul
Oasis

Kurkur
Oasis

Qertassi
Sandstone

Chephren's Quarry
Anorthosite gneiss,
Gabbro gneiss
• Korosko

Nile River

Copper,
Malachite

Wadi Allaqi

Wadi Gabgaba

NUBIAN DESERT

0   50 miles

SYRIA AND PALESTINE: WOOD, GOLD AND SILVER

From the Levant (Syria, Lebanon, and Palestine), Egypt took prisoners of war, cattle, fine wood such as cedar and pine, and the wood resins so essential for mummification. A portion of Egypt's copper came from Syria and Cyprus, clearly identifiable in the later second millennium in the form of oxhide-shaped ingots. Often Egyptian garrisons were stationed on key routes along the coast. At several settlements, Egyptian scarabs have been found, and it is possible that in some places Egyptian craftsmen were engaged in stone carving. Of all settlements in this region it was Byblos that had a particularly close relationship to Egypt. Byblos had a natural spring and a safe, small harbor, fertile land for agriculture, and mountain slopes covered with cedars, firs, and pines just a short distance away. Here, too, was an Egyptian temple of the goddess Hathor—small groups of Egyptians were probably resident here from time to time. Inscribed objects (often stone cups

Left and facing page right: Egyptian gold from the Eastern Desert and Nubia was famous, silver less so, and vessels and jewelry with advanced techniques of crafting were probably influenced by other cultures and found mostly at Tanis in Lower Egypt.

Above: Linen dresses and cloth, made from Egyptian flax, were commonly exported to Byblos and neighboring countries.

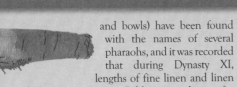

and bowls) have been found with the names of several pharaohs, and it was recorded that during Dynasty XI, lengths of fine linen and linen clothes were sent to Byblos to exchange for wood. Near Byblos, a metal axe inscribed with an Egyptian name was found, which suggests that it was the Egyptians who did the actual tree felling.

In the foundations of the temple of Monthu at Tod, south of Luxor, bronze chests containing a rich treasure were found. The chests were inscribed with the name of Ammenemes II (1932–1896 BCE), who elsewhere records the receipt of large quantities of silver from Syria. The artifacts of silver, gold, and lapis lazuli in the treasure that Ammenemes dedicated to the god are not of Egyptian workmanship, and many scholars think it was a gift from the prince of Byblos.

New Kingdom pharaohs must also have enjoyed a flourishing trade with cities around the eastern Mediterranean. Recent excavations have uncovered a fort, Zawiyet Umm el-Rakham, of Ramesses II on the Mediterranean coast 186 miles west of the delta, which has yielded fine pottery from Cyprus, Syria, Palestine, Crete, and Greece. The reason for such a fort would have been to protect Egyptian sea trade from marauding Libyan pirates.

benefactions to the temples of the Apis and Mnevis bulls.

222–04 BCE During the reign of Ptolemy IV, a debauched individual, a military and economic decline sets in—Egypt faces an attack in Syria and a rebellion at home. Upper Egypt secedes (206 BCE) and is thereafter ruled by a collateral branch. After this time dynastic feuds, court intrigues, and murders gather momentum and foreign intervention is encouraged.

204–180 BCE Ptolemy V Epiphanes ("God Manifest") is proclaimed joint king with his father; after the latter's death the regency of this infant passes through many hands. He marries a daughter of Antiochus of Syria called Cleopatra.

196 BCE A decree is issued by Ptolemy V on what is called the Rosetta stone: citing Egyptian gods, it shows that the king (Ptolemy V) is now crowned at Memphis. Because several revolts have occurred in this region, this is an act of appeasement of native Egyptians. The decree is written in hieroglyphics, demotic, and Greek on the Rosetta stone.

180–64 BCE At Kom Ombo, north of Aswan, Ptolemy VI begins the construction of a temple on sand dunes overlooking the Nile. Dedicated to Sobek the Crocodile and Harer the Elder Horus, it has columns with lotus and papyrus carvings symbolizing the north and the south.

180–164 BCE After Ptolemy VI, Philometor ("Mother-Loving God"), a young boy, takes the throne. There is an invasion by Antiochus in 170 BCE and again in 168 BCE, when the latter is crowned king of Egypt at Memphis. This does not last, however, because of Roman intervention.

The temple of Hathor at Dendera.

ROYAL CORRESPONDENCE

At Tell el-Amarna in 1887, a peasant woman happened upon clay tablets written in the Akkadian cuneiform of Mesopotamia. These were bought up by various dealers and were scattered across the world. Even so, painstaking scholarship has pieced together, from a total of about 350 letters, a fairly coherent picture of dealings among the various powers of the day, from the reign of Amenophis III to that of Akhenaten and then Tutankhamun (approximately between 1360 and 1340 BCE). It is now known that all the letters had been stored in the scribal archive east of the king's house in the ancient city of Akhetaten.

The letters were written in Akkadian rather than Egyptian, and many scribes in Anatolia, Syria, Palestine, and Egypt would have had to learn a foreign language and script. Akkadian was the common language of the entire region, but not as a bazaar or soldiers' colloquial speech—it was a vehicle of upper-class communication and high culture. While the letters between the great powers were written in Akkadian, with a marked Hurrian (north Syrian) input, those from the vassals of Syria and Palestine were heavily influenced by Canaanite, especially in grammar.

Pharaohs depended almost entirely on scribes to write both personal and public documents.

LETTERS OF ROYALTY

There was a standard beginning and ending to formal letters from the pharaoh. They usually ended with the words: "Know that the king is wholesome like the Sun in heaven. His numerous troops and chariots, from the rising of the Sun to the setting of the Sun, are well." A ruler of another large state might address him: "To A, the King of Egypt, my brother, say, 'Thus speaks B, the King of C. May it be well with your house, your wives, your sons . . . with everything in your land.' " If a ruler were too churlish to start his letter with this display of good manners, he might have received a reply saying that since on his side there had been no salutation, he would receive none either. This was for letters among equals.

LETTERS FROM VASSALS

A letter from a vassal in Palestine leaves us with the vivid impression of someone bowing and scraping, if not groveling: "To the king, my lord, my Sun-god, say, 'Thus A, your servant. At the feet of my king, my lord, and my Sun-god, seven times and seven times I fall.' " Other examples are the salutation from one who is a "servant, the dirt under your two feet." Or else: "I fall at the feet of the king, my lord, my sun, my divinity, the breath of my life, seven and seven times." The greetings and declaration of submission to the pharaoh often take up the largest part of the letter, the actual message coming at the tail end. For example, one vassal tells the pharaoh he has become an empty bronze cauldron, having been milked dry by the Sutu people, but was now reassured—presumably the pharaoh had sent him assistance.

164 BCE Rome, gathering momentum as the most formidable military power, begins active intervention in the affairs of Egypt.

163–45 BCE Ptolemy VIII, also known as Euergetes II, who was in charge of ruling Cyrene (Libya), returns to become pharaoh. He is remembered in tradition as a monster who made his subjects suffer.

150 BCE The Dendera temple for Hathor is begun; it is completed in 60 CE.

145–51 BCE There is a succession of later Ptolemies, who are unpopular with the people—one of them even sold the gold coffin of Alexander the Great in order to settle his debts.

118 BCE A decree of Ptolemy VIII clarifies that Egyptians making contracts with Greeks should appear before the higher judiciary, whereas matters among Egyptians themselves are to be taken to lower-ranking judges.

100 BCE The Syrians invent glassblowing, which markedly reduces the time and costs of production.

100 BCE The archive of the priest Dionysius

Image of an Egyptian queen believed to be Cleopatra.

LETTERS FROM CLIENTS

The contents of the letters from Palestinian clients, about three hundred in all, range from requests for goods or military help, to complaints about military threats and the treachery of their peers. The client kings freely accused their own personal enemies of allying themselves with the nomadic and destructive Hapiru people, who were given to frequent raids on towns and garrisons. A large number of the Amarni letters (about sixty) to the pharaoh came from Rib-Addi of Byblos, complaining about treachery and the seizure by enemies of his towns and villages—why did his lord do nothing about it? Where were the Egyptian and Nubian contingents that Rib-Addi had repeatedly requested?

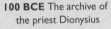

Egypt and Rome

Due to internal strife, the Ptolemies after 130 BCE become clients of Rome.

66–63 BCE Mark Antony's eastern campaigns make him—and Rome—powerful.

60–51 BCE There is ever-increasing Roman interference in Egypt.

47 BCE Cleopatra flees from Alexandria, alleging a plot against her, and puts together an army that fights on the eastern frontier of Egypt. (See also page 173)

46 BCE Julius Caesar, in pursuit of Pompey at the time, reinstalls Cleopatra as joint ruler with her younger brother. Cleopatra dallies with Caesar on a journey up the Nile, and possibly bears him a son, Ptolemy Caesarion.

MARITAL ALLIANCES

A sign of Egypt's supremacy in the Amarna Age (Akhenaten to Ay) is the fact that marital alliances among royalty involved foreign women marrying Egyptian royalty, never the other way around. For example, there were the marriages of Amenophis III and Akhenaten with three Mitannian princesses, a Hittite princess, and a princess from Babylon. Though Kadashman Enlil of Babylon received as gifts from Egypt inlaid ebony furniture, he wrote to Amenophis III voicing his anxiety as he had had no word from his sister since she had been given to the pharaoh in marriage. Was she even alive? As the Babylonian messenger read out this letter, Amenophis singled out one woman from the crowd, who said to the Mesopotamian messengers, "Behold your mistress. She stands before you!" But the messengers departed in doubt. Kadashman Enlil, on being told this, wrote back that the woman who spoke could have been "the daughter of a beggar." It is possible that foreign women did not settle into Egyptian court life: the Babylonian prince was clearly concerned for his sister. There is also the case of the Mitannian wife of Akhenaten, who was called "beloved wife" for a few years, but who then completely disappeared from the records.

ANATOLIA AND BABYLONIA: MILITARY AGGRESSION

Around 1550 BCE, western Asia was divided into several states, large and small, in perpetual conflict over borders, clients, and resources. Around 1470 BCE, Tuthmosis III launched his military aggression, destroying Megiddo and later reaching the Mitannian frontier. The Mitannian king fled, and the rulers of Anatolia (the Hittites) and Babylonia sent Tuthmosis rich gifts and pledges of loyalty. Yet, thereafter, Egypt did not set up its administrative institutions in Asia—pharaohs were content with exacting tribute, raising troops of fighting men for the garrisons, and welcoming the sons of Asian chiefs to be brought up in Thebes. Ultimately, Egypt had to contend with intrigue, and Tuthmosis IV had to take to the field. After a successful battle he married a Mitannian princess, and after his reign Egyptian imperialism was effectively at an end. Pharaohs would now concentrate on diplomacy, gift exchange, and marital alliances.

Right and overleaf: As the pharaohs increasingly ventured beyond their capital cities, they had to confront their neighbors, either militarily, as seen by this image of foreign captives, or through diplomatic negotiations.

44 BCE Julius Caesar is assassinated.

41 BCE Mark Antony summons Cleopatra to Tarsus in Cilicia. She sails up the river Cydnus, says Plutarch, on an exquisite gilded barge, with purple sails and silver oars, reclining under a gold-spangled canopy and attended by musicians. Once lovers, Antony and Cleopatra neglect affairs of state.

31 BCE At Actium in Greece, Antony is defeated by Octavian and Cleopatra withdraws her navy, followed by Antony. Both flee to Alexandria and Octavian follows them there. Antony is killed, and Cleopatra commits suicide by letting a snake bite her.

27 BCE Octavian becomes emperor of Rome, using the name Augustus.

of Akoris contains tenancy and sales documents in demotic and Greek.

80–51 BCE The Romans seize Cyprus from Ptolemy XII, who is then deposed.

51–30 BCE The reign of the beautiful Cleopatra VII, who begins to rule at the age of seventeen with Ptolemy XIII, her elder brother. She is the only Ptolemy who speaks Egyptian. She loses her kingdom to Rome.

30 BCE–395 CE Across Egypt there is worship of the old Egyptian deities (such as Hathor, Thoth, Osiris, Horus, and Amun); of Greek gods such as Apollo; of the Roman Jupiter; of the Jewish god; and also, in a shrine in a large temple at Memphis, of the Syrian Astarte. Many temples are joint shrines for several gods (e.g., Isis, Sarapis, and Thoeris shared a temple).

Bronze figure of the god Horus portrayed as a Roman soldier.

30 BCE–395 CE Peace and relative stability come to Egypt, with a new administrative system, new economic and political institutions, and three (later two) Roman legions to ensure law and order. Egypt is the only province of the Roman Empire to be ruled by a prefect of equestrian rank, rather than a viceroy of senatorial rank (which was the highest). Directly appointed by the emperor, the prefect has a limited tenure of office.

• Egypt is the chief supplier of grain to the

Roman heartland. Josephus (75 CE) writes that Egyptian wheat sustained Rome for four months in the year.

• Egyptians have to bear the cost of Roman rule in many ways; for instance, an imperial visit in 130 CE cost a small town 13,228 pounds of barley, 3,000 bundles of hay, 372 suckling pigs, and 200 sheep.

• Egypt supplies papyrus to the entire Roman Empire, and also exports (mainly from Alexandria) glass and linen. Prophyry and fine granite from Egypt are used for monuments in Rome.

30 BCE–296 CE Coins are minted in Alexandria but it is against the law to take them out of Egypt. They are called drachmae. After this period, Egypt uses the general currencies of the Roman Empire.

27 BCE Octavian becomes ruler of Rome and thereby assumes sovereignty over Egypt.

24 BCE Perhaps the earliest Latin document in Egypt is poetry left behind by a soldier stationed at Qasr Ibrim (Nubia).

0–200 CE In private houses, the figures of gods are painted on walls. Statues of various deities are also kept.

0–200 CE Farmers are regularly in debt, based on the value of their expected

The Roman Style

In the Roman period, some Egyptians adopted Greco-Roman clothes and hairstyles, especially those associated with the elite in Rome.

• Many Romans were mummified and buried with gilded masks.

harvests. Because of monetization, the spiral of debt can be unending.

• Caracalla grants citizenship to all people in the Roman Empire. Until 212 CE, other citizens have decidedly greater legal and fiscal privileges over the local Egyptians.

0–200 CE Collections of love spells in Greek constitute a part of the popular literature of the time.

0–300 CE Unlike the practice in Egyptian temples,

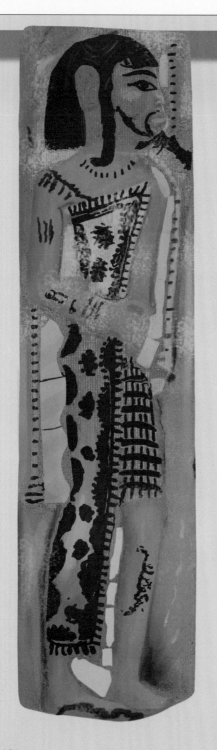

COSMOPOLITAN CULTURES

Embassies arriving from different regions must have added color to the pharaoh's court, which was mainly held in vast open courtyards. Paintings show a wide variety of nationalities present at court, with different physical features, hairstyles, and dress, such as the patterned robes of some visitors and the tasseled skirts of Palestinian chiefs.

Long after Egypt lost her political control of Asia, the prestige of her culture lingered. As the Assyrian kingdom grew in military strength and expanded toward the coast of the Mediterranean, Phoenician ivory carvers were carried off to Assyrian capitals to work for their kings. At the Assyrian capital of Nimrud, many carved ivory pieces were found, once attached to numerous pieces of royal furniture (c. 900-650 BCE). These are mostly exotica. The preponderance of Egyptian motifs—the sphinx, the lioness killing a Nubian, clothes, wigs, jugs—is astounding. Egyptian culture must have been the rage, and the upstart Assyrian elite would have wanted to emulate it.

CLIENT CHIEFS

The Egyptian state did not really maintain law and order in Palestine. There were many complaints of corruption. One Egyptian garrison official at Joppa was accused of using the men who reported for guard duty for his own work. Moreover, the pharaoh was informed that this official released these men only when a ransom had been paid. And whereas the mountain bandits charged thirty shekels of silver as ransom, this Egyptian demanded a hundred! There are many signs in the Palestinian letters of what was to come in 1200 BCE: the number of landless and lawless peoples—of varying ethnic affiliations—grew. Ultimately, many bronze-age states would be swamped by hordes of land and sea migrants. Only the Egyptian state under Ramesses III would survive.

Greek and Roman cult centers allow laypersons to pour libations and make sacrifices in temples.

- The Egyptian goddess Isis becomes popular across the Roman Empire. The mysteries of Isis figure in one of Plutarch's narratives (c. 150). Images of Isis, the mother with a suckling infant Horus, are said to preempt images of Mary and the infant Jesus.

0–300 CE Numerous Greek temples exist during this time in Egypt, dedicated to gods such as Apollo and Demeter, at places like Karanis and Theadelphia.

0–300 CE After their incorporation into the Roman Empire, Egyptians gradually take to the Christian faith.

- Early Christian practices include the exorcism

Isis and Horus provide the universal image of mother and child.

Surveyors assessing the wheat harvest; supplies of grain for towns were carefully measured.

187

ometimes we forget that Egypt is not only the valley of the Nile, but also a large area of desert, and that the Eastern Desert, crossed by numerous seasonal wadi beds, had an array of mineral resources such as copper, gold, limestone, granite, amethyst, tuff, alabaster, and some iron. So, this desert was traversed by Egyptians from earliest times. As the Nile makes an eastward loop below Luxor it comes closest to the Red Sea coast, and from here (more precisely from Coptos on the right bank) went the most important route, eastward to Quseir on the sea, following the Wadi Hammamat. (This wadi had important gold reserves.)

Boats and ships became increasingly more sophisticated as the need to traverse large expanses of water beyond the kingdom arose.

THE PTOLEMIES — TO ARABIA AND INDIA

During the Ptolemaic period (300-30 BCE), the Red Sea trade between Egypt and Arabia/India resumed in force. This was inspired partly by military need—the Ptolemies required a port for the import of African elephants for their army to use against the Indian elephants of the Seleucids—and partly by the general strategic planning of the

EXOTIC EXCHANGES

In general, besides Arabian incense and spices, the sea traffic comprised Indian and Sri Lankan pepper, nard, bdellium, sapphires, diamonds, ivory, pearls, and tortoiseshell; and from the Horn of Africa and Egypt came cloth and garments, glass, wine, and olive oil. There was a great demand for red coral (found on the Red Sea and Mediterranean Sea shores) in India.

various rulers. Ashoka, the great Mauryan emperor of India (c. 268-233 BCE), who converted to Buddhism, received an embassy from Ptolemy II Philadelphos (this is recorded by Pliny). In his turn, Ashoka recorded in his Thirteenth Rock Edict the fact that his men took the message of his religion abroad to five Greek kings, among whom was "Tulamaya."

Ptolemy II had an old canal opened, linking the lower Nile with the Gulf of Suez. On the southern Red Sea coast the port of Berenike was established, supplanting the existing ports of Quseir and Myos Hormos (the latter at the mouth of the Gulf of Suez) in order to save ships the struggle of battling with the winds on their return journey from the Arabian Sea, for Egypt of the Ptolemies had begun trading with the Sabaeans and Nabateans of Arabia in frankincense and myrrh. As sea transport became more widely used, Ptolemy VII appointed an official to be in charge of sailings.

TRAVELER'S SEA GUIDE

So busy must the sea lanes have been that a Greek-speaking Egyptian wrote a handbook, *The Periplus of the Erythraean Sea*, in the middle of the first century CE. This was a guide to the ports, sailing conditions, and cargoes of the coasts of the Red Sea, northeast Africa, Arabia, the Gulf of Suez, and southern Asia to Sri Lanka, and even the eastern coast of peninsular India. Knowledge of trade goods of the period draws largely from this tract.

There is supporting archaeological evidence as well. Recent excavations at Berenike have unearthed Ptolemaic and Greek coins, locally made rope, metalware, pottery and basketry, the coconut, batik-printed fabric, a large cache of pepper, carnelian beads, and huge quantities of teak wood, the preeminent product of peninsular India. In India, one of the southernmost coastal sites, Alagankulam, has yielded Egyptian-looking objects, and peninsular India has been known for decades to have turned up amphorae, glass, and hoards of early Roman coins near its beryl mines, and also along major land routes.

Coffins in the Roman period followed the Egyptian style and were richly decorated and gilded.

of demons that are supposed to cause disease, but Christians do not perform animal sacrifices or pour libations to the gods, nor do they worship the emperor. For these reasons they are often singled out for persecution, and many are martyred.

• They keep a low profile in Egypt and there is little documentary or archaeological evidence of them.

0–400 CE The cult of Sarapis, the Apis bull that was absorbed at death by Osiris, is very popular across Egypt, with important centers at Alexandria and Memphis, where bulls are buried in gigantic sarcophagi.

0–400 CE There are libraries at Alexandria and also in the Serapeum of Memphis. Thousands of papyri, written in hieratic (for temple texts),

---

HYPALUS — A SAILOR OR MONSOON WIND

In an older version of the legend, a Greek pilot named Hypalus (or Hippalus), by studying various ports and observing the stars, hit on a way of crossing the high seas with the southwest monsoon winds behind him—a dangerous undertaking, as the Arabian Sea is rough at this time—so that he could bypass the Arab ports, and prove that a direct journey between the Red Sea and the Malabar coast of southwestern India was feasible. In another version, pieced together from ancient Greek testimony, Hypalus is not the name of a person, as the ancients thought, but refers to the southwest monsoon wind. Someone, perhaps an Arab, had learned how to leave a certain Red Sea/Arabian port and sail along one parallel by watching the stars, in order to make for a particular port on the west coast of India.

How did this knowledge come to Egypt? A romantic Greek legend goes that some soldiers on patrol on the Red Sea coast found a shipwrecked Indian sailor, nursed him back to health, and took him to their king. Once he was able to converse in Greek, this sailor told them that his ship had been blown off course on the high seas and capsized. Then in gratitude, he guided an Egyptian crew chosen by the king across the sea to India.

Once the Romans annexed Egypt, the trade gathered momentum. In the first century, Strabo wrote that 120 ships sailed from Myos Hormos to India each year. Berenike was also a busy port, and in rock shelters along the route to the Nile are inscriptions, one of which states: "X [an Italian name], returning from India, stopped here in the twenty-eighth year of Augustus." In the Ptolemaic and Roman periods, surfaced roads were constructed between the coast and the Nile for goods to be taken by animal caravan to the river and then downstream to Alexandria and perhaps further, by sea, to Rome itself.

THE LAND OF PUNT

Along the Red Sea coast, Middle Kingdom boat remains (planks with mortises) have been found at Marsa Gawasis, southeast of Quseir, with inscriptions in the area that refer to the land of Punt.

In the time of the New Kingdom, Hatshepsut of Dynasty XVIII (1472–1457 BCE) sent an expedition to the land of Punt, in or near present-day Eritrea on the Horn of Africa. This expedition took the Wadi Hammamat route and then boarded sailing ships with unusually broad sails to go south down the Red Sea, a distance of more than 620 miles. Hatshepsut's carvers, in documenting this event, carefully portray the physical features of the chief of Punt and his wife, their round huts with ladders for access, the short-horned cattle, and the palm trees and birds in their land. They then describe the Egyptian boats leaving with gold, myrrh trees for planting, as well as myrrh itself (it was needed during sacrifices in the temples), baboons, leopard skins, and ivory. From the Egyptians, Punt received meat, fruit, beer, beads and other ornaments, and weapons. The voyage to Punt would have been relatively easy, with winds behind the sails, but for the journey back, it was necessary to row the narrow craft up the Red Sea coast. *(See also page 94)*

demotic, Greek, and Coptic (Egyptian written in the Greek alphabet), are known from this period.

0–400 CE Hundreds of brick houses exist in the grand city of Alexandria; the water is supplied by a network of underground cisterns, and there are catacomb burials. Also here, besides the great Caesareum built by Cleopatra, with porticoes, courtyards, groves, and obelisks in front of the structure, there is a theater with columns of Italian marble, and churches.

0 CE (onward) Obelisks and Egyptian-style buildings are constructed in Rome and the cult of Isis spreads outside Egypt.

41–44 CE Legend has it that Saint Mark visits Egypt and evangelizes.

45–50 CE Papers in the office of the local administration at a small town in the Faiyum record 113 contracts about the lending of money.

65 CE There is an unbroken succession of patriarchs (bishops) at the head of the Egyptian church in Alexandria. The Coptic (literally "Egyptian") Church is thus one of the oldest Christian churches. Today, Christians in Egypt are known as Copts.

65 CE The prefect of Egypt makes Meroe a part of the Roman Empire, but soon withdraws and for some time the frontier lies five miles south of the First Cataract.

The Chief of Punt and his wife, graphically depicted on Hatshepsut's temple at Deir el-Bahri.

Up until the period of the New Kingdom, the largest towns were Memphis and Thebes. Akhetaten (Tell el-Amarna) flourished briefly in the lifetime of Akhenaten of Dynasty XVIII. Then, in later periods, towns such as Tanis, Bubastis, Sais, and Alexandria rose to prominence in the delta. Through the ages, Coptos and Elephantine were also important—even if only "provincial"—centers.

An Abydos palette shows the king as a ferocious animal, in the style of early depictions of the pharaoh.

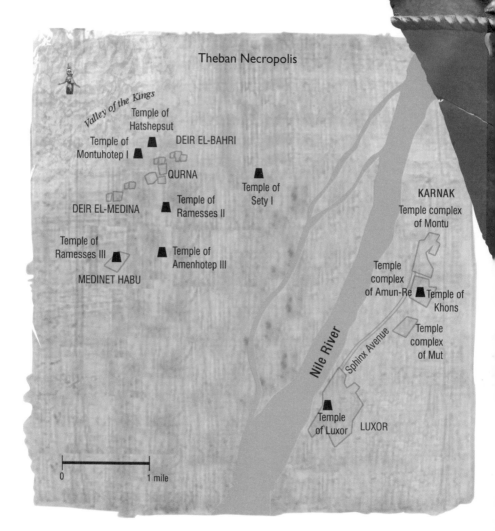

Theban Necropolis

Valley of the Kings

Temple of Hatshepsut

DEIR EL-BAHRI

Temple of Montuhotep I

QURNA

Temple of Sety I

KARNAK

Temple complex of Montu

DEIR EL-MEDINA

Temple of Ramesses II

Temple of Ramesses III

Temple of Amenhotep III

Temple complex of Amun-Re

Temple of Khons

MEDINET HABU

Temple complex of Mut

Nile River

Sphinx Avenue

Temple of Luxor

LUXOR

0   1 mile

100 CE (onward) Toward the end of the century, the technique of covering stone statues with silver or gold spreads from Egypt to Rome.

100 CE A village (Karanis, Lower Egypt) with a population of about 4,000 has two major

Painted linen funerary shrouds in the first and second centuries CE used Egyptian conventions but borrowed from the artistic traditions of ancient Greece and Rome.

temples, one of these made of stone.

- The town of Tebutnis, with a population of about 3,000, has fifty men officiating as priests in the Egyptian tradition.

100–200 CE Highly decorated mummy cloths are used at burial, together with realistic portraits of the dead, painted in encaustic (the color burned into wooden boards with the use of melted wax).

100–200 CE The oldest known fragment of the New Testament (The Gospel According to St. John) is found in Egypt.

100–200 CE The Greek compilation referred to as the *Corpus Hermeticum*, the founding document of the Hermetic tradition (a system of magic that is associated with Gnosticism), is written in Greek and draws elements from Egyptian, Greek, and Jewish practices.

100–300 CE The town of Oxyrhynchus, with a perimeter wall and five gates, has a Serapeum,

CIVIC AMENITIES

Water: The Nile was the main source of water for domestic consumption in towns and in villages. At Kahun and Deir el-Medina we know from written sources that water was carried to the houses on the backs of donkeys. However, there were alternate sources as well.

Akhenaten's capital at Tell el-Amarna was located less than a mile from the river, and this is usually the reason offered by archaeologists for the large number of wells discovered in that town. It would not have been easy to sink a well in that region: the aquifer is about 23 feet below the level of the plain, and since the geological stratum is particularly sandy, well shafts could easily collapse. One solution

might have been to line the well pit with stone or baked brick masonry, as was regularly done in the bronze-age city of Mohenjo-daro (2600–1800 BCE) in Pakistan. At Tell el-Amarna and other pharaonic towns, however, the largest of the wells were sunk in the center of wide shafts.

The shaft was much larger than the actual pit that was sunk down to the water, and workmen would have had to descend down the sides of the shaft to fetch the water, carrying it up in large jars placed on their shoulders. At Deir el-Medina, in Dynasty XX times, a continuous staircase descended spirally 170 feet to reach the water. There might have been a group of skilled well-diggers who specialized in this task.

Drainage: All around the world, hygiene is a feature that only appeared in urban centers long after the excesses of the Industrial Revolution. So, ancient Egyptian towns would not have been clean. Even in spacious and well-built towns such as Tell el-Amarna there were open drains, and archaeological evidence shows that garbage piled up steadily in the streets. Apart from clouds of flies, there would also have been mosquitoes, since some skeletons show evidence of malaria.

Toilets: Some ancient Egyptian town houses had bathrooms, paved with thin stone slabs that sloped either toward a drain that ran down the outer wall of the house, or else into a large container set into the floor. Occasionally, in a rich house or even in a noble's tomb, we find a lavatory with a wooden seat set on a low wall over a large jar. In some of the Amarna houses that have been excavated, supplies of sand were kept next to these toilets.

Roads: The only roads in towns that were given a proper surface were for ceremonial use, as well as for day-to-day use. Either the ruler or the bark of a deity would process along these routes on festival days.

There was no dearth of water, even for the commoner.

two churches, three sets of baths, and a theater that can hold 11,000 people. One documented event describes hot water falling into a bath, scalding a man's belly and leg.

100–400 CE An ordinary rural house has about three rooms; storage facilities; ovens and grain mills; cauldrons; courtyards for the geese, pigs, or poultry; wooden tables and chairs; beds; terra-cotta lamps; children's toys; and more.

100–300 The Serapeum at Memphis is said to have had gilded ornamentation.

100–500 This is the period of an early religious movement we today call Gnosticism, which believes in salvation through personal knowledge—not facts, but knowledge as insight and enlightenment. One of its founding texts is written in Egypt.

106 CE When Arabia becomes part of the Roman Empire, Egypt loses a clearly delineated frontier on the east.

115–17 CE A Jewish revolt, triggered by a religious cause, spreads across Egypt. There is much bloodshed, and hostility toward the Roman rulers only increases. The event is long remembered in Jewish tradition.

117–38 CE In Hadrian's reign, a small brick shrine is built at Karnak.

150 CE (onward) Private letters are commonly written, many by ordinary people living in small towns. These provide detailed information on life outside Alexandria.

200 CE (onward) Certain sites come to be revered and associated with miraculous cures, such as the tomb of St. Menas in the desert near Alexandria. The tomb has a mosaic decoration and the walls are covered with carved plaques; there are columns in this structure.

200 CE With the monetization of agricultural output—fodder, fuel wood, and manure—there is also wage labor, when people with small holdings work on specific tasks on the land. A

A glass theatrical mask.

contract records that two men have been paid to produce 65,000 bricks for a builder.

200 (onward) Even small towns now have bakeries, scribes, carpenters, donkey-drivers, prostitutes, and entertainers. Construction workers and glassworkers often travel, seeking employment. A potter can lease premises to fulfill an order for thousands of jars for a vineyard.

200 (onward) Not only does the Church grow in wealth and influence and thus become a matter of political contestation but Church office is considered a source of advantage.

SOCIAL RELATIONS

It may be inferred from the Middle Kingdom maxims of Ptah-hotep, a senior minister, that life in towns required social skills that no peasant was required to exercise in his village. Ptah-hotep instructed his son: "Do not be proud of your knowledge—consult the ignorant and the wise. The limits of art are not reached, no artist's skills are perfect. Good speech is more hidden than greenstone, yet may be found among maids at the grindstones . . . If you meet a disputant in action, a poor man not your equal, do not attack him because he is weak. Let him alone, he will confute himself."

He continues: "If you are one among guests at the table of one greater than you, take what he gives as it is set before you. Look at what is before you, don't shoot many glances at him—molesting him offends his ka. Don't speak to him until he addresses you . . . If you are a man of trust sent by one great man to another, adhere to the nature of him who sent you: give the message as he said it."

ABYDOS

Located in one of the agriculturally rich parts of Upper Egypt, on the west bank between the alluvium and a semicircle of cliffs at the desert's edge, Abydos was a large settlement. It had royal residences, ritual enclosures, and royal brick tombs, including those of the ancestors of the first pharaohs—and cemeteries that were built anytime between 5000 BCE and 400 CE. For a long period between 3100 and 2500 BCE, only members of the royal family had access to Abydos because it was a sacred center. It then lost some of its ritual importance to Saqqara, and attracted a wide spectrum of settlers up to about 2050 BCE, so that in time many nonelite burials were located here. By Dynasty XII times, the royal burial area took on associations with Osiris, the god of the dead, and many votive stelae were set up in the cemetery. Abydos was also a place of pilgrimage for all Egyptians to the "grave of Osiris," actually the cenotaph of Djer, third ruler of Dynasty I.

Facing page: Abydos became a cult center of Osiris, the deity identified with the pharaoh in the Old Kingdom; Egyptians made pilgrimages to Abydos or made sure their coffins were carried there.
Left: A large stone jar, dating to about 2600 BCE, found at Saqqara, one of the main cemetery sites for the town of Memphis.

200 At Kom Ombo in Upper Egypt, on an important land route from Nubia, a Roman chapel for Hathor is built in a major temple complex, in which several mummified crocodiles are stored.

200–450 CE Demotic gradually goes out of use.

285–303 CE The prefect of Egypt is vehemently

Entrance to the temple complex of Isis at Philae.

anti-Christian and launches a wave of persecutions.

285–325 CE On a journey up the Nile to the southern frontier, Emperor Diocletian founds an outpost on the small island of Philae at the First Cataract. The temple of Isis is the chief temple here, begun by the Ptolemies, completed by the Romans. There are many other shrines and gateways on the island.

300 Inflation rises steadily in Egypt. The price of glass, for instance, rises five and a half times in less than twenty years. This may be connected with the depreciation of Roman coins.

300 An inscribed altar in the main temple at Karnak and wall paintings (depicting Roman emperors as if they are pharaohs) in one of the halls may mark this as a cult center and reception center for early emperors.

300 (onward) Coptic, simpler than the demotic script, is the last phase in the development of the written form of the Egyptian language. Because it is mainly used by Christians, Coptic also has the connotation of "Christian Egyptian." Associated with the use of Coptic is the development of the codex, individual sheets of papyrus/parchment/paper that are bound together as a book, that gradually replace the scroll of papyrus.

300 Some paintings are on tombs and chapels

197

MEMPHIS

An early residence of the pharaohs, Memphis grew to occupy an area stretching nineteen miles from north to south. Its palace and temple of Ptah were surrounded by the White Wall, said to have been built by Menes.

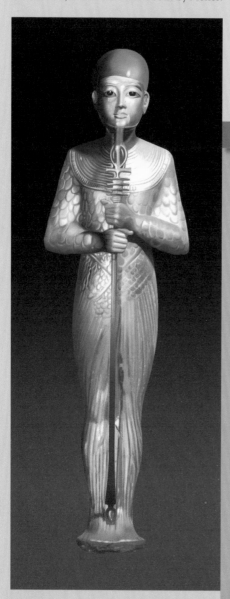

As it was a center of craft production of the highest quality, the high priest of Ptah bore the title "Greatest of Craftsmen." However, the buildings of Memphis became sources of construction material once Cairo became an important city. The site of the temple is now a village and even larger parts of ancient Memphis now lie under the alluvium of the Nile. The cemeteries of this early political capital were Saqqara and Giza.

Ptah was the god who created Memphis, Egypt's first capital after it was unified in c. 3100 BCE.

KAHUN (EL LAHUN)

Excavated by Flinders Petrie, this town was founded by the Middle Kingdom pharaoh Sesostris II (1900–1880 BCE) near the entrance to the Faiyum depression, on the sloping desert edge. It was a large town for the valley temple of the ruler, its priests and staff responsible for the cult, as well as agriculturists, gangs of men employed to drag large stone blocks, soldiers, scribes, and singers and dancers, male and female. The town was also named Hetep-Senusret ("Senusret Is at Peace").

As it was an implanted town, Kahun was built on a grid, whose spine was a wide, east-west street flanked by blocks of houses. The larger houses had several rooms and some courtyards, sometimes with stone-lined water pools and trees. The walls were often painted in bands of blue, yellow, and white. There were pillared verandas and extensive storage facilities. Small finds indicate that spinning and weaving were done in the homes, both large and small.

The small houses were built in rows, back to back. About 220 have been excavated, each with a round and plastered bin for its grain.

The town had a temple and a building in which oaths were administered and legal proceedings conducted. Masses of papyri were found in Kahun, especially in the later buildings. There is written evidence for a prison. Among excavated finds are house furniture, and a variety of tools and personal ornaments.

Chapel of Hathor at Kom Ombo.

Christianity's Success

At the popular level Christianity succeeded because it cared for the poor and the sick, and gave social support that Roman institutions could not. Another reason for its success was that the ancient Egyptian religious beliefs and Christianity had many similarities, especially the belief in judgment after death, and resurrection. The cross, a symbol of Christianity, was not much different from the Egyptian ankh, which symbolizes life.

(walls, ceilings) in the Kharga oasis. Later there are also illuminated manuscripts on papyrus.

300–500 A popular subject for relief sculpture is the Acts of St. Paul.

300–600 The Christianization of a large proportion of the Egyptian population means that there is now intense focus on the written word in the Bible—Christianity is one of the religions of the Book (the Bible).

300–600 The Bible and related manuscripts are translated into Coptic as the Church grows; many manuscripts are circulated at any one time.

300–600 Coptic art, in contrast to the art of the pharaohs, has limited themes that are monotonously repeated. Much of it is a nonverbal complement to biblical narratives for those who cannot read. It is characterized by frontal presentation of the human figure and lack of proportion in the body. Rather than outer appearance, it is the meaning of the image that is of primary importance.

• There are "Faiyum portraits," painted on wood, in a special technique called encaustic—which is as much inlay as painting.

305 St. Anthony is credited with the founding of monasticism.

312 CE (onward) Many churches are built across the Roman Empire, and Christian symbols—the cross and the letters XP—are inscribed on

330 (onward) Constantinople, the newly founded capital of Byzantium or the eastern Roman Empire, drew wealth, trade, and scholars away from Alexandria. Yet, as Alexandria developed ties with Constantinople, the cultural and economic gulf between it and the rest of Egypt only grew.

tombstones and artifacts of everyday use, and are also present in mosaics of the period.

312 CE The persecution of Christians ends after the conversion of Emperor Constantine.

AKHETATEN

"Horizon of Aten" at Tell el-Amarna, this was the city of Akhenaten (fourteenth century BCE).Built as a perfect residence of Aten, the disk of the sun, the city was long (about six miles) but narrow. It served as the capital of Akhenaten and Smenkhkare, and for the first few years of Tutankhamun's reign. Akhetaten was excavated by Petrie in 1891–1912, by Borchardt in 1911–1914, and then by several British archaeologists.

The city was bounded by fifteen stelae set up by Akhenaten. At its northern end were two brick palaces on one side of a royal road, one of these with porticoes, trees, and pools. There was another palace in the city center, where the king would occasionally make public appearances on the balcony. Offices for scribes lay to the east of this house. The gigantic temple for Aten was, naturally, unroofed and open to the sun.

The city had more or less self-contained craftsmen's quarters on the east, and residential areas for the well-to-do on the north and south. There were an exceptional number of wells. Houses had circular clay ovens, animal enclosures, brick silos for grain storage, and also shrines.

Simple graves of workmen have been discovered recently. The royal tombs were robbed in the nineteenth century.

Aten shines down on Tutankhamun (thought to be Akhenaten's son) and his wife, shown on the backrest of a chair. Tutankhamun's original name, Tutankhaten, is carved on the reverse and arms of the chair.

319 CE The Edict of Milan restores to the Church the properties that had been confiscated from it. From this date the Church gains many privileges as regards taxation, public service obligations, and property.

348 The longest personal letter known in ancient Egypt is written by a man of Upper Egypt, on a trip to Alexandria, to his brother. The Greek language of the letter is flawless.

350 According to historians, by now more than a third of the land in one nome is owned by two percent of the population.

350 Perhaps the earliest monastery in Egypt is that of St. Antony in the Eastern Desert, where this saint lies buried.

350–400 A map is made by one Claudius Ptolemy of hundreds of stars in the sky. Ptolemy also attempts to explain the movements of planets through the sky.

378 Emperor Theodosius bans the pagan religions.

385–91 Many Egyptian temples are closed and sacrifice is banned. When a temple in Alexandria is converted into a church there are riots; a statue is desecrated; then a swarm of rats appears, taken as a sign of encouragement by the Christians, who destroy the temple.

389 The Serapeum at Alexandria is destroyed on Theodosius's orders.

395 The last known hieroglyphic inscription.

395–640 Under Byzantine rule the administrative divisions of Egypt become units smaller than the nome. After 500, other than the civil, military, and ecclesiastic officials, there is a district officer in charge.

400 By now there are imposing churches and large monasteries all over Egypt.

400 (onward) Christian ideology shows no interest in the body after death, and once forced to give up their old religious practices, people lose interest in mummification and gradually forget how it was done.

400 (onward) Christianity now influences life and thought in Egypt.

400 Soon after this date, the Julian calendar, a solar calendar that accommodates the leap year, is introduced.

400 (onward) Under the emperors of Byzantium, Christians by far outnumber the Egyptians following the old religious system. Simultaneously, the population becomes increasingly Greek, with a steady immigration from various parts of the Mediterranean world. There is increasing documentary evidence of police activity and imprisonment.

400 The early Egyptian church takes the form of the Roman basilica: a hall with an apsidal end, with colonnades dividing the space longitudinally into central nave and side aisles.

• Some of the earliest Egyptian churches are in Old Cairo, such as the Basilica of Abu Sarga (St. Sargius), with marble columns in classical style. The early church at Dendera is also built on the plan of a basilica, with a trefoil-shaped sanctuary at one end.

400 (onward) The three-dimensional statue is no

THEBES

From the time of the Middle Kingdom, when it was a small town, Thebes functioned as the political center of the country, but most of the houses of this period are buried beneath New Kingdom structures. The heart of the city was the temple of Amun at Karnak, encircled by a brick enclosure (built in Dynasty XXX times). During the later New Kingdom period, many of the existing buildings, including the Dynasty XVIII palace, were demolished and built over. The city expanded, with a probable population of 40,000, and much of the residential area was on a lower level than the temple complex.

From Dynasty XVIII to the end of Dynasty XX, the west bank opposite this great city was the locale of burials and funerary cult temples, the former cut into the desert cliffs as catacombs. The cult temple of each ruler was separate from his rock-cut tomb, lying closer to the cultivated alluvium.

In the center of the east bank settlement would have been the great royal residences, but the modern town of Luxor has covered these up. The area to the north comprised the Karnak temple complex, to the south the Luxor complex, and between them was the residential area on both sides of the Avenue of the Sphinxes that links Karnak with Luxor. East of the Karnak temple enclosure were houses of the Old Kingdom; southeast of these were houses of the Ramesside period

The ruins of Karnak at the center of the Theban kingdom; the city contained the magnificent temple of Amun.

Monastery of St. Catherine.

(Dynasties XIX and XX). At the end of Dynasty XX (c. 1060 BCE), and again after 350 BCE, large areas of Thebes were abandoned.

During the New Kingdom, fresh temple constructions emphasized the supremacy of Amun, with the royal mortuary temples also dedicated to Amun, to whom the pharaoh was believed to have fused in death. At an annual festival the bark of Amun, containing his image or symbol, was taken to the west bank of the Nile for a ritual at Deir el-Bahri.

Wall paintings indicate that sometimes a house could have two stories above the ground floor, with grain receptacles on the roof, a reception room, and activities such as weaving and weighing on the ground floor.

longer a favored art form.

400 The temple of Hatshepsut at Deir el-Bahri is perhaps in this period converted into a church, but does not function for long as such.

• The Greek Orthodox monastery of St. Catherine is built in the Sinai desert, at the foot of Mt. Sinai. It is relatively well preserved today.

400 A text called the "Life of the Desert Fathers" is written in either Greek or Latin. (It is known to us from a Latin copy of the seventeenth century.) It describes the lives of men like

St. Augustine

Ruins of the auditorium of the Roman theater at Alexandria, probably built in the third century, with later modifications.

Founded in 331 BCE by Alexander the Great on the north coast of Egypt at the western edge of the delta, Alexandria remained a Greek city on the soil of Egypt. It was populated by Greeks, except for the Egyptians in the old village of Rhakotis nearby. Little remains today of this wonderful city in which Alexander was laid to rest.

Before 331 BCE it was Memphis that had functioned as the religious and political headquarters of Egypt, but from 330–640 CE, the administrative center was at Alexandria. This city flourished economically because of its location: the wealth of Egypt in its hinterland promoted a healthy trade principally in papyrus, glass, and linen. Local industries included textiles, cameo carving, glass, mosaic work, and shipbuilding. The harbor had an emporium and warehouses, as well as shipbuilders' yards. Canals were built so that craft could move from the Mediterranean into the Nile delta and then upstream. But the marvel at Alexandria was its lighthouse, known as the Pharos, built by the Ptolemies at the end of a long causeway bifurcating the harbor. The first story of the lighthouse was rectangular; above it was an octagonal stage; the highest story was cylindrical and in total height was about 394 feet. With the use of magnification and reflectors, the fire burning on the top was visible for miles. The Pharos is known as one of the seven wonders of the ancient world.

The city, with a perimeter wall on three sides, was laid out on a grid plan of streets wide enough to take a two-way carriage traffic that met at right angles. A large proportion of the area was occupied by grand residences and public buildings; the remaining space contained a few groves, but was mainly divided into residential quarters crammed with ordinary houses with just one foot of space between them. A small residential area that was exposed was found to have modest houses facing each other across narrow lanes. They were built of limestone, and had upper stories. The water supply came from a network of underground cisterns.

Among the public buildings was a theater built in the first century BCE, of which a substantial portion remains today. The palace of the Ptolemies, subsequently used by the prefect of Egypt, was destroyed by Asian invaders in 272 CE. Among the temples was the Serapeum complex, with colonnades providing the facade for the library and marble columns, later broken down and converted into the Church of John the Baptist.

The Caesareum, an ostentatious temple for Caesar built by Cleopatra, was converted into the Church of St. Michael, which was later to be the seat of the patriarch (bishop) of Alexandria. There were dozens of baths and, in the Byzantine period, an amphitheater or hippodrome for chariot races that attracted the masses in much the same way that professional sports events do today. Supporters of rival teams often fought against each other, and champions were folk heroes in the city.

The Alexandrian mobs were notorious. A Roman was lynched in 59 BCE when his chariot ran over a cat. In 80 BCE, Ptolemy X was dragged from his palace to the gymnasium and slain—the mob was a tool in the hands of any unscrupulous faction at court. A major spate of rioting occurred in 250 CE, and in 415 Christians, in full sight of their church, stripped the mathematician and philosopher Hypatia, who attempted to teach a non-Christian philosophy, and dragged her down the streets until she died.

It was, however, in its role in promoting and perpetuating the Greek—not the Egyptian—intellectual tradition that Alexandria made its most lasting contribution to history. The Ptolemies were great patrons of writers, thinkers, and scientists. Alexandria's Great Library was founded soon after the city was created and as its collection grew, it spilled over into rooms in the Serapeum around 250 BCE. Among its most popular manuscripts was a copy of the *Iliad*. (Owning a book was considered prestigious in ancient Egypt—hence the papyri that are found in the tombs.) The Great Library was destroyed, together with the palace, by the invasion by Palmyra in 270 CE. The Serapeum and its treasure of literature was destroyed in 391 CE.

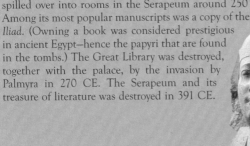

The misnamed "Pompey's Pillar" still stands in front of the Serapeum at Alexandria, where it was erected in c. 299 CE in honor of the emperor Diocletian.

With the aid of Roman garrisons, a prefect ruled Egypt, answerable to none other than the Emperor at Rome. As an outsider, this prefect, a man of equestrian rank, had few vested interests in Egypt. A military man, the prefect also had judicial responsibilities, making an annual tour to hear lawsuits and grievances at the assize centers. Needless to say, he was also responsible for fiscal matters. Those in second rank below him were his legal adviser, chief priest and administrator of temples, finance officer, and military commanders. Below these, there were regional administrators in four subdivisions of the province of Egypt.

The army maintained law and order in the countryside, supervised the transportation of grain along the river, and supervised mining or quarrying that was let out to contractors. The billeting of troops meant that a local community had to provide them with food and fuel, and this often became oppressive.

With increasing monetization in the agrarian sector, some farmers grew wealthy while others were impoverished. In contrast to the Ptolemaic system that is believed to have generally consisted of peasant farmers, class differences widened in the Roman period. This had repercussions in other aspects of life. In a short span of time, the administrative system in the valley of the Nile lost the old institutions and became Roman. No longer did a ruler send a team out to procure metal or stone from a distant region. Such work was now contracted out to a wealthy entrepreneur.

This new system was especially marked at the local level, where the monarchy or state withdrew from its welfare duties and expenses, leaving these to the propertied people of the area. After 200 CE, town councils, comprised of dozens of adult men owning a minimum amount of land, met each month to organize the collection of various dues and taxes, to keep records of property, to regulate the markets and the town's food supply, to raise funds for the impending visit of an emperor, and to organize various festivals. The principle behind the Roman system was that to be wealthy meant that a person had to spend for the public good, be it the import of grain during hard times, the building of a theater, or the expenses of a festival.

An urban administration layout shows the insignia of various officials in charge of towns of the delta and their nome symbols.

ISIS IN THE ROMAN WORLD

Isis was one of the oldest deities of the Egyptian pantheon, and was worshipped everywhere in Egypt. She was the beautiful protector figure, a mother goddess, and mistress of magic, whose son was the young sun, Horus. A daughter of Nut, the sky, she was married to her brother Osiris. According to the legends, when Osiris was killed by his evil brother Set, or Seth, Isis searched unceasingly for his body until she found it washed up on the shores of Byblos. She freed Osiris from his coffin and helped him then become the god of the underworld. There is a striking parallel here to the Mesopotamian myth of Ishtar and Dumuzi. Like Dumuzi, Osiris is one who has overcome death: his symbol is the rising water of the Nile.

The population of the Roman Empire was mainly polytheist, at least into the third century, and there were, among the dozens of cults, "mystery religions" offering salvation to only those who were initiates. Among these was the worship of Isis, not only in Alexandria and Athens, but also in Asia Minor and Rome—obviously the cult was carried far by sailors and soldiers. Caligula (37–41 CE) raised a temple for Isis in Rome. There were statues of her, and her symbols were carved on jewelry. A second-century papyrus from Oxyrhynchus gives the names under which she is worshipped in Arabia, Syria, Cyprus, Caria, Persia, India, Rome, and elsewhere.

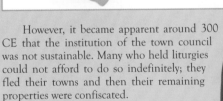

Raised relief believed to be a portrait of the goddess Isis.

However, it became apparent around 300 CE that the institution of the town council was not sustainable. Many who held liturgies could not afford to do so indefinitely; they fled their towns and then their remaining properties were confiscated.

Bust of a late Roman emperor.

207

CHRISTIANITY IN EGYPT

The Coptic Church is the Christian church of Egypt; a "Copt" is an Egyptian Christian. The English word "Coptic" is derived from the Arabic *Gibt*, from the Greek *Aigyptos* ("Egypt"). In the Christian tradition, Egypt is the land where Joseph, Mary, and the infant Jesus took refuge from Herod, and the faith appears to have reached Egypt in its early days. The first converts may have been Hellenized Jewish people, the most numerous residents of Alexandria. Some historians state that Christianity came to Egypt with St. Mark (40–68 CE), whose first convert, a shoemaker, became the patriarch of Alexandria. From then on a continuous succession of patriarchs has headed the church in Egypt.

A relief frieze from Christian Egypt depicts the ancient Egyptian *ankh* sign that became the prototype for the Christian cross; the frieze belongs perhaps to Middle Egypt, the location of many Christian monasteries and places of worship.

COPTIC LITERATURE

Fragments of papyrus of the early second century have been found with portions of the Bible—including parts of the Gospel according to St. John—written on them in the Coptic script. Coptic writing, a late development of Egyptian writing, is largely associated with Christianity. It uses the Greek alphabet to write Egyptian with a heavy Greek input. It is possible that Coptic developed as a written language during the conversion of Egyptians to Christianity. The Coptic Bible was translated from the Greek, and Coptic literature contains religious discourses and tracts about community life in the monastery as well as about conflicts between pagans and officials of the Roman Empire. There are also sermons, accounts of the lives of the saints, and essays on the dangers of disobedience in the monastery and church. A large collection of Coptic manuscripts on Gnosticism, a trend that was important until about the fifth century, was found at Nag Hammadi, by which time large rolls of papyrus had given way to bound books or codices.

This Byzantine-period stela shows the Egyptian ankh on either side of the Coptic cross.

Monasteries

Monasteries were true hermitages, out in the desert. Simultaneously with monasteries for men, monasteries for women were also founded, many set up after 350. Men and women who renounced marriage and procreation withdrew from the everyday world to contemplate or write, or sought refuge in the monastic establishment. Monasteries in Egypt were places where the inhabitants were either solitary hermits, or lived a communal life. Vows of chastity were taken, fasting was common. After 400 those who joined the monasteries were not only the impoverished but often persons with a genuinely religious temperament. Christianity was now a mass religion, and the native Egyptian temple and its cults died out. Monasteries that had as many as 500 monks were on the whole self-contained economic units. Life in them was marked by austerity, discipline, and group activity.

St. Antony (d. 356) and Athanasius, and, most interestingly, their "sayings"—a new genre—on envy, greed, jealousy, and sexual desire.
- The rule of St. Augustine is a guide to religious life in the monastery, concerning prayer, moderation and self-denial, the care of the community and the sick, forgiveness, governance and obedience, and the

GOSPEL OF JUDAS

In 2006, the results of the examination of a text, now called the Gospel of Judas, were publicized and caused a worldwide sensation. The papyrus, which was found decades ago in Egypt and dates to about 300 CE, contains a Coptic translation of an original Greek document that was probably written around 200 CE and which purports to be part of a lost gospel, that of Judas. Close inspection of the handwriting and the ink used, as well as radiocarbon dating, confirmed its antiquity.

CHRISTIANITY IN EGYPT

THE SPREAD OF CHRISTIANITY

Scholars have cited several reasons for the early spread of Christianity in Egypt. Centuries of Ptolemaic and Roman rule undermined the Egyptian language and then the religion. Besides, many early Christian ideas would not have been totally alien to the Egyptians: death followed by resurrection (the pharaohs of past times had been believed to rise at death and dwell eternally with the divine); the idea of judgment after death; and also the legend that the infant Jesus had to be hidden from the evil intent of the ruler of the day. In addition, images of Mary holding the infant Jesus were similar to images of Isis holding the baby Horus.

Catacombs such as the Kom el-Shaqufa complex were used as burial chambers for Egyptians who converted to Christianity; they were among the last of the major constructions of the ancient Egyptian religion.

DEBATE ON THE NATURE OF CHRIST

In 451 CE, Church doctrine took a divisive turn. At the Fourth Ecumenical Council, the nature of Christ was debated. Was he human or was he divine? The understanding arrived at in this Council of Chalcedon was that Christ was both fully human and fully divine. But this was not acceptable to Christians in Egypt. Here the understanding was Monophysite: there could be no duality. The Copts held that divinity and humanity unite in the Christ. Today, the Armenian, Coptic, Ethiopian, Syrian, and Syrian-Indian churches are Monophysite in doctrine. Christ's divinity and humanity were never separate; they were united from the start. Because of this doctrinal difference Copts were not always welcome in the church circles of important centers such as Constantinople. Perhaps such ideological confusion helped the Arabs convert the Egyptian masses to Islam after 641.

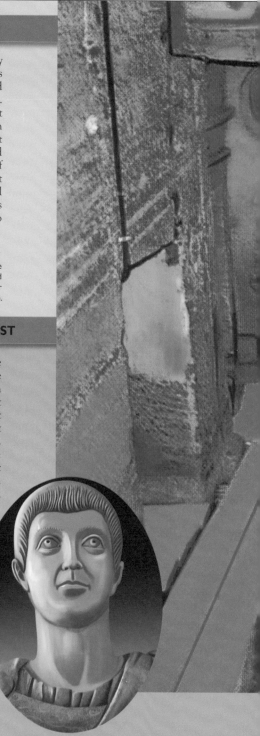

Although Christianity came to Egypt in the first century, it was only given legal status by the emperor Constantine, himself a convert to the religion in 313, when he united the Roman Empire, which included Egypt.

210

MONASTERIES IN EGYPT

Egypt's most important contribution to Christianity is the monastery. Perhaps monasticism was sparked by early Roman persecutions but so many were established that a document of the fourth century says the Thebaid was crowded with hermitages. Legend has it that Egyptian monasticism was founded by St. Anthony in the early fourth century CE, but it had already been instituted in Egypt—what Anthony did was to set the institution in a desert environment. The idea was to live an ascetic life, in self-denial if not poverty, and in solitude. In some monasteries monks lived as hermits, in others the community of monks was important and the monastery could have extensive lands and live in a self-sufficient way.

St. Anthony's: 350 CE. Eastern Desert near the sea. St. Anthony is believed to be buried in a cave nearby. It is one of the earliest monasteries.

St. Catherine's: Foot of Mount Sinai. Greek Orthodox Christians.

St. Macarius's: Wadi el-Natrun, Lower Egypt. Significant leader of the Coptic Church.

St. Simeon's: Sixth century CE. Near Aswan. Housed hundreds of residents and had its own wine press, stables, oil press, bakeries, kitchen, and dining halls.

St. Shenouda: The White Monastery in Sohag, Upper Egypt, was founded in the 440s. It

The monastery of St. Simeon; monasteries were centers of the Egyptian Monophysite doctrine, where both men and women lived. They became more organized at the end of Constantine's reign.

EARLY CHURCHES

In Alexandria, Christians celebrated mass daily. They crowded into churches to hear the sermons; charismatic bishops and patriarchs were cheered on the streets. During Christian feasts and festivals, there were revels and the city was illuminated. While some churches had been located in caves, others were built in the fifth century in the form of the Roman basilica, originally a secular building. A good example is the church at Dendera, a basilica with an apse at the far end, rectangular columns marking the aisles at the two long sides, complex niches in the two long outer walls, and two side entrances.

Painted fresco in a Coptic church.

housed thousands of monks and nuns, and ran agriculture on a huge estate. Much of the stone used for the construction of its various buildings came from ancient temples in the vicinity. Its land came from generous private endowments. St. Shenouda, himself a prolific writer, is important not only for having founded this monastery, but also as one of those who instituted the use of Coptic—not Greek—as a literary language that came to acquire a literary style.

ANCHORS IN ALEXANDRIA

As in Asia and Rome, in Egypt too, early Christians were persecuted by the Roman rulers. If they refused to pour libations, offer incense, or make sacrifices to the emperor, they were thrown to wild animals; this was a period when martyrdom took root. Inevitably, early Christianity did not leave either architectural or textual testimony of its importance—Christians met and worshipped in secret. Some did not even take Christian names. It was from the late third century that the emperors began to realize that persecution would not stem the tide and, after the conversion of Constantine and the Edict of Milan in 319 CE, the trend was reversed. This set the background for the development of Christian theology in Alexandria, which was one of the largest, wealthiest, and most cosmopolitan cities in the Roman Empire.

St. SARGIUS CHURCH

The Oldest Church in Egypt

WHERE THE HOLY FAMILY LIVED FOR SOME TIME DURING THEIR STAY IN EGYPT

After 385 CE, it was illegal to practice the old Egyptian faith and old temples were either plastered over and converted into churches, or taken apart for building stones.

purpose of common life.

400 A papyrus illumination shows Theophilus, patriarch of Alexandria, walking on the ruins of the Serapeum.

400 Egyptian poetry is written within the milieu of the old religion. Many tales are set in the period of the ancient pharaohs.

400–600 The many monasteries of Egypt are autonomous and there is no central authority.

400–600 Some of the early churches have extensions to accommodate pilgrims, baths, and graveyards. Monasteries for their part are complexes around two to four courtyards, with refectories, sleeping and working rooms, and adjoining churches.

400–600 In the ruins of the St. Shenouda monastery in Upper Egypt, popularly known as the White Monastery, monks' cells, storage units, and kitchens are found.

400–600 In spite of the advance of Christianity, written documents reveal the prevalence of oracles, spells, and amulets among the people.

400–600 Hippodromes are built in even small towns like Oxyrhynchus, as chariot races are popular with the masses. It becomes customary to stage circus acts between races.

• Both the Egyptian and Greek systems of medicine are in use.

400–600 The Monastery of St. Macarius in the Wadi el-Natrun in Lower Egypt produces many leaders of the Coptic church.

400–650 The Faiyum and the metropolis of Alexandria continue to have the densest populations in Egypt.

Coptic painting of "Christ in Majesty".

30 BCE–395 CE Egypt fascinates the world from the time of its conquest and annexation by the Roman Empire. Legionnaries return from Egypt as devotees of Isis. Various emperors transport thirteen obelisks to Rome.

30 BCE–395 CE It is the fashion in Rome to have house frescoes and mosaics that incorporate landscapes of the Nile and representations of Isis. People have fake hieroglyphs carved on their furniture and small pyramids erected in cemeteries; an aristocrat could have himself portrayed as a pharaoh.

1200 (onward) Many medieval Europeans believe that Egyptian mummy parts have healing properties, so mummies are taken by merchants to Europe, where they are sold to apothecaries.

1550 For Europe, Egypt has become a fabled land of wonders, excitement, and magic.

1600 Dominican friars, Parisian artists, Italian dilettantes, and those in search of the profound meanings behind the "mysterious and mystical" hieroglyphs travel to the fabled land.

1714 The scholarly rediscovery of Egypt may have begun when Claude Sicard, an Arabic-speaking French Jesuit, identifies the site of Thebes. He describes the remains on Philae and Elephantine.

1700–1800 Travelers publish accounts of their tours with illustrations.

1790, 1793 Jean-François Champollion and Thomas Young are born. Champollion was one of the early Egyptologists; Young was well known as a polymath.

1798 Napoléon invades and temporarily occupies Egypt, then part of the Ottoman Empire. He sets up the Institut d'Egypte and sends 167 experts south from Cairo to make systematic studies of the land. Among the latter is Dominique Vivant Denon, an aristocrat, artist, and writer.

1798–1799 The French are defeated by the British Navy under Nelson. During their retreat, a French army officer discovers, in a dump at Rashid, also called "Rosetta," a stela of basalt or granite inscribed in hieroglyphics, demotic, and Greek. In Cairo, impressions of the inscribed surface are made for decipherment.

1801 The Treaty of Alexandria gives the British title to all the major archaeological finds collected by Napoléon's army.

1802 Denon publishes his travel notes with some exquisite drawings.

1802 The Rosetta stone arrives in England.

1803 Bernadino Drovetti arrives as consul-general of France in Alexandria; he builds up a relationship of trust with Mohammad Ali Pasha and the latter's son and successor and collects antiquities for his personal enrichment and for trade abroad.

1809–1829 Napoléon's expedition publishes its findings in nine volumes of text and eleven volumes of illustrations.

1815 Giovanni Belzoni comes to the notice of the pasha by offering him an "invention" for raising irrigation water faster than the traditional wheel. He also dabbles in archaeological surveys and trades in antiquities.

1816–1827 Henry Salt, as the British consul-general in Cairo, actively collects antiquities from the regions that Drovetti leaves to him.

1818–1819 The great temples of Abu Simbel are discovered and drawn.

1821 An exhibition of Belzoni's discoveries is held in London and draws 2,000 visitors on the first day.

1821–1833 The scholar John Gardiner Wilkinson makes a systematic survey of the Valley of the Kings.

1824 Champollion publishes his *Précis du systeme hieroglyphique des anciens Egyptiens*, in

Napoléon Bonaparte   Mohammad Ali Pasha   Henry Salt   John Gardiner Wilkinson

Obelisk in the Place de la Concorde, Paris.

1880s Many tombs and mummies are discovered in the Theban necropolis, as is Hatshepsut's temple. The mummies of Sethos and Tuthmosis III are found and unwrapped.

1890s It has become the custom to open tombs officially and ceremonially in the presence of high officials.

1881 Mariette dies and is buried in a sarcophagus in the grounds of the Cairo Museum. He is succeeded by Gaston Maspero.

1882 The Egypt Exploration Fund is established to finance fieldwork.

1886–1961 Hassan Selim, an Egyptian scholar, develops teaching and research in Egyptology at the University of Cairo.

1890–1892 The Pyramid Texts inscribed on the walls of the chamber of the pyramid of Pepy I are discovered. Kurt Sethe will publish them in 1908.

1900s Ludwig Borchardt founds the German Archaeological Institute in Cairo; he finds the Nefertiti bust in the sculptor Tuthmose's house at Amarna.

1922 King Tutankhamun's tomb is opened by Lord Carnarvon and Howard Carter.

which the principles of the decipherment of hieroglyphic Egyptian are soundly established.

1826 Champollion is named curator of Egyptian antiquities at the Louvre.

1829–1832 Champollion makes his first visit to Egypt and dies in his early forties.

1830s Richard Howard Vyse, working at Giza, analyzes the structure of the Great Pyramid.

1836 The obelisk from the entrance to the Luxor temple, presented by Muhammad Ali to Louis XVIII, is set up in the Place de la Concorde in Paris.

1837–1841 Champollion's *Grammaire Egyptienne* is edited by his brother and published posthumously. It will be the base from which scholars such as Richard Lepsius begin their studies in Egyptology.

1837 Wilkinson publishes *The Manners and Customs of the Ancient Egyptians*.

1849–1858 Richard Lepsius publishes his monumental *Denkmaeler aus Aegypten und Aethiopien* in twelve volumes.

1850 François Auguste Ferdinand Mariette (b. 1821), a curator at the Louvre, is sent to Egypt to procure Coptic papyri but instead begins to excavate. He finds the Serapeum at Saqqara with several of the sphinxes that had formed an approach avenue, plus several sarcophagi.

1878–1880 The obelisk of Tuthmosis III is set up on the Embankment (along the Thames) in London. The partner of the London obelisk is erected in Central Park in New York City.

Obelisk on the Embankment, London.

In 1799, as Napoléon's army was retreating from Egypt, a French officer found a basalt or granite stela inscribed with three different sets of writing at a place called Rashid ("Rosetta") in the delta. The lowest inscription was in Greek, and the two versions above the Greek were two different ways of writing the Egyptian language: hieroglyphic and demotic. Scholars found this to be an inscription of the priests of Memphis made during the reign of Ptolemy V Epiphanes concerning endowments to certain temples.

By 1802 the Rosetta stone was in England but several scholars had taken impressions of the inscriptions, and over the next few years in western Europe scholars competed to become the first to decipher the beautiful hieroglyphic script. Jean-François Champollion began his endeavor to decipher the Rosetta stone in 1808. Before him, a Swede named Johann Akerblad had recognized that the demotic script is a precursor of Coptic, a language many in Europe still knew.

Champollion realized that besides the hieroglyphics and the demotic script, there was also a hieratic script and that the latter and demotic were cursive versions or developments of the picturelike writing. He began by studying Coptic and was able to match fifteen Coptic signs with their demotic equivalents on the Rosetta stone.

Champollion soon came to the realization that the hieroglyphic writing had signs with phonetic value and were not exclusively logographic—there were more than 1,410 hieroglyphs on the Rosetta stone, whereas the Greek text had only 486 words. Also, by studying the cartouches on dozens of inscriptions in Turin, he was able to read names and gain some idea of the phonetic values of the respective signs.

Champollion's findings brought him recognition as the foremost of the decipherers. Thomas Young, a rival of Champollion, had also worked on the Rosetta stone texts and on a bilingual inscription at Philae, where he had deciphered the name of Cleopatra. It was Young who had, in 1814, told the world that the cartouches enclosed the names of kings and queens.

The Rosetta stone dates from 196 BCE. It is about 45 inches high, 28 inches wide, and 11 inches thick.

400–700 Themes in Coptic painting are "Christ in Majesty," reborn and triumphant rather than suffering; the Virgin with child; and the lives of certain saints who are held in great reverence by the common people. Some beautiful images in vivid colors (green, yellow) are woven into tapestries, of which a few fragments survive— such woven bands were attached to garments or else hung in houses.

- Tombs and affluent homes are some of the structures with mosaic decoration.

412–15 Olympiodorus, a Greek from Thebes, was sent as the emperor's ambassador to the Huns and to the Blemmyes. He always traveled with his parrot, which could call his name, as well as sing and dance.

421 Trouble brewing in the Eastern Desert near the First Cataract comes to a head. A bishop calls for protection against the desert tribes, the Blemmyes (Beja) and Nubades.

442 The monastery of St. Shenouda near Sohag begins with about five acres of land but within

The Countryside

400-600 Brickmakers and carpenters are employed on large estates when necessary; estates buy matting and rope from monasteries; rural potters supply the pottery. Rural people begin to specialize in skills such as treading grapes, pruning vines and carrying olives. All kinds of tasks require wage labor: breaking clods, watering fields, weeding, and tending pigs. At the bottom of the peasant class are debt-ridden farmers who sell the standing crop to spectators. Increasing poverty in the countryside and growth of the Church together usher in charitable institutions and donations to the poor. The large agricultural estate is an important and new factor in the rural economy, requiring a manager to supervise all the leased sectors, and to organise the collection and marketing of the produce.

a few generations it occupies an area of 12,000 acres, with hundreds of cells for its 4,000 residents.

450 (onward) With legacies, land grants, land rents, and tax privileges, the wealth of the Church expands greatly and after 500 the

JEAN-FRANÇOIS CHAMPOLLION

(1790–1832) Born to a librarian, Champollion acquired a fascination for Egypt at an early age. His definitive work, *Précis du systeme hieroglyphique des anciens Egyptiens*, on the decipherment of the Rosetta stone script, was published in 1824. In 1826 he was appointed curator of the Egyptian collection in the Louvre. In 1829 he was able to visit Egypt, where he made detailed studies and some quite masterly drawings. He died soon after, in 1832.

Jean-François Champollion
(1790–1832)

GIOVANNI BATTISTA BELZONI

(1778–1823) A huge Italian, Belzoni traveled energetically in Egypt, Nubia, and the Red Sea littoral. Like other adventurers of the day, he was given to ransacking tombs and temples, and did not hesitate to write his own name on the entrances of tombs and pyramids. Belzoni had a colossal statue of Ramesses II ("Ozymandius") uncovered in Thebes and transported down the Nile. On occasion, his documentation of a tomb was meticulous. He died at the age of forty-five.

Giovanni Battista Belzoni
(1778–1823)

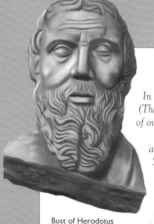

Bust of Herodotus

HERODOTUS

In Anatolia, Herodotus of Halicarnassus (484–430 BCE) *wrote the Historia (The Histories). In Greek, historia means "research" or "inquiry," but it is the origin of our word "history."*

Herodotus was an energetic traveler, keenly interested in different countries and other peoples. He traveled to Egypt, the Levant, Mesopotamia, and the Black Sea, and described their geographies and cultures, and what the local people told him of past happenings. His underlying theme was to get to know the cultural causes of the conflict between Greeks and easterners.

In Book II and Book III 1–38, the Historia describes the Nile and the land of Egypt, the pyramids and legends about the pyramid builders, the invasion of Cambyses, mummification with the use of natron, and more. He gives some interesting snippets about Egyptian manners and customs. He was intrigued that Egyptian women attended the market while the men stayed at home to weave; that dough was kneaded with the feet, but clay with the hands. He found the Egyptians "the most learned of any nation" he had seen. People greeted others on the street not by calling out their names but by bowing low; younger people rose and gave their seats to elders when the latter entered a place.

Church is entitled to a share of all land taxes. Correspondingly, bishops become powerful men.

450 A book (codex) illustration may now depict charioteers (champions) rendered in the Greek rather than Egyptian style.

451 The Council of Chalcedon discusses the ideological schism (the main issue being the human and divine aspects of Jesus Christ) between the patriarch of Alexandria and the bishop of Constantinople. Although largely Christian, Coptic Egypt hereafter comes under the rule of a different branch of Christianity than Constantinople, which was under the Hellenized Orthodox or Chalcedonian Church.

453 The Byzantine army suppresses the Lower Nubian tribes and raids Upper Egypt. Once the area is settled, the tribes are permitted to visit the temple of Isis on the island of Philae.

500 A deed bestowing land on the monastery of St. Shenouda indicates that this institution is important even in the sixth century.

500–80 The rich are now extremely wealthy, and eligible for public office: a affluent family from Oxyrhynchus has members in high military, civil, and ecclesiastic posts.

• By about 550, temple estates, royal land, and public land are not conspicuous categories: in their place

Above: Emperor Justinian.
Left: Section of the temple of Isis at Philae.

AUGUSTE MARIETTE

(1821–1881) Mariette made his name in Egyptology by discovering the Serapeum at Saqqara, a catacomb where sacred bulls were buried when they died. He did not hesitate to use explosives to clear his way through the catacombs. In 1858, he founded the Egyptian Antiquities Service, and a year later the Egyptian Museum in Cairo. The plot for the opera *Aida*, which opened at the Cairo Opera House in 1869, was devised by him. He is buried in a sarcophagus in the garden of the Cairo Museum.

Auguste Mariette
(1821–1881)

Howard Carter
(1874–1939)

HOWARD CARTER

(1874–1939) Son of a British artist, he began work in Egypt, recording the art at Beni Hasan, and then learned excavation with Flinders Petrie at Amarna. In 1908 he met Lord Carnarvon, a dashing millionaire who hired Carter to dig with him at Thebes, where Carter discovered Queen Hatshepsut's tomb, among others. Carter continued his explorations at Carnarvon's expense, finally discovering the tomb of Tutankhamun. Thereafter, Carter took ten years to catalog all its contents. He died in Cairo.

WILLIAM MATTHEW FLINDERS PETRIE

(1853–1942) A British archaeologist whose measurement of the Great Pyramid remains one of the most authoritative, he brought precision and the system of classification and typology of antiquities to the relative dating of tombs in large cemeteries. He is remembered in the lore as an eccentric, remarkably tight-fisted man, keeping his teams on minimal field rations and even selling off the bricks of his temporary shelters to his Egyptian workmen at the close of an excavation.

PETRIE'S DISCOVERIES AT NAUCRITUS

Naucratis was located on an eastern branch of the Nile Delta, near Alexandria. It was a Greek settlement in the seventh century BCE, but not a typical Greek colony. From about 750 BCE the Greeks had been emigrating to other parts of the Mediterranean because of population increase and land shortages, setting up independent governing bodies that engaged in trade. But Naucratis was not such a settlement.

Some shipwrecked Greek pirates who had turned mercenaries and helped Pharaoh Psamtik I were given land to settle at Naucratis around 660 BCE. (Later, the pharaoh Amasis employed Greeks against his internal enemies, taking Greek soldiers to Memphis—where Greek pottery is occasionally found in graves.) The town traded with Greek centers such as Mycenae.

Naucratis was excavated by Flinders Petrie and was found to have, besides local wares, pottery in the styles of Sparta, Rhodes, and Chios. A possible warehouse has been identified. Here scarabs in Egyptian style were manufactured in faience for the Greek market, where they had become an item of consumer demand.

William Matthew Flinders Petrie (1853–1942)

there are estates of the great nobles.

516 Riots occur after some chariot races.

527–63 Emperor Justinian has the temple of Isis (on Philae) closed and its idols carried away.

530 Subsidies are paid to the tribes of the Eastern Desert.

537–38 Justinian overhauls the Egyptian administration, leaving the prefect with less power. Egyptian villagers can directly petition the emperor himself with pleas and with complaints about local officials.

- In the administrative reforms, civil and military authority are brought together in one office as a counterweight to the growing power of church officials. The district officer's appointment is made at the highest level.

565–78 Justin II, the Byzantine emperor, stops subsidies to Arab chiefs (an attempt to stop their raids on Syria), which only causes further trouble.

569 The agricultural economy is in chaos: some people become extremely wealthy while others spiral down into poverty. A man disowns and disinherits his children for attempting to kill him.

600 By now the old aristocrats of the nomes are hardly visible in the records—the Roman system of liturgies has impoverished most of them.

600 At Deir Abu Hinnis near Malawi is a church of John the Short, carved out of the living rock at an ancient quarry, which has wall paintings.

600 The Monastery of St. Simeon near Aswan is distinguished by its fortifications.

600–10 The military commander in Cyrene (northern Africa) develops personal ambitions and invades Egypt with the aim of cutting off the supplies of grain to Rome.

618 The Persian army of Khusraw II captures Alexandria. Egypt surrenders in 619.

628 After settling a treaty, Persia withdraws.

639–41 After the death of the Prophet Muhammad, his general leads an Arab army against Egypt. There is a battle near Heliopolis, and the Byzantine army is routed. The Arabs then take Alexandria, and load ships with tribute.

c. 641 A treatise on Aristotelian physics is written after the Arab conquest. Hellenistic thought and science will be absorbed by Islamic scholars in due course.

641 (onward) The Arabs rule Egypt from a new capital city called Al Fustat (now part of Cairo), leaving the Egyptians the right to worship in the

The Museum of Egyptian Antiquities, Cairo.

■ THE LOUVRE, PARIS, FRANCE

1753 The palace of monarchs such as Louis XIV is made a national museum for the arts.

• The Museum Central des Arts acquires Egyptian statues in the collections of former kings of France.

1798-1801 Napoléon's expedition to Egypt is not the direct source of the Louvre's collection of Egyptian antiquities. After the naval defeat by Nelson, it is the British who claim most of the antiquities collected by Napoléon's expedition.

1826 Henry Salt sells an important collection to the Louvre, including the sarcophagus of Ramesses III.

1827-1830 Acquisitions through gifts and purchases: Bernardino Drovetti (French consul at Cairo) sells his second collection with eighty gold ornaments, sixteen stelae, hundreds of papyri, and some fine sarcophagi.

1830s The domed ceiling painted with the signs of the zodiac from Dendera is detached with the use of gunpowder and then hacked out of the shrine. Bought by Louis XVIII, it is ultimately lodged in the Louvre.

1850s Auguste Mariette sends almost 6,000 antiquities to Paris. Up to the 1950s, the Louvre receives bequests of Egyptian objects.

■ MUSEO EGIZIO DI TORINO (THE TURIN MUSEUM), TURIN, ITALY

The Museo Egizio is devoted exclusively to pharaonic Egypt. It has one of the largest and finest of all collections in Europe (other important ones are in Munich and Berlin). It holds the Royal Canon of Kings papyrus, the Gebelein painted linen, and paintings from the tomb of the official Itimisure in Gebelein.

1824 The core of the collection comes from the king of Sardinia, who purchases Bernardino Drovetti's best collection of 102 mummies, 169 papyri, 485 metal artifacts, 98 stone statues, and 2,400 amulets.

1903-1920 The museum acquires various objects excavated by the Italian Archaeological Mission in Egypt.

1930-1969 Further acquisitions. The Temple of Ellesias (from Nubia) is gifted as a token for Italian help in the rescue of monuments threatened by the Aswan High Dam.

■ AEGYPTISCHES MUSEUM, BERLIN, GERMANY

1830s The museum purchases Drovetti's third collection.

1842-1845 The museum acquires thousands of antiquities from Egypt and Nubia from Karl Richard Lepsius.

1865 Lepsius is appointed keeper of Egyptian antiquities and makes further explorations and excavations in that capacity.

1911-1914 Excavations of Ludwig Borchardt at Tell el-Amarna reveal the exquisite bust of Nefertiti.

■ THE BRITISH MUSEUM, LONDON, ENGLAND

1753 Established with the purchase of the huge art collection of Sir Hans Sloane as well as the Harleian and Cottonian collections of manuscripts. Dozens of Egyptian antiquities, including *ushabti* figures and scarabs.

1802 The museum acquires the Rosetta stone.

1802 The core collection of Egyptian statues is the result of the naval defeat of Napoléon at the Battle of the Nile in 1801 and seizure of the loot gathered by the French army.

1817 Henry Salt, the British consul-general in Cairo, hires the services of Giovanni Battista Belzoni and transports a giant granite bust of Ramesses II from the Ramesseum to Cairo and then presents it to the British Museum.

1818-1838 The British Museum buys several art pieces from Salt, including large statues from the Thebes area and important Nubian antiquities. Later museum acquisitions from Salt include the huge sculptures of Tuthmosis III, Amenophis III, Ramesses I, and Sethos I.

1839 Giovanni Anastasi, the Swedish consul in Cairo, sells 107 stelae and 50 papyri.

1914 Flinders Petrie discovers the Lahun Treasure: five boxes of a Middle Kingdom princess's jewels and cosmetic aids. He offers it for £8,000 to the British Museum, which, after inspection, makes a counteroffer of £2,000.

1916 The Lahun Treasure goes to the Metropolitan Museum of Art in New York (established 1870).

1900s British excavations at Abydos and Saqqara find carved palettes and labels, a key source for political developments in the pre- and early Dynastic periods. Also found is the bronze case for the mummy of a cat of the early Roman period, with gold rings in its nose and ears.

■ MUSEUM OF EGYPTIAN ANTIQUITIES, CAIRO, EGYPT

1858 Said Pasha, the khedive or ruler of Egypt, establishes the Egyptian Antiquities Service with Auguste Mariette at its head.

1858–1859 The museum is founded with the collection of Mariette as its core. It is the first national museum of archaeology in all of western Asia and northern Africa.

1863 Mariette is the first director of ancient monuments in Egypt, and also the head of the museum. Only he can excavate sites.

1880 The collection is transferred to Ismail Pasha's palace (the Boulaq Palace) and a store in the citadel and then brought to a new building in 1900.

1902 The current building of the Museum of Egyptian Antiquities is inaugurated.

1902 Gaston Maspero, a French archaeologist, as director of the new museum, publishes fifty volumes cataloging the various holdings. The museum now has about 136,000 items on display and many more in store. The Tutankhamun gallery displays the gold mask, coffin, and about 3,000 objects from the tomb of the young pharaoh. The museum also has a library that is a major research center for Egyptologists around the world. The body in charge of archaeology in Egypt is called the Supreme Council of Antiquities.

1908 The Coptic Museum is founded in Old Cairo, and is expanded in 1947. It houses about 14,000 papyri, textiles, ceramics, icons, metal artifacts, and seventh-century frescoes from monasteries.

■ RIJKSMUSEUM VAN OUDHEDEN, LEIDEN, NETHERLANDS

Founded in 1818 by King Wilhelm I, this museum has mainly private collections of the early nineteenth century. The best art was acquired in the 1840s.

■ METROPOLITAN MUSEUM OF ART, NEW YORK, UNITED STATES

Contains more than 36,000 objects from the Stone Age to the Roman period, many of them from the museum's own excavations, which began in 1906.

THE ANTIQUITIES LAWS OF EGYPT

1805 Muhammad Ali Pasha takes charge of Egypt after the Ottoman forces are routed by Napoléon. Keen on modernizing the country, he finds that Egyptian antiquities make good gifts for European kings and visiting engineers and scientists.

1810 (onward) Muhammad Ali keeps his own collection of antiquities, housing it in a place on the Citadel of Cairo, and gives away items as gifts. He gives Bernardino Drovetti, the French consul since 1803, blanket permission to excavate sites and take antiquities to France. He cares little for the heritage of Egypt and allows ancient buildings to be taken down for the stone.

1897 Khedive Abbas Helmi passes a decree that anyone taking antiquities belonging to the government will be fined and jailed.

1909 Khedive Ismail Seri passes a law that all ancient buildings and artifacts are the property of the government of Egypt. Those who hold licenses, however, are allowed to purchase ancient objects from the Antiquities Service.

1923 All excavated finds must now remain in Egypt; this replaces a system of sharing antiquities between the excavator and the Egyptian Antiquities Service.

1951–1952 The rules are altered but in general the purchase of ancient artifacts is still allowed.

1983 A law is passed that stops the purchase and sale of heritage objects and bans their export. Thereafter, Egyptian art dealers are required to register their holdings.

223

Much of the learning and science of pharaonic Egypt was transmitted to Europe through the Greeks. Some Greeks were early migrants to Egypt; in the Ptolemaic and Roman periods, others resided as natives of Alexandria and interacted with the priests of the old centers of learning.

Flora and fauna are shown in profusion in much of Egyptian art, conveying the importance given to natural life, as is also evident from the extensive lists of plant and animal names that were compiled.

THE EGYPTIAN CALENDAR

Among the intellectual achievements of the priests of ancient Egypt was the creation of a calendar that, with adjustments made in the Roman Empire and then in medieval Europe, has come down to us today.

In the ancient Egyptian temples, the observation of the night sky was a routine affair, when a specialist priest would announce the time to begin the predawn rituals. The officiating priest would go through purification, begin reciting spells, and open the shrine doors as the sun came up over the horizon. Timekeeping was essential in order to observe particular tasks during the day.

The Stars: Certain stars were only visible at particular seasons, while others—the "stars that never rest"—could be seen throughout the year, such as the planets Venus, Jupiter the Resplendent, Saturn the Horus Bull, and Mars the Red One. From Middle Kingdom times, the stars were painted on temple ceilings and on the inner lids of coffins. The names of ancient Egyptian constellations (the Leg, the Crocodile, the Hippopotamus) are different from those of the modern world, which have been derived from Late Babylonian astronomers.

The Seasons: Of much greater importance was the connection of the position of certain stars with the seasons. At Heliopolis, the center of the cult of the sun, the priests noted the appearance of Sirius or Sopdet (called Sothis by the Greeks) after an absence of about seventy days in the summer. Its first appearance coincided with the rise of the Nile, and was taken as the commencement of the year (thus the "Sothic calendar"). The year was divided into three seasons of four months each. The month (based on the movement of the moon) consisted of thirty days, and was divided into ten-day weeks. The day began at sunset.

The Civil Calendar: Early in Egyptian history, the civil calendar was established, following the solar rhythm. Five days were added at the end of the year, which became feast days for celebrating five gods. In 237 BCE, Ptolemy III issued a decree for the addition of a sixth day.

The Church adopted this calendar in such a way that Christmas, for instance, fell on the festival day of Isis, and saints' days supplanted many old festivals.

Then Julius Caesar, after consulting an astronomer in Alexandria, replaced the lunar Roman calendar with the Egyptian but added an extra day every fourth year. This, the Julian calendar, remained in use in western Europe until the sixteenth century, when it was calibrated even more finely, so that March 21 is always the vernal equinox. The Gregorian calendar that thus came into being is in use in much of the world today.

THE NATURAL WORLD

A unique aspect of ancient Egyptian civilization was the compilation of onomastica, or lists of words in different categories. These were compiled from the Middle Kingdom onward, and were probably used to train scribes in vocabulary and spelling. The subjects listed— plants, liquids, birds, fish, animals, breads, cereals, parts of the human body, forts, and towns—reveal how the Egyptians classified the world. Art and texts commenting on the habits of animals and birds also show that the Egyptians celebrated the richness of the natural world.

MEDICINE

The Egyptians had an intimate knowledge of the properties of plants and the behavior of various animals. Also, the long tradition of mummification of human bodies had given them a knowledge of anatomy that was rare in the ancient world. In hieroglyphic texts, scholars have found about a hundred anatomical terms. The Egyptians had realized the importance of the heart as the seat of the person and his emotions, so it was not removed for mummification. The Egyptians also knew that the brain is enclosed in a membrane, and that its complex convolutions are connected with different functions. Purgatives, enemas, and regulated diets were common. Yet there was no understanding of the circulation of blood, or of the nervous system. The medicine included a long list of plant leaves, flowers, roots, and fruit; animal bones; tortoiseshell; and ox fat, plus minerals such as natron, alum,

and malachite. The medicines were given as powders in a grease medium of ointment, or in dew, water, milk, or honey if to be taken orally. They generally tasted terrible.

One reason for the taste was that, however well the causes of certain ailments were understood, it was still believed that demons inhabited the bodies of the sick and they had to be expelled with repulsive medicines. Medical papyri also incorporated the use of spells, amulets, knotted strings, and other devices as integral to the healing process. Even so, the systematic procedures that some texts prescribe are testimony to the beginnings of a true medical science. Meanwhile, knowledge of anatomy was transmitted, via Greek studies on medicine, to Europe. The ancient Egyptians were also probably the first people to use compresses, bandages, and splints.

MATHEMATICS

The Egyptian language used the same word for "to count" and for "to nod." There were no special signs for the numbers from 1 to 10—the object concerned was written the requisite number of times. There was no zero, either. Where fractions were concerned, 1 was the only numerator, with the sole exception of $\frac{2}{3}$.

The way the Egyptians simplified their sums was to either halve or double. For instance, to find out what 15 x 13 is, one went as follows: 1 x 15 = 15; 2 x 15 will be twice that, 30; 4 x 15 will be twice the last, that is, 60. And the double of the last, 8 x 15, is 120. Then add 1, 4, and 8 to get 13 and add up the corresponding 15, 60, and 120 to get 195 as the final answer.

One could also proceed by halving. How do you distribute 5 loaves between 6 persons? Halve the loaves and give one half to each person; 4 halves are left—halve those, and give each piece (a quarter) to the 6 persons; 2 quarters are left: give $\frac{1}{12}$ of each to the 6 persons. So each person gets $\frac{1}{2}$ + $\frac{1}{4}$ (=$\frac{3}{4}$) + $\frac{1}{12}$ pieces of a loaf.

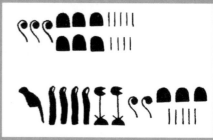

Above: A unique system of counting.
Facing page: Ointment jars in wood or stone were used to store medicines.

Mathematical exercises also included the calculation of squares and square roots. Much of the sophisticated mathematics of pharaonic Egypt, and equally that of Babylonia, passed to the Greeks, and then to the Arabs and medieval Europe.

Ancient Egyptian traditions developed and flourished for an immensely long period: from about 3000 BCE to at least 400 CE, if not later—a period of more than three thousand years. This cultural continuity was only realized because:
- Religious ideologies offered the framework for artistic and literary creativity, and the royal institutions that gave the organizational support to such creativity, themselves backed by religious norms, remained robust.
- Agrarian and administrative stability. No one called the basic assumptions into question.
- Political unification of the Nile valley below Aswan for a very large part of the ancient period. The land was not subjected to perennial warfare between contending city-states and their rulers in the way that Mesopotamia was in the third and second millennia BCE, so that periodic destructions of city walls, city temples, and large-scale loss of life were not facets of the early history of Egypt.

The king list from the temple of Ramesses II at Abydos records names of his predecessors in a row of cartouches, except for those from Amarna, the "heretical" kingdom.

A SENSE OF HISTORY

Several pharaohs completed the construction projects of their predecessors, or added pylons, stelae, or statuary to their temples. Sesostris I of Dynasty XII, who ruled between 1974 and 1929 BCE, built a statue commemorating the intellectual Imhotep, who had lived in the early third millennium BCE. Even in the Late Period (indicated by an inscription at Gebelein), when Smendes (1064–1038 BCE), the founder of Dynasty XXI in the delta, was informed that a colonnade built by Tuthmosis III about 400 years previously was getting flooded, he sent 3,000 men to cut stone for the restoration.

REUSE OF OLDER MATERIAL

Stone blocks belonging to existing buildings were removed, turned around if they bore inscriptions, and used for new building projects.

A narrative of Tuthmosis IV (Dynasty XVIII) inscribed on his "Dream Stela" records Horus exhorting Tuthmosis in a dream to restore the Colossus, in return for which Horus will make him, a younger son, the next king. Tuthmosis had the sand cleared. He then boasted that he had the Colossus painted in many colors. The stela on which this event is recorded was itself lifted from the mortuary temple of Khafre (Dynasty IV).

THE KING LISTS

King lists and annals were documented at the command of various pharaohs between about 2430 and 250 BCE at Abydos, Saqqara, Karnak, and on unprovenanced stelae such as the Palermo stone or on a papyrus inscribed in hieratic called the "Turin Canon of Kings." These were tabulated histories of events in the reigns of previous kings, which gave a sequence of past kings with the length of their reign. What is significant is that on the Abydos stone document, the sponsor of the inscription, Sethos I of Dynasty XIX, is shown making offerings to the seventy-six previous kings, whose names are written in cartouches.

Because of the cults of dead kings and the endowments created for these cults, historical records were kept through the pharaonic period and into the Ptolemaic. These provide the sources from which our main dynastic knowledge is composed.

A wooden coffin decorated with inscriptions; at the head are two eyes that enabled the mummy to look out from behind a painted door through which the spirit could pass.

MAJOR KING LISTS

■ **Palermo Stone**
c. 2470–2360 BCE: Dynasty V. A diorite stela in at least three pieces. Records the time between Menes, the first king, and Dynasty V.

■ **Table of Karnak**
1550–1300 BCE: Dynasty XVIII. Gives the names of sixty-one past kings, but the order is not correct and names of Hyksos rulers, not considered legitimate, are omitted.

■ **Abydos King List**
1296–1279 BCE: Dynasty XIX (Sethos I). It gives (selectively) the names of seventy-six past rulers in their cartouches, beginning with Menes. Originally carved in the Abydos temple with a relief. Hacked out of the wall in the nineteenth century.

■ **Saqqara King List**
1279–1212 BCE: Dynasty XIX (Ramesses II). Names fifty-seven past pharaohs whom Ramesses honored. Inexplicably found in Memphis, in the tomb of an official.

■ **Turin Canon of Kings**
1279–1212 BCE: A papyrus in hieratic commissioned by Ramesses II, it lists names of past kings, giving the length of rule in detail. It documents early history up to the fifteenth century BCE.

■ **Chronicles of Manetho**
c. 300–200 BCE: Early Ptolemaic period. These remain our most complete source, listing the sequence of kings of thirty-one dynasties until Alexander.

THE CIVILIZATION DECLINES

Egyptian civilization gradually lost its coherence under foreign occupation, and drew to an end. Ancient Egypt's culture disappeared not because of inherent contradictions or abuse of the environment, nor due to a great natural calamity, but because of historical circumstances originating elsewhere.

Hyksos and Sea Peoples: Foreign rulers from Asia, the Hyksos ruled in Egypt from 1650 to 1535 BCE but adapted to Egyptian culture, and also made their own contribution to it. Around 1200-1190 BCE, the Sea Peoples attacked northern Egypt. They were repulsed, and did not bring state institutions to an end or provoke the desertion of Egyptian cities. The Greek migration was different.

Greeks: As early as 750 BCE, land shortages in Greece and western Anatolia drove Greek families to regions fringing the Mediterranean, including Egypt. After about 660 BCE, the pharaohs of Dynasty XXVI granted to Ionian Greeks the right to settle at Naucratis in return for having helped as combatants in an internal dispute. Very slowly, certain strata of Egyptian society became Hellenized, with people learning Greek and even taking Greek names.

Persians and Alexander: From 525 BCE onward, Egypt was subjected to invasion and subjugation by the Persians and no indigenous elite could gain independence. Achaemenid Persian rule was followed by the invasion of Alexander in 332 BCE. The rate of immigration of Greeks, Persians, and Jewish people increased thereafter.

Ptolemies: Although devotees of Sarapis, the Hellenic-Egyptian god, the Macedonian Ptolemies (332-30 BCE) were portrayed in monumental art as pharaohs in the old way. The official language for three centuries was Greek. Only Cleopatra spoke Egyptian. Egyptians who could not speak or write Greek could not find posts in the administration. The political center was Alexandria, which, by its location, looked out more on the Greek world than the Egyptian.

Romans: After 30 BCE Roman law and administration prevailed. The Romans employed slave labor. Women were employed to grind rocks and wash gold. Close on the heels of this system of production and distribution, which introduced a new degree of poverty, came Christianity, and a patriarch was installed at Alexandria.

Christianity: Christians placed no importance on the body after death, so the reason for mummification was lost. Many Egyptians converted around 312–640 CE. Christianity became the official religion, and later, Theodosius banned pagan religions: old Egyptian temples were closed, idols desecrated, and many existing temples were converted into churches. Egypt became a predominantly Christian country.

A foreign tribe, probably the Sea Peoples, being led away after defeat by Ramesses III.

RESCUE AND RESTORATION

In 2005, Dr. Zahi Hawass, Secretary-General of the Supreme Council of Antiquities of Egypt, traveled to Europe to reclaim a Dynasty V stela from the Musées Royaux d'Art et d'Histoire in Brussels. He was successful because this piece, purchased in the 1970s, had been illegally taken out of Egypt. Previously, dozens of antiquities had been restored to Egypt; for instance, the mummy of Ramesses I, which was stolen 150 years ago, came back to Cairo from Atlanta, Georgia. Meanwhile, Egypt has claimed the Rosetta stone in the British Museum, as well as the statue of Nefertiti in the Berlin Museum.

A tomb painting with a vine-leaf patterned ceiling shows Anubis and Osiris, gods of the underworld, in front of tables piled high with offerings (c. 1186–1070 BCE).

PILLAGE IN THE NINETEENTH CENTURY

After the Napoleonic attack and research expedition in the nineteenth century, many Europeans took advantage of the absence of protective legislation to trade in stelae, statues, mummies, sarcophagi, and other items, looting Egypt of its heritage. The "discovery" of Egypt by the West occurred in the heyday of imperialism, and early archaeology—if it may be called that—suffered the combined outcome of a "collector's mentality," Egyptian apathy, and the absence of laws to protect the heritage. European and American tourists cruising along the Nile in the nineteenth century would purchase a mummy, but, as it began to rot, throw it into the river. (Even a "modern" archaeologist like Flinders Petrie saw it fit to buy a mummy to carry to London for one of his sponsors.)

Because of political rivalries among the Europeans in Egypt, it was possible for the lid of Ramesses III's pink granite sarcophagus (from the Valley of the Kings) to be taken to Cambridge while the rest of the sarcophagus was sold to the Louvre. Around 1817, the Italian explorer Giovanni Belzoni coveted a red granite Ptolemaic obelisk lying on the ground on Philae Island. He decided he would have it cut into thin slabs of a size suitable for transport by boat to Alexandria. However, when he returned to Philae he found that someone had maliciously hacked the blocks into small pieces.

The gateway to the temple of Amun at Luxor was extended and altered by a succession of later rulers even until the time of the Roman emperors Hadrian and Diocletian.

233

UNETHICAL OPPORTUNISM

In the 1820s, when the English explorer William Bankes excavated Abydos at his own expense and found the invaluable king list inscribed on the walls of the temple of Ramesses II, he copied the list and left it intact. However, subsequent "archaeologists" actually came in and cut the inscribed stone slab away from the temple wall for sale to the British Museum. Even worse, antiquities were removed from their settings either with the use of a battering ram or with dynamite. Richard Lepsius was responsible for the removal by force of faience tiles that had decorated the Step Pyramid of Djoser at Saqqara. We have to be thankful for the detailed notes and drawings made by some of the antiquarians, which in many cases are the only evidence for the existence of certain data. (William Bankes erected an obelisk from Philae on the grounds of his own property in southern England.) When mummies were discovered and unwrapped with great drama, this was done with such speed that invariably the physical remains of the dead Egyptian were doomed to immediately rot away.

In Sinai, ancient reliefs and rock engravings of the pharaohs were destroyed around 1850 when British companies attempted to reopen the copper mines near Serabit el-Khadim.

Right: A fallen obelisk symbolizes the fate of many ancient Egyptian monuments and statuary that were carried away in parts or in whole to other countries; several obelisks were taken to Italy and France.
Below: Cruises on the Nile and vacations in Egypt were widely advertised in the nineteenth century.

THE ROSETTA STONE

The hieroglyphic signs on the upper panel of the Rosetta stone had originally been filled in with powdered red pigment, but no one knew this until recently. In Cairo, after its discovery, three teams worked to make readable impressions. One scholar filled the carved letters with water and then applied ink to the surface in general. The letters repelled the ink and an impression was made: white letters on a black ground, the letters showing up as mirror images of themselves. Another filled the letters with grease and made a rubbing with graphite. Another scholar used sulfur to make a cast. In the British Museum, the letters were whitened and the stela coated with wax for protection. Only recently has the original surface been restored, with a small area deliberately left untouched to show the deleterious effects of repeated tampering.

ANCIENT EGYPT: DESTRUCTION OR CONSERVATION?

Some degree of destruction occurred even in antiquity. More than one New Kingdom pharaoh, in the course of "rebuilding" and "restoration" at Karnak, would dismantle large blocks of some of the most beautiful parts of a complex, for example, the White Chapel built in Dynasty XII times, or Hatshepsut's Red Chapel. (Modern archaeologists have been able to retrieve some of these blocks that had been reused or dumped, and have restored them to their original structure.) The Romans removed some of the thin slabs of Tura limestone that gave a sheen to the Giza pyramids—in order to grind the stone for construction mortar! Residents of medieval Cairo subsequently took care of the remaining slabs.

However, pharaohs were often aware of the importance of the buildings of their predecessors; many added portions (gates, pylons, stelae) to such monuments, and

some pharaohs took steps to conserve older monuments. A report made at the time of Ramesses IX (1123–1104 BCE), on an official tour of inspection of some past royal tombs, states that the pyramid tomb of one of the kings of Dynasty XI, in a particular place, was found with its "pyramid fallen over it . . . Its stela stands in front with the image of the king . . . Examined this day and found intact."

The Saites were especially concerned with protecting the mortuary constructions of Khafre, built centuries before their rule. Around 1060 BCE, when the high priests of Thebes realized that constant pillaging of tombs was occurring across the river, they decided to hide away all the remaining coffins and mummies, adding labels in hieratic stating who it was in the coffin, when he or she was being reburied, and by who. The entire "Cache of Deir el-Bahri" was then sealed, in Year 10 of King Smendes, 1054 BCE.

The pharaohs' own cultural practices sometimes helped conserve Egyptian heritage. Many monuments and rituals were specifically concerned with providing for a dead king in the netherworld. So, when there was a change in dynasty and newcomers were in danger of being considered usurpers, it was actually in their interests to claim a connection with earlier kings by maintaining their memory. This gave them a degree of continuing political legitimacy. For example, the pharaohs of Dynasty XII showed pious regard for the memory of those of Dynasty XI.

Despite their solid structures, even pyramids did not escape pillaging by plunderers, robbers, and zealous archaeologists in the nineteenth century.

EXPLORATION AND EXCAVATION

Today, the Supreme Council for Antiquities in Egypt is as active organizing conservation and restoration as it is supervising exploration and excavation. The council's work includes:
• Clearing villages from nearby tombs and temples such as Meidum and Luxor.
• Restoring the head of a statue from the Cairo Museum to its original site in the colonnaded Sun Court at Luxor.
• Cleaning and replacing Hatshepsut's beautiful temple at Deir el-Bahri.
• Occasionally closing the pyramids to tourists for restoration and cleaning.
In 1843, when Karl Richard Lepsius found the tomb of Maya, the treasurer of King Tutankhamun, he excavated it and drew the reliefs. In 1975, a joint Dutch and British team set out to rediscover the tomb. Each year they spent a season at Saqqara, finding the tombs of Horemheb, of an architect, and of a musician—until finally, in 1986, they struck gold and found Maya's tomb again. Later, they discovered the tomb of a high priest of Aten, the sun god, adding to our understanding of the cultural styles of the Amarna period. A tomb of an unknown Dynasty II pharaoh was also found at Saqqara. Other recent conservation projects include:
• The preservation of the gilded cartonnage mask of Yuya, the father of Queen Tiy (Dynasty XVIII), whose final resting place, along with that of his wife, Thuyu, is now in the Cairo Museum.
• The cleaning and recording of several major groups of papyri.
• The restoration by Ahmed Youssef Moustafa of a cedarwood ship broken in antiquity into 651 pieces, discovered in 1954 in a pit near the Great Pyramid. This is now displayed under glass in its original pit.

237

RESCUE AND RESTORATION IN MODERN TIMES

In 1925, when George Reisner of Harvard University was working at Giza, one of his colleagues almost stumbled into a 98-foot shaft east of the Great Pyramid. Here he discovered some of the royal furniture of pharaonic Egypt. The wood of the chairs, canopy, and litter had disintegrated but the outlines were discernible because they had been coated with layers of gilt, and had been inlaid. Ahmed Youssef Moustafa, chief conservationist of the Antiquities Service, pieced it all together and now the furniture is displayed in the Cairo Museum, with replicas in the Museum of Fine Arts, Boston.

ASWAN HIGH DAM

The most spectacular project for rescue and restoration was the Aswan High Dam project, coordinated by UNESCO. Actually two dams were built, the first in 1902 and, after it overflowed repeatedly, a later dam almost four miles upstream, in 1964. From 1960 onward, twenty-four major monuments were moved to safer places (small temples were transplanted to countries that had helped with the rescue work). Some of these include:
• Temple of Ramesses II, Abu Simbel: moved just 650 feet away from the river, reerected together with its cliff side; 3,000 staff involved in dismantling it into 2,000 blocks of stone; reassembled five years later on its new site.

The ruins of the temple of Isis were painstakingly removed slab by slab to its new destination to prevent submersion by the waters released by the Aswan Dam project.

• Isis temple complex, island of Philae; at the First Cataract (first and second centuries); later, in the sixth century, it was transformed into a church.
• Pharaonic temples at Amada and Qasr Ibrim and forts at Buhen (Dynasty XVIII) and at Semna. These and other monuments were taken apart and moved away, to be reassembled, block by block and slab by slab, in six groups, either at higher levels out of the reach of floodwater, or in the desert, short distances upstream or downstream.

MOVED ELSEWHERE
A small stone shrine dedicated by the Roman emperor Augustus to Isis, converted into a church in 710, and falling into disuse after 1200, was taken apart and sent to Leiden to be rebuilt in the Rijksmuseum van Oudheden (Netherlands).

RAMESSES II RESTORED

Perhaps the most dramatic of all modern explorations was the ceremonial visit in 1976 of the mummy of Ramesses II to Paris, where this former monarch was given a ceremonial guard of honor. Ramesses's skin was deteriorating and beginning to show signs of fungus and infection. But at the Musée de l'Homme, the wrapping and the body were carefully cleaned and sterilized with gamma rays. Eight months later, a rejuvenated mummy was back in his modern home in Cairo.

Ramesses II, a great king of Dynasty XIX, ruled for sixty-six years and was a prolific builder.

Archaeology in Egypt was long plagued by too heavy an emphasis on the deeds of pharaohs and their families. This emphasis was partly because the alluvium of the Nile does not preserve unbaked brick and other remains of villages and towns, whereas mortuary constructions on the edge of the desert have preserved organic remains as few other archaeological sites do, and partly because artifacts belonging to ordinary people were ignored. It was not until the 1880s that the archaeologist Flinders Petrie introduced the systematic study of small finds and developed dating systems based on these everyday objects used by common people.

EPIGRAPHY

Recording and publishing the hieroglyphic inscriptions of Egypt is immeasurably more difficult than dealing with rock inscriptions in India, or clay tablets written in cuneiform in Mesopotamia. Hieroglyphic inscriptions could cover an entire tomb wall, and as nineteenth-century Egyptologists discovered, recording them requires not inconsiderable drawing skills. With only pencils, paper, and simple measuring tools, the archaeologists had to patiently draw the inscriptions, showing with shading whether the signs were sunken or in low relief, and faithfully copying the ancient styles of drawing.

Writing was equally important in a temple or tomb. It was integral with representational painting; often there were labels or snatches of speech identifying the people in a narrative scene, so writing and art were a combined channel of communication. Few inscriptions can be adequately understood unless we know where they are located within a structure, which itself could have been constructed over long stretches of time, and can identify the paintings or reliefs in that structure.

Photography came into use in the early twentieth century, but if the surface was reflective or slightly dirty, the signs were not sharp enough to be read from the photographs. Additionally, an individual inscription might be so large as to require several photographs. So, it is still necessary to use color photographs as the base of facsimile drawing. It is not surprising that very few people can become accomplished Egyptologists.

EMPHASIS SHIFT

Petrie worked in Egypt from 1880 onward, establishing accurate measurements of the Great Pyramid but also digging settlement sites such as Naucratis, Hawara, and Kahun, and Tell el-Amarna. Petrie broke new ground in several ways. First, he moved away from the grand monument, instead digging ordinary habitations and scrupulously retrieving all artifactual material, not just major objects in which museums and sponsors would be interested. Second, during fieldwork at the early sites of Naqada and Abydos, he developed the methodology of typology and seriation and worked out a relative chronology of the graves. Yet even Petrie, when he came upon the timbers of discarded boats in his excavations at Kahun (these timbers had been used for the construction of ramps during the building of the pyramid of Sesostris II of Dynasty XII), did not see anything wrong with using up the wood for the needs of his own excavation camp!

Facing page: The Giza pyramids and the Great Sphinx are icons of ancient Egypt.
Right: Models of the working class, singly or in groups, were commonly made.

RADIOLOGICAL INVESTIGATION

Whereas late nineteenth-century dilettantes opened up mummies and studied the bones for fun, since the 1960s most investigations of mummies have been nondestructive, using technologies that were originally developed in modern hospitals. These include:

- Radiology or X-rays
- Total body imaging using CT or CAT (computerized axial tomography) scans, which take cross-sections without needing to unwrap the linen bandages

The liberal use of preservative natron in antiquity ensured that little soft tissue survives (for DNA identification), but investigations on bodies have found that there was tuberculosis, smallpox, leprosy, malaria, arthritis, and perennial problems with tapeworms, guinea worms, and schistosomiasis (snail fever).

TELL EL-AMARNA

At Tell el-Amarna, archaeologists sought to verify the inferences that had been made from texts and figurative art about the functioning of their economy. The understanding had been that when people worked for the king or a temple, a major part of their subsistence came from the state sector, so the archaeologists tried to decide whether the workmen at Tell el-Amarna obtained their own meat or whether it came from state supplies. They found mud-brick pigpens in one quarter of Amarna, and established that pig bones at the site came from all ages and both sexes. This indicates that pigs were kept by the workers. In contrast, cattle bones were all from one part of the animal, suggesting that beef rations were supplied by the state system. Meanwhile, other aspects of this settlement, such as the technology of its glass production, are also being studied in the field.

QASR IBRIM

At this site on the edge of Lake Nasser, the exceptionally dry soil has preserved hair, fiber, cloth, papyrus, paper, rope, wood, and other materials very well. In the course of excavation of this long-lasting settlement, archaeologists have come up with significant discoveries on the way a habitation mound builds up.

GIZA

Here, not far from the large pyramids, excavation work has been concentrated in the workmen's living area and in a nearby cemetery. A huge cooking and baking area has been found, animal bones are being studied, and flotation is being carried out for plant material. Surprisingly, there is also clear evidence for copper smelting here: slag, charcoal, and small furnaces.

WEST DAKHLA

This rare village of the Old Kingdom has yielded pottery, stone tools, and plant remains.

HELIOPOLIS (CAIRO)

Excavations conducted in 2006 at the site where Ramesses II built a huge temple for Re have turned up huge broken statues, including one of Ramesses in a leopard skin. This might have been an earlier statue of a pharaoh of Dynasty XII, which Ramesses simply adapted.

Figure of a man carrying a back-pack and chest.

INSTITUTIONS OF ANCIENT EGYPTIAN RESEARCH

IN EGYPT

Institut Français d'archeologie orientale du Cairo
37 rue el-Cheikh Ali Youssef
BP Qasr al-Ainy 11562, Cairo

Centre Franco-Egyptien d'Etude des Temples de Karnak
63 BP Luxor

Deutsches Archaologisches Institut
Abteilung Kairo

Netherlands Flemish Institute (NVIC)
1 Mahmoud Azmi Street, Cairo

OUTSIDE EGYPT

British Museum
Great Russell Street, London WC1B 3DG, United Kingdom

Egypt Centre
University of Wales, Swansea, Singleton Park, Swansea, SA2 8PP, United Kingdom

Egypt Exploration Society
3 Doughty Mews, London, WC1N 2PG, United Kingdom

Griffith Institute, Oxford
Sackler Library, 1 St. John Street, Oxford, OX1 2LG, United Kingdom

McDonald Institute for Archaeological Research
University of Cambridge, Downing Street, Cambridge, CB2 3ER, United Kingdom

The Oriental Institute, University of Chicago
1155 East Fifty-eighth Street, Chicago, Illinois 60637, United States

Besides the above, several academic institutions of the United States, Italy, Belgium, Austria, Canada, Switzerland, and Australia have Egyptology programs.

RESEARCH JOURNALS ON ANCIENT EGYPT

Cahiers de Karnak (Cairo, Franco-Egyptian Centre)

Journal of Egyptian Archaeology (Faculty of Archaeology, Cairo University; previously published by the Egypt Exploration Society, London)

Mitteilungen des Deutschen Archaeologischen Instituts, Abteilung Kairo (Cairo)

Chronique d'Egypte (Brussels)

Revue d'Egyptologie (Louvain and Paris)

Beiträege für Bauforschung und Altertumskunde (Wiesbaden)

Zeitschrift für Ägyptische Archäologie und deren Nachbargebite (Vienna)

Adams, Barbara, and Cialowicz, K. M. *Protodynastic Egypt*. Princes Risborough: Shire Press, 1997.

Aldred, Cyril. *The Egyptians*. 3rd ed. London: Thames and Hudson, 1998.

Arnold, Dieter. *Building in Ancient Egypt: Pharaonic Stone Masonry*. New York: Oxford University Press, 1991.

Assmann, Jan. *The Search for God in Ancient Egypt*. Trans. D. Lorton. Ithaca: Cornell University Press, 2001.

Badawy, Alexander. *A History of Egyptian Architecture*. Berkeley: University of California Press, 1968.

Baer, Klaus. *Rank and Title in the Old Kingdom*. Chicago: University of Chicago Press, 1960.

Baines, John, and Malek, J. *Atlas of Ancient Egypt*. Oxford: Oxford University Press, 1980.

Bowman, Alan K. *Egypt After the Pharaohs*. London: British Museum, 1986.

Breasted, J. H. *Ancient Records of Egypt: Historical Documents*. 5 vols. Chicago: University of Chicago Press, 1906-1907.

Butzer, Karl W. *Early Hydraulic Civilization in Egypt*. Chicago: University of Chicago Press, 1976.

Cook, J. M. *The Persian Empire*. London: JM Dent, 1983.

David, A. R. *The Pyramid Builders of Ancient Egypt*. London: Routledge and Kegan Paul, 1986.

Edwards, I. E. S. *The Pyramids of Egypt*. Rev. ed. Harmondsworth: Penguin, 1985.

Edwards, I. E. S., Gadd, C. J., and Hammond, N. G. L. eds. *The Cambridge Ancient History*. 3rd ed., vols. I and II. Cambridge: Cambridge University Press, 1970.

Faulkner, R. O. *The Ancient Egyptian Book of the Dead*. London: British Museum, 1985.

Gardiner, Alan. *Egypt of the Pharaohs*. Oxford: Clarendon Press, 1966.

Herodotus. *The Histories*. Trans. A. de Selincourt, rev. by A. R. Burn. Harmondsworth: Penguin, 1977.

Hoffman, Michael A. *Egypt Before the Pharaohs*. New York: Dorset Press, 1979.

Jenkins, Nancy. *The Boat Beneath the Pyramid*. London: Thames and Hudson, 1980.

Jones, D. *Boats*. London: British Museum, 1995.

Kemp, Barry. *Ancient Egypt*. London: Routledge and Kegan Paul, 1989.

Lichtheim, Miriam. *Ancient Egyptian Literature*. 3 vols. Berkeley: University of California Press, 1973-80.

Lucas, A. *Ancient Egyptian Materials and Industries*. 4th ed., rev. by J. R. Harris. London: Edward Arnold, 1962.

Nicholson, Paul T. *Egyptian Faience and Glass*. Princes Risborough: Shire Press, 1993.

Oren, E. D., ed. *The Hyksos: New Historical and Archaeological Perspectives*. Philadelphia: University Museum, 1997.

Parkinson, R., and Quirke, S. *Papyrus*. London: British Museum, 1995.

Parkinson, R. *Voices from Ancient Egypt*. Norman, Oklahoma: University of Oklahoma Press, 1991.

Raven, Maarten, and Taconis, Wyben. *Egyptian Mummies (Leiden Museum)*. Turnhout: Brepolis Publications, 2005.

Redford, D. B., ed. *Oxford Encyclopaedia of Ancient Egypt*. 3 vols. New York: Oxford University Press, 2001.

Robins, Gay. *The Art of Ancient Egypt*. Cambridge, Massuchesetts: Harvard University Press, 1997.

Said, Rushdie. *The River Nile*. Oxford: Pergamon Press, 1993.

Sasson, Jack, ed. *Civilizations of the Ancient Near East*. 4 vols. New York: Charles Scribner, 1995.

Scheel, Bernd. *Egyptian Metalworking and Tools*. Princes Risborough: Shire Press, 1989.

Shaw, Ian, ed. *The Oxford History of Ancient Egypt*. Oxford: Oxford University Press, 2000.

Siliotti, Alberto. *The Discovery of Ancient Egypt*. Cairo: American University in Cairo Press, 1998.

Spencer, A. J. *Early Egypt: The Rise of Civilization in the Nile Valley*. London: British Museum, 1993.

Tiradritti, Francesco. *Ancient Egypt: Art, Architecture and History*. London: British Museum, 2002.

Trigger, Bruce, Kemp, B. J., O'Connor, D. B., and Lloyd, A. B. *Ancient Egypt: A Social History*. Cambridge: Cambridge University Press, 1983.

Tyldesley, Joyce. *Nefertiti: Egypt's Sun Queen*. London: Penguin Viking, 1998.

——. *Hatchepsut: The Female Pharaoh*. London: Penguin, 1998.

——. *Private Lives of the Pharaohs*. London: Penguin Viking, 2000.

——. *Egypt: How a Lost Civilization Was Rediscovered*. London: BBC Books, 2005.

Uphill, E. *Egyptian Towns and Cities*. Princes Risborough: Shire Press, 1988.

Vinson, S. *Egyptian Boats and Ships*. Princes Risborough: Shire Press, 1994.

Watterson, Barbara. *Women in Ancient Egypt*. London: Sutton, 1991.

Wilkinson, A. *Ancient Egyptian Jewelry*. London: Methuen, 1971.

Woldering, I. *The Arts of Egypt*. London: Thames and Hudson, 1967.

ba: the visible form of a human personality or soul after death, which appeared as a human-headed bird, able to fly between the tomb into the afterlife.

benben: the primeval mound believed to have been formed at the time of Creation.

Book of the Dead: ancient funerary texts and spells developed at the beginning of the New Kingdom and partly based on the earlier Pyramid Texts and Coffin Texts; inscribed in tombs and coffins or placed with the dead to guide them through the afterlife.

canopic jars: four containers to store the preserved organs—stomach, liver, lungs, and intestines—removed from the body before mummification. After Dynasty XIX, the lids took different forms associated with deities: human for the jar containing the liver, baboon for the lungs, jackal for the stomach, and falcon for the intestines.

cartonnage: layers of linen or papyrus stiffened with gypsum plaster and painted.

cartouche: ornamental oval-shaped frame surrounding royal names and occasionally those of gods, and believed to provide symbolic protection; also used in furniture or other objects.

Coffin Texts: funerary texts developed from the earlier Pyramid Texts; written on coffins during the Middle Kingdom.

corvée: the obligation to perform free labor for the sovereign.

cult temple: the standard religious building(s) designed to house the spirits of the gods, accessible only to the priesthood; usually located on the Nile's east bank.

deshret: "red land," referring to barren desert.

false door: in a tomb, the means by which the soul of the deceased could enter and leave the world of the living to accept funerary offerings brought to the tomb.

funerary temple: usually built on the Nile's west bank, they were religious structures used for ritual commemoration of dead pharaohs.

hieroglyphs: Greek for "sacred carvings," these were ancient Egypt's formal picture writing, used mainly for tomb and temple walls.

hypostyle hall: temple hall densely packed with monumental columns.

ka: "soul" or life energy, this was a person's "double" created at birth, which lived on after death, sustained by food and other offerings by the living.

kemet: "black land," referring to the fertile areas along the Nile's banks.

mastaba: "bench," describing the mud-brick tomb structure built over an underground burial chamber, from which pyramids developed.

nemes: the yellow-and-blue striped headcloth worn by kings, usually twisted into a ponytail at the back; the most famous example was found on Tutankhamun's golden death mask.

nomarch: local governor of each of Egypt's forty-two nomes.

nome: Greek term for Egypt's forty-two provinces, twenty-two in Upper Egypt and twenty in Lower Egypt.

obelisk: monolithic stone pillar tapering to a pyramidal top, often placed around temples and gilded to reflect sunlight; usually set in pairs and extensively inscribed.

Opening of the Mouth: ceremony culminating the funeral, performed on the mummy by the heir or funerary priest, using spells and implements to restore the senses; symbolically represented the god Anubis performing the ritual.

Opet festival: annual celebration held at the temple of Luxor to restore the powers of the pharaoh at a secret meeting with the god Amun.

ostracon: a potsherd or tile, used for writing on in ancient Egypt.

papyrus: the heraldic plant of Lower Egypt whose reedlike stem was sliced and layered to create paperlike sheets for writing.

pharaoh: term for an Egyptian king, derived from the ancient Egyptian word for palace, per-'o ("great house").

pylon: monumental gateway with sloping sides that forms the entrance to temples.

Pyramid Texts: funerary texts inscribed on the walls of late Old Kingdom pyramids and restricted to royalty.

sarcophagus: derived from the Greek for "flesh-eating." Refers to the large stone coffins used to house the mummy and its wooden coffin.

scarab: the sacred dung beetle believed to propel the sun's disk through the sky in the same way the beetle pushes a ball of dung across the ground.

Sed festival: jubilee ceremony of renewal of kingship, usually celebrated after thirty years' rule.

Serapeum: extensive network of underground catacombs at Saqqara in which the Apis bulls were buried, later associated with the Ptolemaic god Serapis.

serdab: from the Arabic word for "cellar," a small room in a mastaba tomb containing a statue of the deceased, to which offerings were presented.

serekh: an early symbol of Egyptian kingship in the shape of a palace.

shabti (ushabti): small servant figurines placed with the deceased, which would act on their behalf when called upon to undertake any manual work in the afterlife.

shaduf: a simple hand-operated lever in the form of a horizontal pole with a skin or bucket at the long end, used for lifting water for irrigation.

solar bark: the boat in which the sun god Re sailed through the heavens, with actual examples buried close to certain pyramids for use by the spirits of the pharaohs.

stelae: slabs of stone, wood, or plaster, usually funerary, commemorative, or votive. Prayer stelae were inscribed with prayers of gratitude or to gain favor from a favorite god; funerary stelae provided a symbolic door for the deceased to move from the living world to the afterlife; votive stelae were decorated with scenes of the deceased in front of a deity. Certain stelae were thought to have healing powers.

udjat (wadjet) eye: also known as the Eye of Horus, the udjat or wadjet is depicted as a human eye and eyebrow. It symbolized the legend of Horus losing his left eye in his war with Seth to avenge the death of his father. Thoth, god of wisdom and magic, found the torn fragments of the eye and reassembled them into the full moon. The eye was a symbol of protection.

uraeus: an image of the cobra goddess Wadjet worn at the brow of royalty to protect them by symbolically spitting fire into the eyes of their enemies.

wadi: the dry bed of a seasonal stream.

Weighing of the Heart: ceremony where the heart of the deceased was weighed against the feather of Maat with Osiris as judge. If light and free of sin, the person was considered worthy of entering the afterlife; if heavy with sin, the heart was eaten by an underworld monster and the deceased was damned forever.

wesekh: ornamental collar of protective value made of gold, precious stones, and metals; from Dynasty XVIII onward it was given to officials, dignitaries, and soldiers as a mark of honor.

INDEX

INDEX